WAR IN THE MODERN WORLD, 1990–2014

In *War in the Modern World, 1990–2014*, Jeremy Black looks at the most modern of conflicts from the perspective that war is a central feature of the modern world. Arguing that understanding non-Western developments is crucial if the potential of Western warmaking is to be assessed accurately, the book also asserts that knowing the history of conflict can only help future generations. Black argues for the need to emphasise the variety of military circumstances, as well as the extent to which the understanding of force and the definitions of victory and defeat are guided by cultural assumptions. War has a multi-faceted impact in the modern world, and this book shows its significance.

This title takes a global and historical perspective on modern warfare, enabling the reader to approach familiar conflicts through a new analytical framework. This book is an invaluable resource for all students of the history of modern warfare.

Jeremy Black is Professor of History at the University of Exeter. He is a leading military historian whose books include *War and Technology* (2013), *War and the Cultural Turn* (2011), *A History of Diplomacy* (2010), *European Warfare in a Global Context, 1660–1815* (2007) and *Rethinking Military History* (2004), and is editor of the Routledge Warfare and History series.

WARFARE AND HISTORY
General Editor: Jeremy Black
Professor of History, University of Exeter

WORLD WAR TWO
A Military History
Jeremy Black

WAR IN THE MODERN
WORLD SINCE 1815
Edited by Jeremy Black

WARFARE AND SOCIETY
IN EUROPE
1898 to the Present
Michael S. Neiberg

THE PELOPONNESIAN
WAR
A Military Study
J. F. Lazenby

SAMURAI, WARFARE AND
THE STATE IN EARLY
MEDIEVAL JAPAN
Karl F. Friday

WAR, POLITICS AND
SOCIETY IN EARLY MODERN
CHINA, 900–1795
Peter Lorge

THE WARS OF THE FRENCH
REVOLUTION AND
NAPOLEON, 1792–1815
Owen Connelly

INDIAN WARS OF CANADA,
MEXICO AND THE UNITED
STATES, 1812–1900
Bruce Vandervort

WARFARE IN THE ANCIENT
NEAR EAST TO 1600 BC
Holy Warriors at the Dawn of History
William J. Hamblin

THE WAR FOR A NATION
The American Civil War
Susan-Mary Grant

EUROPEAN WARFARE IN A
GLOBAL CONTEXT, 1660–1815
Jeremy Black

WARFARE, STATE AND
SOCIETY ON THE BLACK SEA
STEPPE, 1500–1700
Brian L. Davies

For a complete list of titles in the series, please visit http://www.routledge.
com/books/series/SE0417

WAR IN THE MODERN WORLD, 1990–2014

Jeremy Black

LONDON AND NEW YORK

First published 2015
by Routledge
2 Park Square, Milton Park, Abingdon, Oxon OX14 4RN

and by Routledge
711 Third Avenue, New York, NY 10017

Routledge is an imprint of the Taylor & Francis Group, an informa business

© 2015 Jeremy Black

The right of Jeremy Black to be identified as author of this work has been asserted by him in accordance with sections 77 and 78 of the Copyright, Designs and Patents Act 1988.

All rights reserved. No part of this book may be reprinted or reproduced or utilised in any form or by any electronic, mechanical, or other means, now known or hereafter invented, including photocopying and recording, or in any information storage or retrieval system, without permission in writing from the publishers.

Trademark notice: Product or corporate names may be trademarks or registered trademarks, and are used only for identification and explanation without intent to infringe.

British Library Cataloguing in Publication Data
A catalogue record for this book is available from the British Library

Library of Congress Cataloging in Publication Data
Black, Jeremy, 1955-
War in the modern world, 1990-2014 / Jeremy Black.
pages cm. -- (Warfare and history)
Includes bibliographical references and index.
1. Military history, Modern--20th century. 2. Military history, Modern--
21st century. 3. Military art and science--History--20th century. 4. Military
art and science--History--21st century. 5. War--History--20th century.
6. War--History--21st century. I. Title.
U42.B528 2014
355.0209'051--dc23
2014019110

ISBN: 978-1-138-80360-2 (hbk)
ISBN: 978-1-138-80361-9 (pbk)
ISBN: 978-1-315-75361-4 (ebk)

Typeset in Bembo
by Taylor & Francis Books

Printed and bound in the United States of America by Edwards Brothers Malloy on sustainably sourced paper.

FOR
JOHN AND DIANA CHADWICK

CONTENTS

	Preface	viii
1	Bringing together two narratives	1
2	The Revolution in Military Affairs	6
3	A conventional account, 1990–2000	13
4	Signs of difference, 1990–2000	42
5	The War on Terror	54
6	A multitude of conflicts	82
7	Into the future: the rivalry of major powers?	109
8	Into the future: weak states and 'small wars'?	132
9	Conclusions	141
	Selected further reading	151
	Index	153

PREFACE

This book is written in the conviction that war and the possibility of war are central features of the modern world. This is the world which succeeded the great power, military and ideological confrontation known as the Cold War. It is no longer sensible to begin accounts of the modern world in 1945, or earlier, because much of the agenda of political, economic, social and military activity is now set in a very different environment. The massive demographic growth of the last quarter-century, the rise of China to great power status in economics as well as politics, and the reality across most of the world of a post-imperial politics ensures that the world of the late 1940s and 1950s is as one, for much of the world's population, with earlier ages.

If this ensures a very different context to that of the Cold War, it is still one in which war and the possibility of war are central. To argue this is to go against the arguments and implications of an important body of literature that has suggested that violence and war have become and are becoming less common.[1] Such may indeed be a perspective in a Western Europe that has been largely peaceful since 1945, and, even more, 1990, but it makes far less sense in the Middle East or Africa.

Furthermore, the prospect of war is of great concern in the two most populous parts of the world: East and South Asia. This prospect seems to become more, not less, likely. The possibility of conflict between China and Japan, remote in 1990, came to the fore in international attention in 2013. So did the possibility of a North Korean assault on South Korea. The rise of Hindu sectarian politics in India, and the instability of both Pakistan and Bangladesh, made the situation in South Asia troubling, while a bitter internal conflict in Sri Lanka only ended in 2009.

In these and other areas, alongside the possibility of war between states came that of conflict within them. The number and intensity of such conflicts were affected by the end of the Cold War, notably in Central America. However, they were scarcely vestigial features from that age. Indeed, in some countries, the extent to which the Cold War had really been grafted onto earlier local rivalries, and was exploited for them, became apparent once the Cold War was over and conflict continued. This was readily apparent in sub-Saharan Africa and the Middle East. In addition, some of the civil warfare prior to 1990 had had only an indirect relationship, at best, with the Cold War and this pattern remained the case.

Conflict within countries might well bring the intervention, direct or indirect, of other states. The collapse of Syria in the 2010s into a deadly and lengthy civil war that by February 2014 had cost about 140,000 lives indicated the unpredictability of conflict, as well as the capacity of such conflict to cause regional and, indeed, global tensions. Less dramatically, the outbreak of civil war in South Sudan in December 2013 showed that countries that became independent with high hopes could swiftly descend into mayhem. The murderous brutality experienced by large numbers of civilians, in Syria, South Sudan, the Central African Republic and elsewhere, indicated that the anti-societal potential of conflict was scarcely restrained by the norms of human rights law.

Such conflicts affect not only the lives of those who live in the countries involved, but also their neighbours and countries further afield. The refugee is very much a citizen of the modern world, a product of anti-societal warfare and of the extent to which regimes and others frequently define states in terms of ethnic, religious and social identities, and then apply these definitions to exclude and brutalise others.

Moreover, as another instance of the significance of preparations for war, although the percentage of state expenditure absorbed by the military is lower for most states than that devoted to social welfare or public debt, nevertheless the total figure is still formidable. War has a political, financial, economic, social and cultural impact in the modern world; and this book is written with a conviction of its significance.

Such a goal poses problems for the historian, both practically and culturally. It is difficult to gain historical perspectives on current events, and there is a supposition that historians should tackle the past, not the present, let alone the future. In addition, the politics of historical interpretation – always an issue, but usually a fairly muted one in the study of the distant past – is unavoidable in the discussion of contemporary affairs. The importance of warfare in modern politics highlights this problem. Moreover, the policy implications of the historical analysis and judgement of very recent times are immediate and likely to be hotly contested; even if that analysis is expressed only in terms of what is emphasised in the narrative.

So an explanation is required. First, I see history not only as an engagement with the past, but also as a habit of mind that, while indeed based on the study of the past, can also be applied to present and future. I would describe this habit of mind as a questioning one, sceptical of received truths, and therefore anti-authoritarian. Indeed, I would take this argument further and argue that historians should try to study the present and consider the future, not only in order to acquire perspectives that could be usefully employed in their consideration of the past, but also because this use of their skill is a valuable public

PREFACE

good. If historians do not do so, others will apply the past with probably less understanding and skill.

Secondly, although I am no Postmodernist, I doubt that we can produce definitive accounts of the past, however valuable they might be in theory; while I think that quasi-definitive assessments are perforce on matters of very narrow span. Thus, I am dubious about the validity and extent of the qualitative differences automatically so readily claimed on behalf of historical work on the past as opposed to the discussion of the present.

As far as *War in the Modern World* is concerned, there seem particularly strong reasons why I should engage with present and future conflict. First, such conflict is, and will be, important; and will help define the world of succeeding generations. Indeed, the extent to which war can do so is a revenge of the particular and the moment, against the teleological certainties of models of long-term historical development. Possibly as a result, many historians who do not specialise in military history are reluctant to pay it sufficient attention, or prefer to adopt a simple explanation of developments and their consequences.

Secondly, alongside detailed studies of aspects of warfare, much of my work on military history has deployed a series of related conceptual arguments that are also important for the current situation and indeed for the future. In particular, I have argued for the need to emphasise, for any particular period, the variety of military circumstances and developments, as well as the extent to which the understanding of force, as well as the definitions of victory and defeat, are guided primarily by cultural assumptions. This view has led me to be wary about interpretations of military capability and change based on material culture and, more particularly, technological superiority. Linked to this, I emphasise the need to see tasks or goals rather than capabilities as the central context for, and motor of, change in warmaking.

I have also argued the need to consider non-Western developments, not in terms of some failure to adopt and adapt Western methods and paradigms, but rather as a response to specific circumstances and cultures.[2] It is particularly pertinent to consider these arguments in light of conflict since 1990, and this is a major theme of this book. The understanding of non-Western developments is crucial if the potential of Western warmaking is to be assessed accurately. The conflicts in Iraq and Afghanistan are the most conspicuous instance of a failure to make such assessments. Others will probably follow.

Thirdly, as a related point, there is considerable confusion as to the definition and application of the concept of modern war, and this book is intended to contribute to discussion of the issue. In particular, there is confusion about the relationship between modern and total war, and indeed about the definition and historical location of the latter.[3] In practice, total war is/was not necessarily modern, and modern war is not necessarily total. This point is a crucial critique of the teleological commonplace of the standard narrative and analysis of long-term military developments. I focus here on modern war as war in a

PREFACE

certain period of time, rather than applying some alleged characteristics of modern warfare as a standard by which to judge the variety of conflict that in fact is the case.

In thinking about the topic, I benefited greatly from the opportunity to attend the 2008 conference of the Society for Military History, and would like to thank the Society for inviting me to give the opening plenary lecture and for awarding me the Samuel Eliot Morison prize. I have also benefited from the opportunity to speak at the 2008 Asia-Pacific Conference for Senior Military Officers; the 2008 West Point Summer Seminar in Military History; Singapore Staff College; the 2013 conference on Conflict and Culture held by the Catholic University of Lisbon; the 2013 Oxford University Summer School; and at Adelphi and North Texas universities and the Sorbonne. I have profited greatly from teaching at the University of Exeter, notably for the MA in Strategy in 2013–14 and for that in Military History in 2014.

I would also like to thank Kevin Farrell, Frank Hamilton, Rob Johnson, Tony Kelly and two anonymous readers for commenting on earlier drafts. Their generosity in doing so is much appreciated. None is responsible for any of the errors that remain. Eve Setch has proved a most helpful editor and Janet Fisher an excellent copy editor. Part of this work appeared in a 2009 publication by the Social Affairs Unit and I would like to thank Michael Mosbacher for giving me permission to use this material. It is a great pleasure to dedicate this book to John and Diana Chadwick to mark a quarter-century of friendship.

Notes

1 S. Pinker, *The Better Angels of our Nature: Why Violence has Declined* (London, 2011).
2 J. Black, *Rethinking Military History* (London, 2004) and *War and Technology* (Bloomington, Indiana, 2013).
3 J. Black, *The Age of Total War, 1860–1945* (Westport, Connecticut, 2006).

1

BRINGING TOGETHER TWO NARRATIVES

The present dominates the past because we see the latter through the prism of today, both the events of today and its memories. For Western commentators, everything summed up by the words Iraq and Afghanistan is apt to be particularly imposing and to play a key role in defining modern warfare. This situation has been the case since the American intervention in Afghanistan in 2001 and, even more, the American-led invasion of Iraq in 2003. As Saddam Hussein's unprovoked invasion of Kuwait in 1990 was directly responsible for the Gulf War of 1990–91, the major conventional conflict of that decade, Iraq has played a key role in analysis from the outset of the period covered in this book. Indeed, the word Iraq, like Vietnam earlier, is employed in the West to signify a certain type of war or even the issues and problems of modern warfare as a whole.

Yet, as I seek to show in this book, this focus, while understandable, is also highly misleading, because these conflicts did not launch new developments. Instead, they represented tendencies and, in particular, methods of warfighting that were already present. The parallels between Soviet operations in Afghanistan in 1979–89 and Western operations there from 2001 were instructive, while in Iraq in 1991 the American forces employed Cold War weaponry and tactics against Iraqis armed with Cold War-era Soviet equipment.

Moreover, these wars can detract from the other conflicts of the period. It is instructive, for example, when lecturing on this period, to ask which war has led to the most casualties and to be repeatedly told, in both Britain and the USA, Iraq, meaning the 2003 struggle and its aftermath, when, in practice, casualty figures in both Congo and Sudan have been considerably higher.

This contrast is part of a pattern of underplaying non-Western conflict. Try asking, 'Which war in the period 1946–80 had the most combatants or the highest casualties?' The answer usually given is 'Vietnam', meaning the Vietnam conflict when the Americans were involved, and not, more accurately, the longer pattern of post-1945 conflict in that country. Instead, the answer should be 'the Chinese Civil War of 1946–49'. Or again, asking about the 1980s, and being told, notably, but not only, in Britain, the Anglo-Argentinean Falklands War (1982), and not that between Iran and Iraq (1980–88). The latter conflict did not involve dramatic battles or major advances, and the war did not lead to territorial transfers. Nevertheless, those are not the sole criteria of military effectiveness, purpose or consequences. Alongside heavy casualties, the Iran–Iraq War helped entrench the Islamic Revolution in Iran, and also led Saddam Hussein to invade Kuwait in 1990 in order to try to recoup his costs.

This point about relative attention leads towards the central conceptual argument. Analysts, both historians and, more seriously, those working on the present, have focused on the Western narrative of military history, and, especially, the themes of technological proficiency as deployed in conventional warfare. As a result, analysts have tended to underplay the non-West. Or rather, the latter has been considered largely in terms of opposing Western powers and with reference to the adoption of Western weaponry and methods. This thesis has proved particularly attractive to many military historians, as with the discussion of the period 1450–1800 in terms of a European-based 'Military Revolution'.[1]

This approach, however, is less than a complete account for past or present. In particular, it offers a misleading narrative for non-Western warfare, one characterised by a lack of due attention and an absence of understanding. Indeed, there is a tendency to simplify non-Western military circumstances, and goals and forms of warfare, and to fail to appreciate profound cultural differences within the non-Western world.[2] This tendency can even be seen in some of the literature that argues for the need to reconsider the future of conflict. There is, in particular, a failure to understand the variations within the subsets into which non-Western warfare is commonly broken, notably Oriental, sub-Saharan African, South Asian and Middle Eastern.

The failure to understand non-Western warfare, moreover, is significant, not simply because we ought to try to understand the situation around the world, but also because, as throughout from the early sixteenth century, the effectiveness of Western forces requires such an understanding, as sometimes, more bluntly, does the very survival of Western expeditionary units. Thus, those who are concerned about Western military effectiveness need to support an approach to military environments and conflict as they are, and not as might be wished, whether militarily, politically or both, and whether describing past, present or future.

In backing such an approach, commentators can risk accusations of relativism, of defeatism, and of what in the USA is termed declinism, but that is a misleading assessment. It is in order to avoid defeat that one notes weaknesses and opposing strengths, not in order to welcome it. Ignoring such weaknesses is a sign not of heroism and bravery, but rather of folly. Ignorance will not be the basis for a triumph of the will, and the latter approach is not the best one to waging conflict.

In short, this book is a contribution to military education, by which I mean education about the military as much as education for the military. Indeed, the former is more necessary, because there is, notably, but not only, in the West, a widespread public ignorance about military issues and problems. This ignorance is also apparent in political circles and many military figures complain about such ignorance. A lack of military experience on the part of politicians is part of the equation, and was particularly apparent as the generations that had experienced, first, military service in World War Two and, then, conscription into compulsory military service, retired. Furthermore, a lack of focus on military issues reflects the emphasis on domestic issues and social policy in political concern.

Moreover, this emphasis is an aspect of the expeditionary warfare mindset that has been dominant in the West since the Cold War ended. With troops dispatched to distant tasks, war somehow seems separate and detachable from more urgent domestic concerns. This situation is a recipe for poor military morale and for failures in policy-making. The situation is different in countries where conflict has been more common and where military service is still compulsory, notably Israel.

The period since 1990 has seen a particularly abrupt shift in the discussion of Western military proficiency. In the 1990s, alongside the misleading claim that nuclear weaponry and, subsequently, the end of the Cold War had made war obsolete,[3] there was a triumphalist focus on high-spectrum capability. This was a focus that continued the Cold War emphasis on such weaponry and related doctrine, especially on the part of the USA. In the 1990s, this focus was linked to an assertion that, in the shape of a supposed Revolution in Military Affairs (RMA, see chapter 2), this capability had changed, indeed transformed, the nature of current and future warfare, and that understanding this change, and transforming the military accordingly, would ensure victory.

This thesis received powerful support from the role in particular of American air power in the defeat of Iraq in 1991 and of Serbia in 1995 and 1999, and in the rapid overthrow of the Taliban in Afghanistan in 2001. The thesis appeared to reach a new level of validity with the rapid overthrow of Saddam Hussein in 2003, as the Iraqi military was speedily routed, and by an American-led Coalition force significantly smaller (and even more focused on American strength) than that deployed against Iraq in 1991. Moreover, the task in 2003 was far more ambitious, as operations in 1991 had been restricted to an attempt to drive Iraqi forces from Kuwait and, once achieved, there was no exploitation in terms of a conquest of Iraq.

The aftermath of the 2003 invasion as the conquest of Iraq rapidly faced large-scale opposition, however, suggested that much of this triumphalist discussion had been misplaced. This reconceptualisation was not a case of complete revisionism, in that the Iraqi military had indeed been totally routed and the regime completely overthrown. Moreover, the insurgency did not prove the basis of a Baathist revanche. Nevertheless, alongside the triumphalist narrative, and greatly compromising the conclusions drawn from it, there was a different narrative that became increasingly prominent about Iraq. This narrative emphasised the limitations of conventional forces and methods. Linked to this came a questioning of the notion of a clear hierarchy of military success, and, instead, an emphasis on the variety of means of effective conflict.

The term effectiveness has to be employed with care, as the insurgents and terrorists in Iraq were scarcely creative politically or socially. However, for a while, particularly in 2006, the insurgents and terrorists were able to challenge the result of the invasion, and, indeed, the confidence that the world's leading military power, the USA, could employ force to secure its purposes.

If this situation suggested the vitality of non-Western military practices, and the challenges they posed, this point was underlined in 2006 by the difficulties the Israeli military experienced at the hands of Hizbullah in southern Lebanon, and, also from 2006, by the resurgence of the Taliban in Afghanistan. In each case, it is possible to debate the extent to which the Western force was actually defeated, and there is a need not to assume a greater degree of success for insurrections than is merited. This is a point more generally true of the post-1945 world, with its romanticism of left-wing guerrillas and, more seriously, the failure to note the military and political limitations of such warfare.

Nevertheless, there is no doubt that each of the above episodes represented a major blow to the use of military means to secure a political response, not least that of creating an impression of success. From that perspective, the Israelis were unsuccessful, and there was significant public disquiet in Israel. In Afghanistan, the impression was created of a situation slipping out of control, which indeed was the case.

In each case, as earlier with the North Vietnamese/Viet Cong in the 1960s and early 1970s, the political prospectus of the non-Western force was vicious, deadly and dangerous, but that provides even more of a reason why their military narrative has to be included. To present modern warfare in terms of a comforting account of Western proficiency, as was particularly the case with coverage in the 1990s and the early 2000s (and possibly in conscious reaction to the pessimistic post-Vietnam situation in the 1970s), will not make us any safer, nor will it help ensure the effective planning and training that is necessary. The conviction that modern, limited warfare could be defined and, then, fine-tuned to achieve victory and suit Western political purposes, not least in terms of liberal interventionism from the 1990s, and its neo-conservative equivalent in the 2000s, proved particularly feckless.

This book therefore seeks to clarify a number of troubling themes for the Western powers. It offers an approach to military history and developments that aims to provide not only a global coverage, but also an analysis that is open to the number of military environments and narratives that are involved and that can interact. As such, this book provides an approach that is also valid for earlier periods. Indeed, looking back, the book encourages a re-consideration of standard narratives of military history, both over the last century and earlier. This re-consideration will probably become more common as the twenty-first century proceeds. As a process and a subject, history involves the interaction of past and present, in part due to the interplay of structure and agency but also because of the shaping of the experience of the past in terms of the perception of the present. War and military history are not exceptions to this situation. Instead, as this book will show, they exemplify it.

Notes

1 J. Black, *Beyond the Military Revolution: War in the Seventeenth-Century World* (Basingstoke, 2011).
2 R.H. Schultz and A.J. Dew, *Insurgents, Terrorists, and Militias: The Warriors of Contemporary Combat* (New York, 2006).
3 J. Mueller, *Retreat from Doomsday: The Obsolescence of Major War* (New York, 1989); C. Kaysen, 'Is War Obsolete? A Review Essay', *International Security*, 14 (1990), pp. 42–69; R.L. O'Connell, *Ride of the Second Horseman: The Birth and Death of War* (New York, 1997); M. Mandelbaum, 'Is Major War Obsolete?', *Survival*, 40 (1998–99), pp. 20–38.

2

THE REVOLUTION IN MILITARY AFFAIRS

Modern technology and total power were key themes in the understanding of twentieth-century Western warfare. If their deadliest manifestation was the American use of two atomic bombs against Japan in August 1945, this was only because the far more extensive, powerful and varied nuclear arsenals subsequently built up by the major powers were not used. These arsenals were to the fore in the Cold War, exciting fear of the nature of any conflict between the USA and the Soviet Union, but also proving the basis of the watchful peace of deterrence, a deterrence based on the reality of Mutually Assured Destruction (MAD).

This theme of the competition of potent and technologically advanced systems, however, appeared less pertinent in the late 1980s as the Cold War eased, ebbed and, finally, ended. The advent of Mikhail Gorbachev as Soviet leader in 1985 was followed by nuclear limitation agreements, by Soviet disengagement, especially from Afghanistan, and by the end of Soviet-sponsored Cuban expeditionary operations in Africa.

The largely unpredicted collapse of European Communism and the Soviet Union in 1989–91 in a course of events not expected, still less planned, by Gorbachev, took this process unexpectedly forward; but also created what was at once a new military landscape, and the need and opportunity for new planning and doctrines. In the USA, which now dominated what was referred to as a unipolar world, that is a world organised round one power, the military discussion was largely in terms of what was described as the Revolution in Military Affairs (RMA).

More widely cited than defined, and meaning too many things to too many people to allow for precision, the RMA in fact had a number of meanings and associations.[1] In combination, these meanings and associations suggested the usefulness of the RMA to its advocates, but also its misleading character. Indeed, the RMA was symptomatic of a set of cultural and political assumptions that tell us more about the aspirations of the 1990s than they do about any objective assessment of military capabilities. In this, the RMA was like other 'constructions' or analytical concepts, such as military revolution and *blitzkrieg*. In particular, the RMA reflected the desire in the 1990s for unquestioned potency without any matching need to accept conscription, a war economy or many casualties. In part, the RMA therefore can be seen as a response to a decline of the warrior ethos which has been discerned as a more general tendency in the sociology of modern warfare.[2] This decline ensured that bellicosity, in the West, but not only in the West, took a different form to earlier centuries, as, in most societies, it did not involve military service by civilians. Another trend in the 1990s was a marked reduction in global military spending.[3]

The RMA also reflected the assertion of Western, more particularly American, superiority, as well as the ideology of mechanisation that had long been important to American military thought. This ideology was crucial, for capability, if not worth, was defined in a machine age in terms of machines. The potency of these machines was then used to assert and demonstrate superiority.[4] Indeed, force projection was a key term and concept for the RMA and in Western tasking and conduct in the 1990s and 2000s.

The focus on machinery also appeared to provide a ready measure of assessing the strength of different states and indeed civilisations. Strength could not only be assessed, indeed measured. It was also apparently possible to shape, indeed define, the changing equations of strength by investing in new capability at the cutting edge of technological progress.

Thus, the RMA was an expression of the modern secular technological belief system that is prevalent in the West, and that easily meshes with theories of modernisation that rest on the adoption of new technology and related concepts.[5] Moreover, it was particularly crucial to Americans that the RMA was an American-led military revolution as it apparently underlined American proficiency and, indeed, became almost a way to validate it.[6] As a revolution, the RMA served the American commitment to break with the past and to lead the future, indeed to make the future.

The RMA also offered a way to look at the world in which this proficiency appeared to be without end or, at least, would be redefined in terms that the Americans were confident they could determine. In accordance with a long-term tendency in American military (and political) thinking,[7] the RMA met the American need to believe in the possibility of high–intensity conflict and of total victory, with opponents shocked and awed into accepting defeat. This was significant in terms of means and outcomes.

Militarily, there would be no need for the costs of attritional warfare, while the frequently ambiguous and qualified nature of modern victory could also be avoided. The RMA also meant that the aftermath of Vietnam could be banished.

In addition, the certainty of the RMA appeared to offer a defence against the threats posed by the spread to more, notably hostile, powers, of earlier technologies, such as long-range missiles and atomic warheads, as well as of new ones, such as bacteriological warfare, and of whatever might follow. Providing invulnerability, the RMA appeared to keep the Americans ahead.

This point was taken on board by politicians who understood the need to offer the public security. Standing for President, George W. Bush, in 1999, told an audience at The Citadel, a prominent American military academy in Charleston, that 'the best way to keep the peace is to redefine war on our terms'. Gaining and using the initiative was a key aspect of military doctrine.

Once elected in 2000, Bush declared at The Citadel in 2001, 'The first priority is to speed the transformation of our military.' Indeed, the sense that already established military structures and systems were part of the problem, and not a key means to the solution, that in fact they stood in the way of the necessary transformation, helped explain the very poor relations between Donald Rumsfeld, Bush's choice as Secretary of Defense from 2001 to 2006, and many of America's senior commanders.

This tension was related to the totalising culture and prospectus offered by the RMA, and by the transformation of the military that was its institutional and doctrinal expression. The belief in clear problem, and obvious solution, proved potent, especially in a political and institutional culture, that of America in the late 1990s and early 2000s, that did not welcome ambiguity or doubt. Ironically, many of those who, from the mid-2000s, later advocated counter-insurgency (COIN) doctrine as the ultimate solution to everything said the same, earlier, about the RMA and Transformation.

Transformation entailed a move from large 'platform-centric' formations and units, such as armoured divisions, to groupings that were orientated on particular missions and that were designed to act in a more agile fashion. These groupings grew on, and were located in, what was referred to as a matrix of networks of sensors, information processors and shooters. Thus, 'network-centric' warfare was the goal as it was believed to take military capability to a new plane of effectiveness. A new language of capability and implementation was important to the new doctrine.

The RMA can be located very much in terms of a particular moment in American strategic thought and military politics, one of post-Cold War boldness of conception about America's ability to act as a force for good, a boldness held in liberal as much as neo-conservative circles.[8] Those who touted the RMA and the quest to achieve it helped, however, to get the USA into the serious military predicament it faced in the aftermath of the Iraq invasion of 2003.

At the same time, the ideas summarised as the RMA could serve to support a range of Western political strategies, including those of both isolationalists and interventionists. In practice, the RMA particularly lent itself to the cause of American unilateralism, and this was most clearly espoused by neo-conservatives, notably figures close to George W. Bush who endorsed the idea of a 'coalition of the willing', in other words those willing to support the policy of the Bush government.

However, unilateralism was more generally a characteristic of American attitudes, and the neo-conservative use of it drew on a long tradition. At the same time, recent and current developments and attitudes were of great importance. As a reminder of the difficulty of fixing meaning, the combination of unilateralism and the RMA can therefore be assessed either in the context of the *relative* American decline in a more multi-centred world, a process that began in the 1960s with the rise in the Japanese and German economies, and that gathered pace from the 1990s with the growth of those of China and India,[9] or as a response to the unipolar American-dominated international system that followed the end of the Cold War.

Moreover, it is important to be cautious about suggesting too much coherence and consistency in the idea of an RMA. This is a point that is underlined by consideration of military revolutions that are supposed to have occurred earlier. A less harsh view than that just summarised can be advanced if the RMA is presented, instead, as a doctrine designed to meet political goals, and thus to shape or encourage technological developments and operational and tactical suppositions accordingly, rather than to allow technological constraints to shape doctrine, and thus risk the danger of inhibiting policy. That is a pertinent conceptual point, but, in reality, much discussion of the RMA, especially, but not only, in the USA, did seem to suggest a technology-driven and defined warfare, one enabled by technology and expressed through it. The impression created was of unprecedented potency.

Much of this technology was focused on overcoming the problems of command and control posed by the large number of units operating simultaneously, and on fulfilling the opportunities for command and control gained by successfully overcoming this challenge, and thus aggregating sensors, shooters and deciders to achieve a precise mass effect from dispersed units. This permitted the delivery of mass effect from overall numbers of troops that did not offer the mass available in terms of numbers alone during the Cold War.

Advocates of the RMA progressed to talking about 'space control' and the 'empty battlefield' of the future, where wars would be waged for 'information dominance' – in other words, control of satellites, telecommunications and computer networks. The American military thus contrasted their information grids and networks, which were to be safeguarded in wartime, with hostile ones that had to be destroyed. Integrated communications technologies were designed to enhance offensive and defensive information warfare capability, while better communications permitted both more integrated fire support and the use of surveillance to enable more accurate targeting. All were to be achieved rapidly in accordance with political and military needs, not least, in the latter case, getting within opposing decision cycles. Surveillance capability also enabled commanders to have greater knowledge of the locations of their own units, as with the use of the American Blue Force Tracker system during the invasion of Iraq in 2003.[10]

The new weaponry was indicative of priorities. There was a stress on cheaper, unmanned platforms or drones, intended to replace reconnaissance and attack aircraft. Whether termed 'unmanned aerial vehicles' (UAVs) or 'remotely piloted vehicles' (RPVs), these platforms were designed to take the advantage of missiles further by providing mobile platforms from which they could be fired or bombs dropped. Platforms do not require on-site crew, and thus can be used without risk to the life or liberty of personnel. As a consequence, they can be low flying and enjoy enhanced accuracy, as the risk of losses of pilots to anti-aircraft fire has been removed. These losses, and the problems they posed, not least the prospect of hostage-type situations with the pressures they entailed, contributed to the priorities for a new air power.

In addition, at least in theory, the logistical burden of air power is reduced with unmanned platforms. So also is the cost, as these platforms are less expensive than manned counterparts, and there are big savings in pilot training. Unmanned platforms should also be more compact and 'stealthy' (i.e. less easy to detect and intercept), while the acceleration and manoeuvrability of such platforms would no longer be limited by G-forces that would render pilots unconscious. These points suggest that the future value of large aircraft carriers is questionable, at least in so far as they carry manned planes. It should be possible, instead, to provide smaller vessels able to launch unmanned platforms.

In 1999, unarmed drones were employed extensively for surveillance over Kosovo in order to send information on bomb damage and refugee columns, and in Afghanistan from 2001 and Iraq from 2003 armed drones were used as firing platforms. They had impressive characteristics. The 26-foot, American-produced Predator drone, with its operating radius of 500 miles, flight duration of up to 40 hours, cruising speed of 80 miles per hour and normal operating altitudes of 15,000 feet, was designed to destroy air-defence batteries and command centres. It can be used in areas contaminated by chemical or germ warfare, and its software is programmed to be able to tell if the intended target has moved close to civilians and to suggest accordingly a change of plan. Drone attacks increased greatly under President Obama from 9 in Pakistan in 2004–7, when Bush was President, to 117 in 2010. At least 2,371 people died in drone strikes in Pakistan in 2006–14. American attacks also increased elsewhere, notably in Yemen. There was a particular emphasis on using drones to kill terrorist leaders. Moreover, the frequency of attacks was employed to signal intentions, as in 2014 when Pakistani attempts to rally domestic support for a new policy towards the Taliban were eased by the marked lessening of these American attacks.

The use of drones rapidly spread, with Israel employing them, while, in 2008, the Russian-backed breakaway region of Abkhazia claimed to destroy seven reconnaissance drones sent from Georgia (the Caucasus republic and not the American state). Israel had provided Georgia with drones. In the 2010s, Britain and France began a joint development of combat drones, while in 2014, Britain unveiled the Taranis, a prototype fighter-bomber drone.

The capability of unmanned platforms is enhanced by designing them to work within systems or networks that bring together dispersed units and different types of weapons, and, moreover, from a number of environments: space, air, land and sea. These systems operate on the basis of high and sustained rates of information. By 2000, American military surveillance satellites, with their digital sensors and their almost instantaneous transmission over encrypted radio links, had a resolution better than 100 millimetres (4 inches). The potential of this surveillance became a major international issue in 2002, as the USA claimed that satellite information made it clear that Iraq was stockpiling weapons of mass destruction and evading the ground search programme being carried out by United Nations (UN) inspectors. This episode apparently highlighted the extent to which it was possible to overcome one of the major characteristics of totalitarian regimes – information management.

America is at the forefront of such technology, although it is not alone in its development goals, and, in order to recoup some of the cost, is likely to sell advanced weapons to allies. It is difficult, however, to control the process of technology transfer. For example, in 2000, the Americans threatened action if Israel, which had benefited greatly from such transfer, sold an airborne radar system to China that could be used against America's ally Taiwan.

In any assessment of the technology, it is necessary to note the contrast that is readily apparent between sea/air power and land capability, a difference in perspective that explains a great deal of how the American military ended up in its position in the early 2010s: one of unrivalled power projection but an inability to determine, or even often dominate, the situation in Afghanistan. Superiority in forms of military technology and military-industrial complexes is more important in sea and air environments, where its effect is fundamental; but precisely the same forms of superiority in technology and industry have a far smaller impact so far as land power goes. A general theoretical conclusion that emerges is that factors that help provide a capability advantage, or cause success (the two are not synonymous), in one context are not necessarily relevant in others. Partly as a result, the RMA as an ideology is, in many respects, an air power ideology and one that also represents the extension of the latter into space. As such, it is an ideology that suffers from the more general problems of air power ideology, namely the tendency always to find strategic value in its use. In particular, air power advocates underrate its deficiencies tactically and operationally, and exaggerate the ability to obtain strategic goals through using air attack. However, it is important not to over-look the extent to which, as part of the RMA, there was also a process of major change, or at least aspirations, in the other services.

Some of the discussion of the RMA, not least the emphasis on network-centric warfare, implied, or even assumed, that the world is an isotropic (uniform) surface, made knowable, pliable and controllable by new technology. The limitations of a technology-driven account of capability and change, however, were pertinent. This account entails the misapplication of tactical capabilities and lessons to operational goals, and of operational lessons to strategic goals, a misapplication that readily stems from the tendency to take an overly optimistic view of technological capabilities and from the disinclination to appreciate the political dynamics and measures of strategic goals and issues.

This view can lead to the illusion that fresh technologies can, and thus will, bring new capabilities, indeed definitions of power, and therefore that problems can be readily banished. That, however, is not an accurate analysis. Thus, picking apart the RMA is not some parlour game, but, instead, is crucial to the assessment of Western capability.

Notes

1 R.R. Leonhard, *The Art of Maneuver: Maneuver-Warfare Theory and AirLand Battle* (Novato, California, 1991); L. Freedman, *The Revolution in Strategic Affairs* (Oxford, 1998).
2 C. Coker, *The Warrior Ethos: Military Culture and the War on Terror* (London, 2007).
3 J. Eloranta, 'Twentieth Century Military Spending Patterns', in G. Kassimeris and J. Buckley (eds), *The Ashgate Research Companion to Modern Warfare* (Farnham, 2010), pp. 158–59.
4 C. Pursell, 'Introduction' in Pursell (ed.), *A Companion to American Technology* (Oxford, 2005), p. 1.
5 J. Black, *War and Technology* (Bloomington, Indiana, 2013).
6 K.L. Shimko, *The Iraq Wars and America's Military Revolution* (Cambridge, 2010).
7 B.M. Linn, *The Echo of Battle: The Army's Way of War* (Cambridge, Massachusetts, 2007).
8 A.J. Bacevich, *The New American Militarism: How Americans are Seduced by War* (Oxford, 2006).
9 F. Zakaria, *The Post-American World* (London, 2008) and, less convincingly, S. Amin, *Beyond US Hegemony? Assessing the Prospects for a Multipolar World* (London, 2006).
10 J.J. McGrath, *Crossing the Line of Departure: Battle Command on the Move. A Historical Perspective* (Fort Leavenworth, Kansas, 2006), p. 225.

3

A CONVENTIONAL ACCOUNT, 1990–2000

The RMA suggested novelty as the key theme of the 1990s, but, in practice, there was more continuity in warmaking, not least because it was Cold War structures, commanders, weaponry, training and doctrine that were employed and tested in the conflicts of the 1990s. This use of Cold War assets was recognisably the case with the USA, and involved in particular the new grasp of the operational dimension of war; a grasp that had developed in the 1980s as a manoeuvrist doctrine was advanced to aid planning for a mobile defence of Western Europe in the event of Soviet attack. This doctrine and planning was linked to the post-Vietnam revitalisation of the American army, a revitalisation that involved a process of transformation or, at least, redirection.

The 1991 Gulf War

Continuity with the Cold War was particularly the case because the major war the USA fought in the 1990s was at the outset of the decade and was waged against a military largely equipped by the Soviet Union. This was the First Gulf War, a conflict set off by the Iraqi invasion of neighbouring Kuwait; of course, this was not the first Gulf War: there had most recently been a major one between Iran and Iraq. A far smaller, weaker and more vulnerable target than Iran, which Iraq had unsuccessfully attacked in 1980, oil-rich Kuwait rapidly fell on 2 August 1990. Six days later, Saddam Hussein, Iraq's dictator, declared Kuwait to be Iraq's nineteenth province. Kuwait offered a major source of wealth after the exhaustion of lengthy war with Iran, and a substitute for grants and loans from other powers, such as the Saudi and Kuwaiti money that had sustained Iraq during the war with Iran.

The response defined high-spectrum warfare for the decade. Concerned about the impact of Iraqi expansion in the centre of the world's foremost region of oil production and, even more, oil exports, George H.W. Bush, the American President from 1989 to 1993, encouraged by Margaret Thatcher, the pugilistic British Prime Minister from 1979 to 1990, rapidly began diplomatic and military preparations for conflict. Iraq's failure to press on to attack neighbouring Saudi Arabia ensured that the initiative thereafter rested with its opponents. However, Saudi Arabia was a far more formidable challenge than Kuwait, particularly due to its far greater size, the strength of its armed forces, and its close political links with the USA, not least with Bush; while the element of surprise had been lost.

On 3 August 1990, two American carrier groups were ordered towards the region, a key display as well as means of support, and on 8 August, in response to a Saudi request, delivered two days earlier, for ground troops, the first American forces arrived. The build-up of substantial (mostly American) Coalition forces in Saudi Arabia in the second half of 1990 benefited from the availability of Saudi oil and bases. This build-up was matched by a blockade intended to hit Iraqi trade, particularly exports of oil, Iraq's major resource.

Saddam suffered from the marked decline of the power and influence of his Soviet patron and traditional arms supplier. This decline made UN action against him easier. In turn, Saddam's refusal to meet a UN deadline for withdrawal from Kuwait led, on 17 January 1991, to the start of a major air offensive on Iraq. Although aircraft from twelve countries were involved, the Americans were central to the offensive, which worked because of the rapid success in overcoming the sophisticated Iraqi anti-aircraft system. Saddam had used French and Soviet technology to produce an integrated system in which computers linked radars and missile; but the system, although advanced for the day, was overcome at once. Moreover, Iraq's heavily outnumbered air force did not intervene in strength. Instead, the MiG-29s flew to Iran where they were added to its air force.

The Allied air offensive benefited from state-of-the-art American weaponry: B-2 stealth bombers able to minimise radar detection bombed targets in Baghdad – one of the most heavily defended cities in the world – and did so with impunity, while the Americans made highly effective use of guided bombs. Thermal-imaging laser-designation systems were employed to guide the bombs to their target, and pilots launched bombs into the cone of the laser beam in order to score a direct hit. The destruction of the air-defence system, with only one aircraft lost (to an Iraqi MiG-29) on the first night, was a triumph not only for weaponry, but also for planning that made full use of the opportunities presented by the Allied weapons, while also out-thinking the Iraqis – for example by getting them to bring their radars to full power and thus exposing them to Coalition attack. This method had earlier been successfully employed by the Israelis against the Syrians in conflict over control and influence in southern Lebanon.

The use of stealth and precision in 1991 had important operational and strategic consequences as it meant that it was possible to employ a direct air assault aimed at overcoming the entire Iraqi air system, rather than an incremental rollback campaign. Moreover, the situation on the ground was totally transformed. As a consequence of the air assault, Iraqi forces were to be short of supplies, their command and control system was heavily disrupted so that they could not 'understand' the battle, and their morale was low.

A CONVENTIONAL ACCOUNT, 1990–2000

Both at the time and subsequently, RMA advocates were to make much of the potential of air power, and to draw considerable attention to the 1991 campaign, not least when discussing how to succeed against Iraq in 2003 while deploying fewer troops. Air power was indeed crucial to the first three phases of the 1991 operation: destroying Iraqi command and control, isolating the battlefield and greatly weakening Iraqi forces in the Kuwaiti theatre of operations.[1]

Phase four, the ground campaign, saw a rapid Coalition success. In February 1991, Iraqi forces were driven from Kuwait. They were out-generalled and out-fought by Coalition forces that benefited not only from superior technology, but also from their ability to maintain a high-tempo offensive in executing a well-conceived plan that combined air and land strength. Allied fighting quality, unit cohesion, leadership and planning, and Iraqi deficiencies in each of these, all played a major role in ensuring a rapid victory. The technology attracted considerable interest due to the importance attached to precise bombardment. The Americans indeed employed satellite surveillance, cruise missiles and guided bombs, as well as Patriot anti-missile missiles against Iraqi attacks.

The ground war began at 4 am on 24 February 1991. The poorly led Iraqis had surrendered mobility by entrenching themselves to protect their conquest of Kuwait, a repetition of the methods they had followed during the Iran–Iraq War of 1980–88 in order to protect their initial gains from Iranian counterattacks. Pessimistic predictions, for example by the former British Prime Minister Edward Heath, that the entrenchments would be difficult to take, and that the Iraqis would force attritional warfare on the Coalition, causing heavy casualties, proved totally mistaken. These predictions had led the Americans to provide a large number of medical units.[2]

While the Iraqis were attacked from the south on the direct route to Kuwait City, their right flank was outmanoeuvred by a rapid American advance from Saudi Arabia through the desert to the west of Kuwait City. This advance put pressure on the Iraqis when the outflanking American forces turned to attack them, destroying much of the Iraqi army on 27 February. The following morning, after a hundred hours of non-stop combat, George H.W. Bush ordered a ceasefire. The Iraqis had suffered over 50,000 dead, as well as 81,000 prisoners and the loss of nearly 4,000 tanks. In contrast, the Americans suffered 143 battle fatalities, 33 of them from 'friendly fire', a figure that reflected the difficulty of supplying in-time information about location and in ensuring action accordingly.

Despite the rapid victory, the American doctrine of AirLand Battle had proved, like other military concepts, more difficult to execute in practice than to advance in theory and to train for. This gap in part arose from the problems of synchronising air and land forces under fast-moving combat conditions. Nevertheless, compared to earlier conflicts, such as the Linebacker II American air offensive on North Vietnam in December 1972, there was unified control

15

over air operations, with a single air manager: the joint force air component commander. Moreover, target acquisition and accuracy were effective, the pace of the air attack was maintained, and this attack was successfully employed to affect operations on the ground.

Although the focus was on new technology, much of the weaponry was well established. Indeed, it was the bringing to higher, or optimal, performance of the latter that was very important. This, for example, was the case with tanks. The Gulf War of 1991 provided opportunities to display the major enhancement of the latter in the 1970s and 1980s, notably as a result of the use of composite armour, high-performance engines and high first-shot-kill capability gun systems, each of which was significant for improved performance. This exemplified the contrast between the weaponry of the last stage of the Cold War, and the World War Two legacy weapons models, and ideas that had been influential earlier. The Soviet-supplied Iraqi tanks were both technically inferior and poorly used, the latter a key point. The Iraqis dug in, believing that this would protect their tanks from air and tank attack, but they failed to understand the capabilities of both precision munitions and up-to-date tank gun technologies that ensured a high first-shot-kill capability even when only part of the turret was visible.

Some of the new technology performed very well. Cruise missiles successfully provided a new capability for surface warships, such as the World War Two battleship USS *Wisconsin*, demonstrating the capacity of the latter for littoral force projection. It was no longer necessary to rely on aircraft carriers for this capability.

In contrast, some high-tech weaponry, such as the British runway-cratering bombs and the American Patriot missile, did less well than was claimed at the time. In addition, important parts of the Allied military did not employ weaponry that was available. For example, the Americans used 9,300 precision-guided munitions, but most of their aircraft were not equipped nor their pilots trained for their use, and instead employed unguided munitions, which made up 90 per cent of the aerial munitions employed. This use of unguided munitions was in spite of the precedent set by the extensive and effective use of precision-guided munitions in the Linebacker I and II campaigns in Vietnam in 1972. The situation was to be different against Iraq in 2003. Similarly, in 1991, although the Americans had developed stealth aircraft, most of their planes lacked this expensive capability.[3]

The understandable focus on the American contribution to the Gulf War, which included over half a million military personnel, has led to an underestimation of the contribution of other states, and indeed of the impact of the war on other states. For all those militaries that took part, and the Coalition was far larger than was to be the case in 2003, the war raised issues of force projection, logistics and interoperability, notably with the USA, although the last was eased by the experience of many militaries in co-operation through the North Atlantic Treaty Organization (NATO).[4]

There was also an important contribution from states, principally Germany and Japan, that did not send troops into the combat zone, but that did provide financial support and/or indirect military help by freeing Coalition forces for operations. This was an instance of the wider pattern of Coalition warfare, an element that, again, was to be far weaker when Iraq was attacked in 2003.

The varied politics of the war had important military implications. The conflict, for example, saw attacks on Israel by Iraqi Scud missiles and, although they did not achieve their desired aim of bringing Israel into the war and thus jeopardising Arab military and political support for the USA, especially from Saudi Arabia and Syria, the missiles underlined Israeli vulnerability. Concerned that their deterrence had been lessened as a result of their inaction, the Israeli government wished to take reprisals on Iraq, but, aside from discouraging weather conditions, they were affected by American opposition to such action. The USA, however, did provide Israel with satellite information and Patriot missile batteries to protect them from Scuds.

The need for the USA and Israel to counter the military and, even more, political threat from Scud missiles, dramatised the implications of the spread of such weaponry. This was an issue that arose repeatedly thereafter, not least in 2013 when Syria used missiles to fire gas into rebel areas. American anti-missile doctrine had long focused on Soviet intercontinental ballistic missiles, but the challenge posed by the Scuds in 1991 indicated that short-range anti-missile defences and doctrine were also necessary, as well as drawing attention to the problems of relying on the Patriot missiles for that purpose.

More centrally to the Gulf War, the failure to keep military objectives and political goals in harmony helped ensure that the conflict did not lead to the hoped-for overthrow of Saddam Hussein. The American decision to end the offensive was taken in haste once Kuwait was cleared, in a war that was very high tempo, without an adequate consideration of how to translate the outcome of the campaign into a durable post-war settlement. The latter situation recurred, albeit in a very different context, in 2003.

This failure was linked in 1991 to military factors, specifically the persistence of 'friction' and 'fog': an inability to distinguish victory from the large-scale operational success which was obtained helped ensure that the wrong decisions were taken. The civilian leadership under George W. Bush permitted the decision to end the war to be governed by military considerations, specifically the expulsion of Iraqi forces from Kuwait. However, the major goal, in fact, was political: the need to create a stable post-war situation in the Gulf, the military preconditions for such stability being ultimately a political judgement.

It was not only with the benefit of hindsight that it became clear that the decision to end the war was taken too soon, jeopardising the prospect for victory: this was also apparent at the time. There were, however, concerns about the legal mandate and international backing for the invasion of Iraq (as opposed to the liberation of Kuwait). In part, the Coalition structure acted as a major constraint, but the UN mandate was also a significant factor.

There was also anxiety that overthrowing Saddam Hussein, the step seen as a necessary outcome to the war, might have unwelcome consequences. It was feared that his overthrow might lead to the dissolution of Iraq, as the Shia rebelled in the south, or, at least, could leave Iran too strong and thus challenge the balance of power in the Gulf. Such a challenge would threaten the interests both of the USA and of its allies. This, indeed, was to happen in 2003. Thus, 'realist' power politics played a significant role in 1991.

Nevertheless, whatever the benefit from liberating Kuwait and weakening Iraq in 1991, the end-result was highly unfortunate. After the Coalition ceased its advance, Saddam was able to employ his forces, particularly the Republican Guard (the army closest to him) and its plentiful artillery and tanks, to smash a rebellion in the south by the country's Shia majority, causing heavy casualties and destroying Shia shrines. This destruction was a key way of damaging Shia cohesion and demonstrating the regime's power. It corresponded to the destruction of churches and mosques in the conflicts in former Yugoslavia later in the decade.

In contrast, in Operation Provide Comfort, a multi-service, multi-national operation that was essentially a continuation of the Gulf War, Coalition forces protected the Kurds in northern Iraq from action by Saddam's forces. This protection was an important continuation to restraining Saddam and, in the longer term, to his overthrow in 2003. The 1991 war was also followed by the long-term use of Allied air power in order to try to prevent Iraq from rebuilding its military, but this proved an expensive commitment that had only limited success – not least because policing the 'no-fly zones' declared over Iraq was easier than influencing developments on the ground.[5] Furthermore, launched in response to the Iraqi refusal to allow in UN inspectors to assess their weapons programme, the Anglo-American Desert Fox bombing campaign in 1998 was not regarded as a success; although it has been argued that this campaign had an important effect on Iraqi decision-making.[6]

After the Cold War

American forces had been increasingly drawn into the Gulf from the end of Britain's 'east of Suez' presence and, more urgently, from the overthrow of the Shah in the Iranian Revolution of 1979.[7] However, the wider political context for Iraq, specifically the 1991 war, was not so much the Middle East, more specifically the Gulf, but rather Europe. The end of the Cold War with the collapse of the Soviet Union, which was dissolved at the close of 1991 as the former republics of the Soviet Union became independent states, was the crucial element.

The end of the Cold War did not lead to the 'end of history' or the 'peace dividend', both of which were foretold by some of the more superficial commentators who believed that Soviet collapse represented a triumph for American-led democratic capitalism, and that there would be no future clash of ideologies to destabilize the world. The military consequences, however, were significant. In what was a transformation in strategic affairs, the Western powers, led by the USA, were now able to intervene more frequently against states that earlier would otherwise have looked for Soviet support, not least because, aside from providing arms and military support, the Soviet Union would have vetoed supportive UN resolutions in the Security Council. Events in the UN did not match American expectations in 2003, but, whatever the situation there, the USA, from 1990, was better able to give effect to its strength. This shift in context proved fatal to Saddam Hussein in both 1991 and 2003.

Moreover, in the 1990s, this greater opportunity for intervention was accompanied by a drive for such intervention. The established parameters within which peacekeeping was generally expected to take place, especially that conflict had already ended and that the government of the state in question accepted the deployment of peacekeepers, were interpreted increasingly generously in favour of action. This change was seen with the use of terms such as 'peace support', 'peacemaking' and 'peace enforcement', instead of peacekeeping. Linked to such rationalisations, the tempo of operations increased after the end of the Cold War.[8]

Within sections of the 'international community', especially among jurists, there was a changing attitude towards the use of force. It was as if bellicosity was reformulated, away from being a justified aspect of the sovereignty of individual states. Instead, bellicosity was seen as a problem in others, and, in response, there was emphasis on a different bellicosity, one that was a necessity in pursuit of the maintenance of international order and the implementation of systemic norms. This view provided the background to ideas about the desirability of interventionist warfare. These ideas are not new, but their application was. It was, however, to become clear that these allegedly normative ideas could not readily overcome the values of opponents for whom compromise is unacceptable, force necessary, and even desirable, and war crucial to identity and self-respect.

Separately, interventionism encountered the problem that the leading Western power, the USA, had an ambivalent relationship with the constraints of collective security, especially with the UN, and not least with the notion of UN direction of operations involving American forces. The resulting tension helped lead to a significant degree of disenchantment with the UN on the part of the Bush administration and, conversely, with American policy across much of the world in the mid-2000s. That had military consequences, notably in the shape of a smaller Coalition involved against Iraq in 2003 than in 1991. As a result, there were fewer troops available for occupation duties than might otherwise have been the case. More troops would not necessarily have brought stability to Iraq, but they would have helped.

American force projection was not seriously challenged in the 1990s and 2000s by a revived Russia, the largest republic in the Soviet Union, because the collapse of the Soviet Union was not followed by a stronger Russia.

Instead, Russia confronted serious economic difficulties as the dismantling of the old command economy exposed the uncompetitive nature of much Soviet-era industry, while it proved difficult to establish effective monetary and fiscal mechanisms. Western loans were necessary in order to prevent a total collapse of Russia in the 1990s and, even so, debt payments caused a severe crisis in 1998, leading to default and devaluation.

From 1989, moreover, Soviet (and then Russian) power collapsed in Eastern Europe, and garrisons were withdrawn. The last Russian troops left the former East Germany in 1994. Moreover, former Russian allies joined NATO: Poland, the Czech Republic and Hungary being the first to do so in 1997. The former East Germany had already become a member of NATO with German unification in 1990, a step that led to the dismantling of the East German *Volksarmee* and the incorporation of some of its members into the West German *Bundeswehr*. As an indication of the geopolitical potential of Communist forces in Eastern Europe, East German military *matériel* was illicitly shipped to Iraq in 1990 by members of the *Volksarmee*.

With Russian weakness, the arithmetic of deterrence, underlined as it was both by the risk of MAD through potent arsenals, and by the threat of a conventional Soviet attack in Europe, no longer discouraged overt Western intervention in the Third World. Indeed, in 1994, the American and Russian leaders agreed not to target each other's states with their strategic nuclear weapons. The end of the Cold War also increased the number of potential allies for the West; and thus deepened its logistical capability (leading, for example, to plans for bases in Romania and Bulgaria), and strengthened its capacity for force projection. At the same time, this capacity was put at the service of a mixture of regional objectives, and a universalist aspiration to secure a more benign world order. This mixture, and, more specifically, the universalist aspiration, posed serious challenges not only to Western military capability but also to related political goals.

In particular, there were acute issues of prioritisation between alternative commitments, and also of how best to devise sensible political missions that matched military capability, and how best to organise and enhance the latter in order to secure missions. A variety of military devices and doctrines, such as American preparation for confronting two major regional crises simultaneously, and the American (from 1992) and British reconceptualisation of naval warfare away from conflict with other navies and, instead, towards littoral power projection, were important. However, these devices and doctrines did not address the issues of the sensible assessment of objectives and the political management of conflict.

Somalia

The specifics of objectives and implementation were, as is so often the case, difficult to cope with. From success in the Gulf War in 1991, attention usually turns to American failure in Somalia in 1993. That, indeed, is a key contrast that requires exposition, but it is one that is mishandled if the contrast is simply in terms of American success or failure. Instead, it is necessary to consider the particular nature of the Somali military and political environment, one that contrasted greatly with Iraq. The latter, in 1991, was a weaker surrogate for the Soviet Union and an opponent for which the American military was prepared by its planning and enhancements during the latter stages of the Cold War. Neither point was true of Somalia.

Moreover, American intervention in Somalia was in fact tangential to a bitter and lengthy period of conflict there, a point that was also the case, on a far greater scale, for the earlier intervention in Vietnam and for the later one in Afghanistan. Following Somalia's failure in the Ogaden war with Soviet-backed Ethiopia in 1977–78, a key episode in regional power politics and a largely overlooked Cold War conflict, a weaker President Barre had faced growing opposition from clans which, increasingly, obtained heavier arms. In addition, the Somali National Movement mounted a serious challenge to Barre from 1978, although, in 1988, the government was able to drive them from the northern towns they had seized, albeit causing heavy civilian casualties in the process. In 1989–90, other resistance movements further eroded Barre's position, full-scale civil war broke out and Barre fled into exile in January 1991, mounting unsuccessful attempts to return that April, as well as in April and September 1992.

Somalia, which had been united only under recent Western imperial rule, was increasingly split into areas uneasily controlled by clan factions. Each of these factions deployed artillery and armoured vehicles, as well as the light lorries carrying heavy machine-guns which were a distinctive feature of Somali warfare. These off-road lorries were more generally used across much of North Africa, for example in Chad, enabling a bypassing of the meagre road network. Such lorries were to be seen again during the Libyan civil war in 2011. Several of the Somali clans, the key element in Somali society, also made use of child fighters. These elements are still the case of conflict within Somalia.

The UN intervened in Somalia in 1992 in order to bring humanitarian relief, although also to resolve immediate security problems. The UN forces, however, were inadequate to the latter task, and the ambiguity of the mission helped to lead to chaos. The Americans, in Operation Restore Hope, initially provided 28,000 men of the 37,000 UN force, their advance guard arriving to great publicity on the beach of the dusty capital, Mogadishu. Mohamed Farah Aideed, whose faction dominated the south of Mogadishu, was a key local figure. The rivalry between Aideed and the Abgal subclan under Ali Mahdi Mohamed, which dominated northern Mogadishu, was an important backdrop to UN intervention as the UN force originally sent to Somalia was, in part, designed to help maintain a ceasefire between the two factions that had been brokered by the UN in March 1992.

In May 1993, the scope of the UN forces expanded when, in pursuit of a secure environment in which to ground the government of Somalia, they were given the task of disarming the factions and controlling all heavy weapons. By then, the forces were 28,000 strong, including an American quick reaction force. Aideed opposed this UN mission, and, on 5 June 1993, his men ambushed a Pakistani unit, killing twenty-four men. This urban ambush led the UN, supported by the USA, to move against Aideed, action which included mounting a helicopter gunship attack on 12 July. In an escalating crisis, attacks by Aideed on US troops in August led the American government to dispatch Special Operations Forces that were intended to capture hostile clan leaders, particularly Aideed.

On 3 October 1993, the American Task Force Ranger captured several Aideed supporters (but not Aideed) in a raid in Mogadishu; but then met opposition, with two helicopters shot down. As a result, the Somalis that day gained the initiative on the ground, while the Americans were spread out and vulnerable. Evacuation needs therefore became far more complex. Helicopters provided vital cover as well as dropping water, but the attempt to provide ground relief that day failed. In the clash that continued until the force was relieved by American, Pakistani and Malaysian ground troops early next day, the Americans lost 18 dead and 83 wounded, while about 500 Somalis were killed.

Most of the Americans were successfully evacuated despite heavy odds, and several key Aideed supporters had been captured, but the operation was perceived as a failure by the relatively risk-averse Clinton government and by an American population not prepared for losses and unclear about goals in Somalia. There had certainly been over-confidence on the part of government and commanders alike.[9] The raid was in practice no more than a check, but it led to serious questions being raised in the USA about the purpose of the American commitment and about the long-term prospect. In reaction to their losses, the Americans abandoned aggressive operations in Somalia, deciding, on 5 October 1993, to withdraw all American troops by the following March.

Bin Laden

This decision was seized on by Osama bin Laden, the Saudi-born leader of the Islamicist terrorist movement al-Qaeda, to argue that the Americans could be forced to retreat as the Soviets had been from Afghanistan in 1989. The fall of the Soviet Union also played an important role in the myth-making that helped encourage bin Laden. Drawing on Egyptian and Saudi Arabian fundamentalist theology and Islamicist political culture, and on Saudi money, bin Laden's movement was a rejection of the West, of modernity and of what were perceived to be the secular allies of both in the Muslim world, as well as an aspect of deep-rooted tensions, for example Sunni hostility towards Shias.

In opposition to the West, al-Qaeda drew on a widespread anxiety, frustration and anger in parts of the Muslim world, and on a rejectionism that was not interested in debate or on what outsiders would perceive as a rational assessment. Believing in mission and inevitability, bin Laden sought to fit events into a panorama demonstrating the truth of his prospectus.

The collapse of the Soviet Union proved a key episode as this was presented as arising from the Soviet failure in Afghanistan in the 1980s, a failure in which future members of al-Qaeda had played a role, including bin Laden. Supposedly the war in Afghanistan demonstrated that faith could overcome an advanced power.[10] In practice, this was a serious misjudgement of the relationship between failure in Afghanistan and Soviet collapse. The latter collapse was largely due to the interaction of Gorbachev's policies with nationalism both in Eastern Europe and within the Soviet Union. Moreover, bin Laden greatly underplayed the role of Western, especially American, support in Afghanistan, notably in the provision of missiles able to curtail the role of Soviet air superiority (although he was keen to acquire such technology for his own use), and also did not note the extent to which the Soviets only devoted a relatively small percentage of their military resources to the Afghan war.[11] Instead, the Soviet military in the 1980s focused heavily on confrontation with NATO and, to a lesser extent, China.

The belief that the Americans could also be forced to retreat helped inspire bin Laden's 'Declaration of War against the Americans Occupying the Land of the Two Holy Places', issued in August 1996. The Declaration called for the expulsion of American forces from Saudi Arabia, where their presence was a legacy of the Gulf War of 1990–91, and for the overthrow of what was seen as the pro-American Saudi government.

Bin Laden's response was a prime instance of the Islamist jihadist internationalism (albeit a bitterly divided internationalism) that became more significant in the late twentieth century. In part, this development was a response to the Iranian Revolution in 1979 (the basis for Shia activism), and, in part, it arose from the opposition to Soviet forces in Afghanistan, which proved the basis for Sunni jihadist revivalism. This ideological radicalisation, which drew on broader currents of hostility to globalisation, Westernisation and Christianity, was a key element in the changing ideological context of conflict in the Islamic world. That the Soviet Union and the USA, whose bitter rivalry had defined the Cold War, could be lumped together in this analysis, indicated the extent to which Islamic jihadist internationalism involved very different conceptions of the international system and, thereby, of the military situation.

From the jihadist perspective, another similarity was provided by asymmetrical warfare. This was seen as providing an opportunity to counter and then overcome the strength of Western conventional forces and their preparedness for symmetrical conflict. Suicide military operations were a particular dramatic version of asymmetrical warfare.

Africa and American caution

Most of the American troops left Somalia in March 1994, while the UN forces withdrew in March 1995.[12] Faction fighting continued, and the number of factions increased, as did civilian casualties. By 2003, the country was divided into about twenty-five warring fiefdoms while clashes continued. Somalia also became a setting for al-Qaeda, with the *Shabab* group formed in 2005. By 2008 Somalia was regarded as one of al-Qaeda's leading areas of operation.

After 1994, in response to failure in Somalia, no American combat troops were sent on peacekeeping missions to Africa. This was a policy that limited the options for international intervention during the Rwanda Crisis in 1994, and in 2003, when pressure built up for UN intervention in the mounting crisis in Congo, the American government made it clear that it would not send troops. Moreover, in Liberia, a state founded by America in the early nineteenth century that was devastated in the 1990s by civil war, the Americans restricted themselves essentially to providing logistical support for Nigerian peacekeepers. American interests in sub-Saharan Africa had been attacked when al-Qaeda directed truck bomb attacks on American embassies in Nairobi and Dar es Salaam in 1998, but, in the aftermath of failure in Somalia in 1993, American military engagement with the continent remained limited. African members of al-Qaeda active in the 1998 attacks were to play a major role in the formation of the *Shabab* in Somalia in 2005. Far from being a failed state of no wider consequence, Somalia was a central location in a wider network of terror.

The culture of the American military

In October 2007, Robert Gates, the Secretary of Defense, told the conference of the Association of the United States Army:

> In the years following the Vietnam War, the Army relegated unconventional war to the margins of training, doctrine, and budget priorities ... This approach may have seemed validated by ultimate victory in the Cold War and the triumph of Desert Storm. But it left the service unprepared to deal with the operations that followed: Somalia, Haiti, the Balkans, and more recently Afghanistan and Iraq – the consequences and costs of which we are still struggling with today.

The culture of the American military played a key role, as notions of self- and collective-worth and institutional culture were closely bound up with regular warfare. Failure in Vietnam and Somalia encouraged this assessment. The equivalent counterpointing of regular and counter-insurgency warfare with hard and soft power contributed to this, as the former was felt to be more masculine. There was also a linguistic tendency to regard regular warfare as real or true warfare, and irregular warfare, and thus counter-insurgency warfare, as a corruption that could, and should, be compartmentalised. In part, this response drew on the reaction within the American military to the Vietnam War, and the strong sense that failure there was a result of inappropriate tasking, a sense that was a means of confronting the memory.

The contrast with success in the 1991 Gulf War underlined this perception. Moreover, within the American army and elsewhere, there was uneasiness about the extent to which a stress on counter-insurgency warfare might lead to a diminished ability to engage successfully in regular warfare.

There was also opposition to military operations other than war (MOOTW), even though they were part of a long-standing pattern in American military activity, for example in the Caribbean.[13] This opposition looked towards the unwillingness of the military to heed advice from the State Department about the need to plan carefully for the aftermath of the conquest of Iraq in 2003.

Haiti

Failure in Somalia did not prevent American action nearer home, where political sensitivities were stronger. In Operation Uphold Democracy in 1994, the USA sent 20,000 troops to Haiti in pursuit of a UN mandate to restore Jean-Bertrand Aristide, the President deposed by a military coup in 1991. This intervention was seen as a way to stop the flight of Haitian refugees to the USA, and was an instance of the extent to which population movements helped prompt military actions. In this case, the pressures of domestic American politics against such immigration provided a key impetus. There was also a long tradition of American intervention in the Caribbean, including Haiti.

In the event, Aristide's restoration was achieved by negotiation rather than force, although it proved difficult to make Haitian society conform to the goals of the subsequent US-dominated UN peacekeeping mission; and the later history of Haiti was far from benign.[14] Indeed, the corruption and violence associated with the Aristide regime culminated with his overthrow in 2004. This overthrow was due to a domestic rising, but was linked to American pressure on the regime and against the associated violence, a violence that, in turn, led to the deployment of American and French troops.

The peacekeeping and humanitarian support goals of the interventions in Haiti and Somalia were correctly described as low-intensity conflict, as any comparison with the wars against Iraq in 1991 and 2003 would demonstrate. However, these interventions were still difficult and dangerous for the troops involved, and the mission culture that stemmed from the nature of peace-keeping added to the difficulty. It proved hard to secure adequate and timely intelligence, both military and political, and to bring the two into line, while the unpreparedness of the American military for operating in urban environments was revealed in Mogadishu. The relative ease of Operation Joint Cause, the rapid overthrow of the regime of the drug-dealing General Noriega in Panama in December 1989, proved no real preparation for the problems, both military and political, of Mogadishu in 1993. As a result of the fate of the latter intervention, Operation Uphold Democracy in Haiti was supported by adequate force. Moreover, it was no accident that American defence expenditure rose in the early 1990s under George H.W. Bush, before falling under his successor, Bill Clinton.

Yet, as always, the adequacy of force depended largely on the political context and on the skill with which the mission was crafted. The American preference for being prepared for warfighting led to a practice of overwhelming force that worked in Panama and Haiti. This emphasis differed from the British preference for minimum necessary force, as well, more seriously, as from the necessity for long-term commitment focused on nation-building.

The former Soviet Union

Action of a very different type characterised the former Soviet Union, as competing interests sought to direct the fate of successor republics or, indeed, to ensure, or prevent, their dissolution. Thus, the army of the newly independent Georgian state used force in an unsuccessful attempt to resist separatism by the Muslim province of Abkhazia, but the latter received crucial Russian diplomatic and military assistance. More than 200,000 Georgians (over half of the population of Abkhazia) were driven from their homes. A Russian 'peacekeeping' force is still there in order to pre-empt any possible action by Georgia, and to demonstrate that Russia can protect its protégés. The lesson was driven home in 2008 when, in a swift offensive, Russia successfully intervened against Georgia in order to protect separatist protégés in South Ossetia. The Russian dominance of the region was a backdrop to the Winter Olympics in nearby Sochi in 2014.

Further east, following the collapse of the Soviet Union, the newly independent republics of Armenia and Azerbaijan fought in the Caucasus, in 1992–94, over control of the region of Nagorno-Karabakh, a struggle won by Armenia.[15] Over 1 million Azerbaijanis became refugees in this bitter war, one in which 'ethnic cleansing' played a major role.

There was also a bitter clan-based civil war in Tajikistan between 1992 and 1997 in which about 50,000 people were killed. There, a 25,000-strong, Russian-dominated peacekeeping force helped ensure the defeat of the southern groups, including Muslim fundamentalists, that had contested the dominance of northerners, although the resolution was not peace but rather a guerrilla struggle. Pressure to end the conflict in 1997 in part reflected concern that Taliban success in Afghanistan would be followed by Taliban intervention in Central Asia, a 'domino effect' similar to that feared by America during the Vietnam War.

At a smaller scale, Uzbeks and Meskhetian Turks fought in the Ferghana Valley of Uzbekistan, a long-standing area of tension. Further west, the 'Trans-Dniester Republic', supported by the forces of the former Soviet 14th Army, sought to break away from the newly independent republic of Moldova. The net effect was of a weakening of the once-powerful Soviet military, and also an increase in the number of states facing insurrections. This was an important aspect of the more general situation in which conflict within states in the 1990s was more widespread than Western expeditionary warfare.

The USA and other Western powers benefited from the collapse of the Soviet Union to establish a degree of military co-operation with some of the successor states, a key instance of the more widespread relationship between military assistance programmes and political, ideological and economic change, if not transformation. For example, from 1994, Ukraine's military was given American money under military co-operation programmes, and some of its officers were trained in the USA.[16] Georgia also turned to the West. Russia, however, bitterly opposed NATO expansion and in 2013 its pressure helped lead Ukraine to reject talks on joining the European Union (EU). In 2014, a change of government in Ukraine in response to popular pressure led Russia to seize Crimea.

The deficiencies of the Soviet military were to be cruelly demonstrated in the accidental sinking of the nuclear submarine *Kursk* in 2000, which dramatised the decline of Russian naval power. The Soviet navy had become the second-largest naval power during the Cold War, but it became increasingly obsolescent in the 1980s and 1990s as it proved impossible to sustain the cost of new units, and in the 1990s the navy was gravely affected by the break-up of the Soviet Union. This break-up was particularly important in the case of the Black Sea naval base of Sevastopol, which came under the authority of Ukraine, and was affected by the tension between pro- and anti-Russian movements there before being seized by Russia in 2014.

More profound problems were revealed in the northern Caucasus, where the Russians encountered serious difficulties from Muslim separatist movements that were able to rely on considerable popular support, in part because of a long tradition of ethnic strife and, specifically, of opposition to Russia. Russian expansion had been bitterly resisted in the nineteenth century, and there had been a series of rebellions against Soviet rule.

The Chechen Republic of the Russian Federation was a centre of separatism, and in 1991 it declared its independence from Russia. The Chechen President, Dzhokhar Dudayev, represented an interesting combination of military traditions. He had risen through the Soviet air force, becoming its first Chechen general and commanding strategic nuclear bombers based in Estonia. In Afghanistan in the 1980s, Dudayev had developed a new bombing strategy against the *Mujahideen*, the Afghans resisting Soviet control. Yet, he had also come to be impressed by the nationalism of the Afghans and Estonians, and adopted the guerrilla tactics of the former. In Chechnya, Dudayev issued a decree giving every man the right to bear arms. In 1993, he used National Guard units to dissolve a provisional supreme council appointed by Boris Yeltsin, the Russian President.

Yeltsin was unwilling to accept separatism, not least because of oil in the area, and his fear of the consequences in terms of encouraging separatism in nearby areas of Russia, notably along the northern Caucasus. Yeltsin was also concerned that political opponents would accuse him of being weak. He therefore responded by invading Chechnya in December 1994. The previous month, a covert attack on Grozny to help pro-Russian groups fighting Dudayev's supporters had failed. In December, the Russians deployed nearly 24,000 troops, including 4,700 from the Ministry of Internal Affairs Forces (a key paramilitary force), as well as 80 tanks and 90 helicopters. Many, however, were poorly trained.

Russian forces captured the capital, Grozny, in January 1995 after lengthy and difficult operations in which they employed devastating firepower, especially intensive artillery barrages and bombing, in a city of near half a million people. This city provided a terrain ideally suited to well-motivated opponents; many Chechens were former Soviet soldiers who understood urban fighting tactics. Rocket-propelled grenades were employed effectively in attacks on Soviet armoured vehicles, while ambushes were frequent. The Russians were eventually successful, although many of their opponents escaped.

Brutality and intransigence, however, encouraged resistance which the Russians were unable to crush. In 1996, they withdrew (and the Chechens occupied Grozny) under a peace agreement, in order to strengthen Yeltsin's position in a presidential campaign. The 1994–96 campaigns revealed the deficiencies of the badly led, badly equipped, badly motivated and under-strength Russian forces. Not least among these deficiencies was the lack of appropriate training and doctrine for counter-insurgency warfare, despite the experience of war in Afghanistan in 1979–88. The Russian preference in Chechnya for large-scale firepower reflected the dominance, in their doctrine and practice, of preparations for conventional war with the West.[17] More seriously, but in a related fashion, the Russians appeared to have no response other than force and yet could not use that effectively, nor really afford it. The Russians added to the usual problems affecting counter-insurgency policies, the difficulty of transforming these policies into peacekeeping; they failed at both.

It is also necessary to emphasise large Chechen numbers and the extent to which the Chechens, while poorly disciplined, were well-armed (if short of ammunition) and determined.[18] Many indeed had also been trained through conscription in the Soviet army. The rebels, moreover, were able to receive support from across the region's borders.

The renewed Russian attack on Chechnya in 2000 was provoked by Chechen moves into neighbouring Daghestan, and by explosions in Moscow blamed on Chechen terrorists. In Daghestan, about 600 members of the

Wahhabi sect, some of them Daghestanis, but many not, sought both to destroy Russian power and also to coerce the population, most of whom were moderate Muslims. Control of the villages was contested, as the rebels were not strong enough to seize the capital, Makhachkala. The rival forces essentially operated in different environments: the rebels on paths, the mechanised Russian forces on roads. This was a long-standing pattern of insurrectionary and counter-insurgency warfare, also seen in Afghanistan.

In practice, the explosions in Moscow, and possibly even the fighting in Daghestan, may have reflected the direct or indirect intervention of the Russian secret police, whose malign influence can be compared with that of the Inter-Services Intelligence Agency (the ISI) in Pakistan. The renewed attack on Chechnya certainly reflected the determination of a secret police product, Yeltsin's Prime Minister, and eventual successor, Vladimir Putin, to assert control. Putin's willingness to turn to the military looked towards the Russian use of force against Georgia in 2008 and Crimea in 2014.

The Russian campaign in Chechnya led to the fall of Grozny in January 2000, but indicated military deficiencies similar to the Russian campaigning in 1994–96. As with other forces battling insurgency, the Russians suffered from the problem of inadequate intelligence, which reflected the limitations of surveillance in such contexts. In such a situation, later seen with Coalition forces in Iraq and Afghanistan, there was an over-reliance on firepower responses, often poorly directed. This point underlines the extent to which Russia can seem part of the West from the perspective of a radical Muslim. Guerrilla opposition in Chechnya, including suicide bombings there and elsewhere in Russia, continued, and, in response, the Russians mounted raids on guerrilla areas and seized suspected Chechens. Opposition was firmest in the mountainous south.[19] The extent to which news could be managed in Russia helped ensure that the apparently intractable nature of the situation in Chechnya received insufficient attention in Russia other than in terms of a dangerous terrorist movement. Western commentators did not make adequate use of comparisons with Chechnya when discussing policies in Iraq and Afghanistan.

Chechnya did not delimit what was a spreading pattern of violent Muslim opposition in Russia, especially elsewhere in the northern Caucasus. This spread even led to concern about the stability of Russia vis à vis a widespread and sustained terrorist movement.[20] The differential birth rates of Muslims and non-Muslims made this issue apparently more acute, as did the extent to which Russian populism could have a racist tinge.

Former Yugoslavia

While the fall of the Soviet Union led to conflict in the Caucasus, the disintegration of Yugoslavia in 1991 into its constituent republics had the same effect in the Balkans. A federal state held together earlier by its Communist dictator from 1945 to 1980, Josip Tito, Yugoslavia was divided between ethnic groups, most prominently Serbs and Croats, that sought independence for the areas they dominated and pursued the widest possible definition of the latter. As, and after, the Yugoslav state collapsed, Franjo Tudjman, the authoritarian President of Croatia from 1991 to 1999, used nationalism to provide both identity and rationale for his power; and the same was true of Serbia under Slobodan Milošević from 1989 to 2000. Moreover, in 1991, in the far north of the country, about 70,000 men out of a population of only 2 million Slovenes mobilised in order to resist attempts to prevent Slovene independence, and the Serb-dominated Yugoslav army did not push the issue to widespread conflict. The threat of large-scale resistance won Slovenia its independence, a process encouraged by its distance from Serbia.

In contrast, the army made a far greater effort against Croatia which, unlike Slovenia, both had a border with Serbia and contained a large Serb minority. This war, which began in the Krajina region in the summer of 1991, with bitter fighting that autumn over the city of Vukovar, spilled over into Bosnia. One of the Yugoslav republics, Bosnia was ethnically mixed, with large Croat (Catholic), Serb (Orthodox) and Bosnian (Muslim) populations. Suffering from both Croat and Serbian expansion, each of the communities in Bosnia formed an army. The Bosnian Serbian and Bosnian Croat forces co-operated with the armies of Serbia and Croatia, pursuing their own and joint objectives. The Bosnian Muslims proved particularly vulnerable.

The conflicts in Yugoslavia were brutal, involving, for example, the killing of prisoners and civilians, but also limited. War there entailed demonstration and negotiation, a politics by military means that were intensively political, a mixture of sudden and brief brutality, with truces and convoluted strategies of diplomacy. Fighting in the Bosnian capital, Sarajevo, from 1992 to 1995 included high-intensity street fighting, but served as much as a tool for propaganda as for military advantage. Bosnian Serb bombardments of the city were aimed at political or psychological targets, rather than at military objectives that could help capture the city.[21] At the same time, the disruption was acute and most of the Bosnian population became refugees, fleeing to areas under sympathetic control or abroad.

Western intervention to end a conflict on Europe's doorstep was weakened by a combination of European weakness and American reluctance to act. The latter was the case with the indecisive President Clinton (1993–2001), but also with an American military leadership concerned about mission creep and the problems of fighting insurgent forces in difficult terrain. The United Nations Protection Force, created in April 1992 in response to the outbreak of civil war in Bosnia, proved too weak and restricted to maintain order and, in particular, to restrain the aggression of the Bosnian Serbs. NATO launched its first combat action, air strikes in 1994, but they were limited in number and affected by restrictive rules of engagement.

Despite this, settlements were eventually imposed in Bosnia in 1995 and in Kosovo in 1999, at the expense of the expansionism and ethnic aggression of a Serbian regime that unsuccessfully looked for Russian sponsorship. The West played a major role, with 3,515 sorties flown and 100 cruise missiles fired (as well as artillery used against the Serbs), in Operation Deliberate Force in 1995, the first large-scale NATO combat mission.[22]

Yet, the ability of Serbia's opponents, especially the Croats, to organise military forces capable of opposing the Serbs in the field was more important than NATO efforts in preventing Serb victory, and then in taking war to the Serbs. This ability was seen in the autumn of 1995 when the Croats and the Bosnian Muslims, who had been brought together in 1994 in part by American pressure, and who received American arms and money, were able to mount successful offensives against the Serbs and the Bosnian Serbs. The Croats overran, first, western Slavonia and, then, the Krajina, while the Bosnian Serbs were driven from central Bosnia. The attacking forces, which were assisted by a private military company, Military Professional Resources Incorporated, may have numbered 200,000 men. Combined with NATO air attack and diplomatic pressure, these offensives pushed the Serbs into accepting the Dayton peace agreement on 21 November 1995. This agreement left Bosnia as a federation of Serb and Croat-Muslim zones, each of which, in turn, were divided into self-governing cantons.

The brutal slaughter of civilians by the Serbs (and, to a lesser extent, by their opponents) was an all-too-familiar feature of conflict in much of the modern world, and reflected the extent to which ethnic groups were seen as the units of political strength, and thus as targets. In July 1995, the Bosnian Serbs murdered about 7,000 unarmed Bosnian Muslim males in Srebrenica, which had been designated a safe zone by UN representatives whose peace-keeping force was too weak and too focused on self-preservation to prevent the massacre. The restrictive nature of the instructions under which UN forces operated was also a serious issue. It became clear that humanitarian inter-ventions required a very robust military dimension, able to provide effective protection and to ensure coercion.

Among the combatants in the former Yugoslavia, what was termed 'ethnic cleansing' – the expulsion of members of an ethnic group – was more common than massacres. Ethnic cleansing was generally associated with the Serbs, but was also used by the Croats on a major scale, for example against Serbs in the Krajina.[23] Croat action does not excuse Serb actions, but it helps explain the paranoia that characterised Serbian policy-makers.

In turn, such action against civilians led to pressure on outside powers to adapt existing views on peacekeeping in order to adopt a proactive policy of peace enforcement focused on humanitarian goals. This new priority over-came earlier hesitations about military action.[24] The NATO Implementation Force (IFOR) sent in to ensure compliance with the Dayton Accords was more powerful than the UN force had been. It included 57,000 troops,

20,000 of them Americans. With the end of the Cold War, they were no longer required to protect West Germany from Soviet attack, but bases there aided a deployment to Bosnia. In December 1996, IFOR became the Stabilization Force. This was a successful deployment, and fighting markedly declined.[25]

Humanitarian goals were central to liberal internationalism, which became more pronounced as a theme in Western policy in the 1990s. Such intervention, however, presupposed that success could be readily obtained, and belief in this intervention relied on the notion of a clear capability gap between the two sides. Indeed, from the humanitarian perspective, the forces of 'good' had to be successful in order to avoid the suffering that could result from military operations. These suppositions helped explain the difficulties faced by Anglo-American representatives when they discussed the numerous Iraqi civilian casualties arising from the war of 2003 and, far more, its aftermath.

Later in the 1990s, in order to suppress separatist demands, as well as to destroy support for the Kosovo Liberation Army, which had begun attacks on the police in 1996, the Serbs also used the tactics of ethnic cleansing in Kosovo. This was part of Serbia with a majority ethnic Albanian and Muslim population where the Serbian regime had long resisted demands for autonomy. The Western response over Kosovo was coercive diplomacy which, in 1999, became a forceful humanitarian mission, Operation Allied Force. Costing over \$3 billion, the resulting seventy-seven-day bombing and cruise missile assault by American, British and French forces (and other NATO countries) was far less effective than Operation Deliberate Force had been in 1995. President Clinton, nevertheless, made public his unwillingness to commit land forces as well.

Yet, the air assault helped lead in 1999 to the Serb withdrawal and acceptance of a ceasefire, which was followed by the establishment of a NATO peacekeeping force headed by Britain, France, Germany, Italy and the USA. Thereafter, the continuing isolation of Serbia, in a successful form of economic and financial warfare, contributed to an erosion of support for Milošević and his fall in the face of Serbian popular action in 2000.

In 1999, George Robertson, the British Secretary of State for Defence (and later Secretary General of NATO), publicly scorned commentators who warned about the difficulty of winning the Kosovo conflict by air power alone, and also about the contrast between output (bomb and missile damage) and outcome. However, the use of air power in Bosnia had already amply demonstrated the problems of managing an air assault when the alliance responsible was divided about its application. The NATO air attack in 1999 suffered the loss of only two aircraft, but the subsequent Serbian withdrawal from Kosovo revealed that NATO estimates of the damage inflicted by air attack, for example to Serb tanks, had been considerably exaggerated. The Serbs benefited in practice from the limitations of NATO intelligence information and its serious consequences for NATO targeting, and from the severe impact of the weather on NATO air operations, a large number of which were cancelled or affected. As a result, despite 10,000 NATO strike sorties, employing simple and inexpensive camouflage techniques that took advantage of the mountainous terrain and the wooded cover, the Serbs preserved most of their equipment.

Furthermore, the air offensive had not prevented the large-scale expulsion of Kosovars from their homes, and this brutal expulsion badly compromised the success of the NATO operation. Indeed, the Serbian ethnic cleansing campaign, Operation Horseshoe, increased as the air attack was mounted.

The Serb withdrawal in 1999 may have owed more to a conviction, based in part on Russian information and the build-up of American forces in Albania, that a NATO land attack was imminent, as well as to the withdrawal of Russian support, rather than to the air offensive. In practice, French, German and, eventually, American rejection of British pressure for such an invasion indicated their doubts of its feasibility. Indeed, a land attack on Kosovo faced serious logistical challenges and was dependent on the willingness of neighbouring countries to provide access and bases. This lack of willingness, especially on the part of Greece which was unwilling to permit the use of the port of Thessaloniki, contributed to the mistake of not preparing adequate options in the event of the air offensive failing. Albania, to the west of Kosovo, represented a far less attractive option as a base, not least for reasons of weak transport infrastructure, limited logistical capability and poor invasion routes into Kosovo.

The 'what if' counterfactual involved in considering the likely consequences of a land attack serves as a reminder that possible conflicts were an important aspect of the military history of the period as they entailed a consideration of effectiveness and likely capability. In turn, the consequences affected decisions on procurement and, in the short term, influenced political perceptions of the possible.

The Kosovo crisis suggested that air power, as so often, would be most effective as part of a joint strategy, rather than as a strategic tool alone. Indeed, ground and air threats were not totally separate: the eventual threat to the Serbs on the ground from a NATO invasion made their forces vulnerable to air attack, as it made dispersal, rather than concentration, a less viable proposition. Moreover, although the damage to the Serbian army from air attack was limited, the devastation of Serbia's infrastructure, in the shape of bridges, factories and electrical power plants, was important, not least because it greatly affected the financial interests of the élite as well as their morale, and the functioning of the economy. Thus, there was a marked contrast between the limited tactical and operational impact of air power, and its possibly more effective strategic consequences.

The issues of the legitimate and effective use of force were prominently raised in 1999 as action and intervention were debated. The majority of the Kosovars expelled returned to their homes in the wake of the Serbian withdrawal. Their return was key to the claims of 'success' for the NATO operation.[26] Kosovo, however, then saw much violence against Serbian civilians by ethnic Albanians. Moreover, Kosovo, like Bosnia, remained tense and in 2004 there were murderous anti-Serbian riots in the Kosovo town of Mitrovica. The perspective on Western intervention varies greatly with some commentators sympathetic to the Kosovars, while others regard their leaders as essentially criminals, and are more sympathetic to the Serbs. Religious affiliations and animosities further complicate perceptions.[27]

So also with Macedonia (the Greeks insist that it is termed the Former Yugoslav Republic of Macedonia) in 1999–2001. A crisis there built up until, in 2001, the interaction of ethnic grievance, political demonisation and security problems led to the escalation of what the government termed a 'semi-criminal battle in a lawless region' into an insurrection by the National Liberation Army. This was a new ethnic Albanian guerrilla group that looked to neighbouring Kosovo. This insurrection, however, was checked by a NATO-backed counter-attack before a political agreement was negotiated. In the fighting, the Macedonians used attack helicopters and artillery, but also found that they could only achieve so much, notably in the fighting around Aracinovo in June 2001.[28]

The strength of the West

The use and experience of Western military power in the 1990s offered different conclusions. On the whole, there was a major burst of optimism about Western prospects, which drew on the combination of the collapse of the Soviet Union, the rapid defeat of Iraq and belief in a revolution in military affairs, indeed the Revolution in Military Affairs. The major growth of the American economy was also very important. Benefiting from the important structural reforms of the late 1970s and 1980s, which, in part, entailed a move away from earlier corporatist practices towards neo-liberalism, and from the speedy diffusion of more efficient economic practices and from large-scale investment, the American economy grew rapidly. International trade liberalisation in the 1990s was also important to American growth, not least as it aided outsourcing.

In contrast to claims about likely decline, most prominently by the historian Paul Kennedy in 1988,[29] America's position in the global economy was indicated by the substantial rise in its share of global exports – from 15.7 per cent in 1993 to 17.7 per cent in 1999 – and that in the period of major growth in world trade. There was also a rise in the American percentage of the world's growing gross domestic product (GDP) and America's contribution to the increasing gap in per capita income between the West and the rest. The dollar continued to dominate foreign exchange trades, accounting, in 2001, for just under 45 per cent of global foreign exchange turnover. The American economy and public finances were the main targets for investment both from the Middle East and from East Asia. America therefore benefited both from growing world demand for oil and from the major expansion in the Chinese economy.

The greater potency of American ballistic missiles offered a hard-edged demonstration of this American power and wealth. The Trident II D-5 sea-launched missile, deployed from 1990, considerably increased the accuracy of such missiles, while the ability to use the W88 warhead with the missile increased its yield and, therefore, capability.[30] Military success in the 1991 Gulf War and in the 1999 Kosovo campaign, moreover, led other states to seek to emulate aspects of the RMA or, at least, the technology involved.

The change with China was particularly instructive, as China had adopted a military ideology of asymmetry during the period of control by Mao Zedong (1949–76), while, in addition, the Communist regime remained in power, unlike in the Soviet Union. Aware of a major capability gap, China departed from Maoist principles and changed the curriculum in the National Defence University in pursuit of a Chinese RMA that could cope with the lack of campaigning experience since the 1978–79 war with Vietnam. The Chinese focused on the need to learn from the American example.[31]

However, at the same time, there were signs of limitations in Western military effectiveness and capability. The setback in Somalia in 1993 and the delay in achieving success over Kosovo in 1999 were both indicative of wider problems. The Israelis, for example, found it difficult to suppress opposition in southern Lebanon and in the occupied Palestinian territories. In 1987, the *intifada*, a rebellion against Israeli rule in occupied territories, and specifically against the pace of Israeli settlement on the West Bank (Palestine west of the River Jordan), began with stone-throwing crowds challenging Israeli authority. The *intifada* was to underline the weakness of imposed political settlements in the Middle East where the bulk of any population felt alienated, and also to expose the limitations of regular troops in the face of popular resistance. The Israeli military encountered problems in dealing with what was to them a novel form of warfare, one far less welcome than conventional conflict with regular Arab armies. The Oslo Agreement of 1993, and the subsequent creation of a Palestinian autonomous territory on the West Bank under Yasser Arafat, was to fail to prevent a resumed escalation of conflict in the 2000s.

In southern Lebanon, Hizbullah, a Shia guerrilla force, offered a stronger opposition to Israeli pressure than that mounted there earlier in the 1980s by the guerrillas of the Palestinian Liberation Organization and by Syrian regulars. Willing to take casualties, Hizbullah enjoyed Iranian support and was able to respond tactically to Israeli advantages, not least by employing surface-to-air missiles against Israeli air power. In Israeli attacks on Hizbullah forces in April 1996, the use of advanced technology, such as American Bell AH-1 Cobra helicopter gunships by the Israelis and of Soviet Katyusha rockets by their opponents, indicated the extent to which modern weapons systems were widely employed. The remarks of a Hizbullah spokesman that month are interesting: 'Do not say because we are weaker we should give in. Israel is not so strong. Look at the Vietnamese. Did they stop because America was stronger?' The spokesman was guarded by a fighter carrying an American M16 assault rifle.[32]

The problems of Western military power were particularly relevant to the gap between output, which could be delivered, and outcome, which was far harder to achieve. These problems were not really related to a failure to maintain military strength, but the latter was also notable, not least in affecting the number of operations that could be mounted. Under President Bill Clinton (1993–2001), the priorities and ethos of the American government were focused on social welfare, notably an abortive attempt to widen health provision. In contrast, the American military was cut by a third and weapons procurement was reduced. Operational pressures on the American military mounted, in large part due to unforeseen circumstances. For example, in 1999, the USA sent the sole aircraft carrier permanently assigned to the Pacific to the Mediterranean in order to contribute to the air assault on Serbia during the Kosovo crisis.

American force reductions made it increasingly likely that a major commitment would be launched with inadequate strength and/or would entail Coalition resources. President George H.W. Bush's intention that the USA would be able to launch two Desert Storm-scale (1991 Gulf War) operations concurrently had to be abandoned. The cutback led to pressure in America for greater effectiveness from smaller forces and also to concern about the ability to call on allies, and indeed about the gap between their military effectiveness and that of the USA, a gap that was held to threaten interoperability. There were indeed serious cuts among the NATO allies, both Canada and most of the European NATO powers. Yet, there were (and remain) tensions between the external constraints that alliance policy-making entails and the nature of political culture in the USA, which tends to be hostile to compromise with foreign powers. American politicians and public opinion instinctively think in unilateral, and not multilateral, terms.

Pressure on the USA for greater military and political effectiveness was in part a matter of the ideas (and ideology) summed up by the RMA, but there was also a more general sense about the need for military development to reflect different goals after the Cold War. This process was to be termed Transformation, but it was not limited to the policies subsequently described with that term. In part, there was a significant continuation of the inclination of the military (non-American as well as American) in the 1980s for more flexible structures as well as doctrine and operational planning that stressed mobility, but there were also important new developments.

In the early 1990s, the American army's interest in employing information technology to enhance situational awareness was linked to a stress on agility and flexibility. The concept, Force XXI, sought to network battlefield information systems. To test the concept, a division-size Experimental Force was designated in December 1994 and adapted accordingly. In the Advanced Warfighting Experiment in 1997, a digitised task force was tested against a conventional opponent. This test proved more successful than the brigade-scale test carried out in 1994. The latter had revealed a lack of familiarity with new computerised equipment as well as the absence of the tactics necessary to exploit new capabilities.

In the late 1990s, the concept changed to the Army After Next Project. In place of adapting information technology to existing systems, the systems of the later years of the Cold War, there was a focus in the American army on a new generation of weapons systems, which were to be ready by 2025. The emphasis was on being able to respond rapidly to all circumstances, and, to that end, a 'Strike Force' was created to test the potential for rapid deployment of a force able to take the initiative. Pushing forward by Eric Shinseki, who became Chief of Staff in the Army in 1999, this policy also entailed a broad front improvement, including different logistical structures and an ability to function jointly with the other military services. Rapid deployment at a distance entailed airlift, and this need encouraged the development of smaller, lighter fighting vehicles which could be used to equip light infantry units. The plan was to be able to field a combat-ready brigade anywhere in the world in 96 hours and a division in 120 hours. This goal represented a key enhancement in American capability, and one that contrasted with the situation in 1990 when Iraq invaded Kuwait. Then the American forces sent to Saudi Arabia had principally gone by sea. They had focused on heavy units, notably armour.

The emphasis in American army planning now was on the brigade as the key unit, rather than the division; and this emphasis looked towards the decision, taken in 2003,[33] to convert the army into a modular, brigade-based force. The Stryker, an eight-wheeled, medium-weight armoured vehicle, became the platform of choice, providing a mobile, armour-protected combat system, and with each vehicle able to connect with all the information systems serving the unit. A sense of greater effectiveness was to be derived from the comparison between the difficulties experienced in Mogadishu in 1993, when trying to rescue two downed helicopters, and the far less costly experience of a Stryker unit facing a similar task at Tall Afar in Iraq on 4 September 2004.[34]

The relationships between effectiveness, expenditure and foreign policy were indirect, but, under Clinton, there was a caution about policy in the Middle East that contrasted with the more assertive and bellicose position under his successor, George W. Bush, in the far more threatening situation after the terrorist attacks on New York and Washington on 11 September 2001. Under Clinton, threats to Saddam Hussein were not matched by sustained action, while the challenge posed by Muslim terrorism (meaning Islamicist terrorism, not terrorism representative of all or many Muslims) was not adequately met.

Cruise missile strikes, however, were launched against terrorist bases in Afghanistan and Sudan in 1998, strikes of which the Republicans were sharply critical, and ironically so given the subsequent War on Terror, which was to be declared by a Republican administration, that of George W. Bush. Mounted in response to deadly al-Qaeda attacks on American embassies in Africa, the launching in 1998 of these seventy-nine cruise missiles represented an impressive display of force, but not one that stopped the terrorists. Indeed, Osama bin Laden, the head of al-Qaeda, was able to raise funds by selling missiles that did not detonate to the Chinese, who were interested in cutting-edge American military technology. The failure of these attacks was a small part of a much wider American inability to understand what was going on in the Muslim world, or, indeed, the complex relationship between cause and effect.[35]

The reliance on cruise missiles in 1998, as that on air power against Iraq that year in the Desert Fox campaign, reflected at once the potential it brought for action without having to deploy ground forces, and yet also the hesitation about committing such forces that the Americans had already shown in the Balkans over Bosnia and were to show over Kosovo in 1999. Although it proved easy to blame such hesitation on a reluctant American public lacking resolve, in practice there were powerful military and governmental factors that encouraged a disinclination to send ground forces. Most significant was the army's unwillingness to become involved in a mission without apparent end unless they had clear goals and readily apparent superiority.

This unwillingness, which was clearly spelled out by Colin Powell when Chairman of the Joint Chiefs of Staff, drew on the legacy of Vietnam as well as on the unsuccessful intervention in Beirut in 1982–84 and in Mogadishu in 1992–94. This attitude, which was dominant in American military thinking, was to pose problems in the aftermath of the Iraq invasion of 2003. It led to a focus on an attempt to use kinetic force in order to settle problems rapidly, rather than on a need to think about what each mission entailed.

At the same time, prior to the al-Qaeda attacks in 2001, there were already signs of American concern about a more dangerous world order, signs that contrasted with optimism earlier in the 1990s. The Strategic Assessment 1999 issued by the Institute for National Strategic Studies of the National Defence University in Washington commented on strengthened and hostile Sino (Chinese)-Russian ties, and later added:

> Of the three U.S. strategic goals – security, economic prosperity, and democracy – the last two have received considerable emphasis in recent years. This pattern reflects a belief that global security affairs have been stable enough to permit an emphasis on the world economy and democratic enlargement. Dangerous international trends now suggest that managing security affairs will need to be given attention and priority in the coming years. Pursuing economic progress and democracy will be difficult, unless security goals are first attained.[36]

The run-down of the military was taken further in Western Europe where there were significant cuts in the percentage of national wealth and government revenues spent on the armed forces. In Germany, the wealthiest European state, in 1999, this percentage dropped to 1.5 per cent of GDP, leading to public complaints from the American Defense Secretary. There was also a reluctance to serve in the German military: 40–45 per cent of Germans who were drafted opted for social service, for example as paramedics. Moreover, as far as France was concerned, the capability of the *Force d'Action Rapide* that took part in the Gulf War of 1991 was affected by the inability to demand that conscripts serve there. This problem encouraged the abandonment of conscription in France and, in 1996, the decision was taken to professionalise totally the armed forces. In Spain, in 1993, when 118,000 of the 146,000-strong army were conscripts, the government decided that it could not contribute a brigade to the UN forces in Bosnia, as conscripts could not be expected to serve there and there were insufficient regulars. At that stage, most Spanish men of draft age never went into uniform. In Italy, in 1999, Carlo Scognamiglio, the Defence Minister, warned that Italy would be unable to guarantee its own security, let alone meet its foreign peacekeeping obligations, unless the number of professional soldiers was doubled from 25,000 to 50,000. He blamed Italy's falling birth rate and a liberal law on conscription allowing people to opt out of military service as conscientious objectors.

The state of the European militaries led to concern both there and in the USA where there were particular worries about interoperability with the Americans within NATO and also about the degree of European resolve. These concerns lay behind the political tensions that were to be far more manifest at the time of the Iraq War in 2003. The same was true of Canada, which had played a major role in both world wars and in the Cold War. Canada cut its defence expenditure in the 1990s and refused to participate in the 1991 Iraq War.

In part, differences between the USA and Western Europe, differences that were to remain an issue into the 2010s, reflected not only contrasting positions in the international order, but also very dissimilar recent histories. The domestic logics of military power were pertinent, not only the location of this power in specific national political cultures, notably the civic republicanism of the conscription without bellicosity seen in Germany, Italy and Spain. The need for this military power to maintain internal stability was exceptional in Western Europe, being seen only with the British army in Northern Ireland.

In contrast to the systems of conscription without bellicosity, the American military, like its British counterpart, relied on volunteering professionals who were willing to serve and risk their lives. Moreover, the American army did not need to devote much effort to domestic policing. Thus, the National Guard was available to guard the frontier with Mexico when doubts were raised about the effectiveness of police units to block routes used by drug smugglers and illegal immigrants. In 1992, in very different circumstances, the deficiencies of the National Guard in responding to riots in Los Angeles led the Governor of California to request federal troops. Four thousand soldiers and marines were deployed, while the National Guard units there were federalised. This deployment led to a sharp decrease in levels of violence. The Los Angeles riots as a whole resulted in 54 deaths, 2,328 injuries and more than $900 million of property damage.[37]

Capability and effectiveness do not exist in a vacuum. Before continuing the discussion of conflicts in which Western powers played the key role, it is necessary to turn to a different account of warfare in the 1990s, one in which the West had a role, but indirectly and without supplying the central narrative.

Notes

1 J. Olsen, *John Warden and the Renaissance of American Air Power* (Dulles, Virginia, 2007).
2 J.J. McGrath, *The Other End of the Spear: The Tooth-to-Tail Ratio in Modern Military Operations* (Fort Leavenworth, Kansas, 2007), p. 42.
3 R.H. Scales, *Certain Victory: The US Army in the Gulf War* (Fort Leavenworth, Kansas, 1993); R.W. Swain, *'Lucky War': Third Army in Desert Storm* (Fort Leavenworth, Kansas, 1994); A.H. Cordesman and A.R. Wagner, *The Lessons of Modern War: IV. The Gulf War* (Boulder, Colorado, 1996); J.A. Olsen, *Strategic Air Power in Desert Storm* (London, 2003).
4 R.M. Connaughton, *Peacekeeping and Military Intervention* (Camberley, 1992).
5 A.J. Bacevich and E. Imbar (eds), *The Gulf War of 1991 Reconsidered* (London, 2003).
6 T. Ricks, *Fiasco: The American Military Adventure in Iraq* (New York, 2006), pp. 8–20.
7 M.A. Palmer, *On Course to Desert Storm: The United States Navy and the Persian Gulf* (Washington, 1992).
8 J. Blaxland, *The Australian Army from Whitlam to Howard* (Cambridge, 2014), p. 357.
9 T. Karcher, *Understanding the 'Victory Disease': From the Little Bighorn to Mogadishu and Beyond* (Fort Leavenworth, Kansas, 2004), pp. 34, 40, 45.
10 L. Wright, *The Looming Tower: Al-Qaeda and the Road to 9/11* (London, 2006).
11 L.W. Grau and M.A. Gress (eds), *The Russian General Staff: The Soviet-Afghan War* (Lawrence, Kansas, 2002).
12 K. Allard, *Somalia Operations: Lessons Learned* (Washington, 1995); M. Bowden, *Black Hawk Down: A Story of Modern War* (New York, 1999).
13 F.N. Schubert, *Other Than War: The American Military Experience and Operations in the Post-Cold War Decade* (Washington, 2013).
14 B. Shacochis, *The Immaculate Invasion* (New York, 1999).
15 E. O'Ballance, *Wars in the Caucasus, 1990–1995* (Basingstoke, 1996).
16 L.I. Polyakov, 'American Defense Transformation: A View from Ukraine', in C.C. Crane (ed.), *Transforming Defense* (Carlisle, Pennsylvania, 2001), p. 18.
17 A. Raevsky, 'Russian Military Performance in Chechnya: An Initial Evaluation', *Journal of Slavic Military Studies*, 8 (1995), pp. 681–90.
18 J. Hughes, *Chechnya: From Nationalism to Jihad* (Philadelphia, 2007).
19 A. Lieven, *Flaying the Bear: Chechnya and the Collapse of Russian Power* (New Haven, Connecticut, 1998); S. Knezys and R. Sedlickas, *The War on Chechnya* (College Station, Texas, 1999); S. Smith, *Allah's Mountains: The Battle for Chechnya* (2nd edn, London, 2001); R. Seely, *Russo-Chechen Conflict, 1800–2000: A Deadly Embrace* (London, 2001).
20 G.M. Hahn, *Russia's Islamic Threat* (New Haven, Connecticut, 2007).
21 C.S. King, 'The Siege of Sarajevo, 1992–95', in W.G. Robertson and L.A. Yates (eds), *Block by Block: The Challenges of Urban Operations* (Fort Leavenworth, Kansas, 2003), pp. 235, 273.

A CONVENTIONAL ACCOUNT, 1990–2000

22 M.A. Bucknam, *Responsibility of Command: How UN and NATO Commanders Influenced Airpower over Bosnia* (Montgomery, Alabama, 2003).

23 J. Gow, 'After the Flood: Literature on the Context, Cause and Course of the Yugoslav War – Reflections and Refractions', *Slavonic and East European Review*, 85 (1997), pp. 446–84; S.L. Burg and P.S. Shoup, *The War in Bosnia-Herzegovina: Ethnic Conflict and International Intervention* (Armonk, New York, 1999); T. Ripley, *Operation Deliberate Force: The Campaign in Bosnia, 1995* (Lancaster, 1999); C. Shrader, *The Muslim-Croat Civil War in Central Bosnia: A Military History, 1992–1994* (College Station, Texas, 2003); M.A. Hoare, *How Bosnia Armed* (London, 2004).

24 M. Melvin and S. Peach, 'Reaching for the End of the Rainbow: Command and the RMA', in G. Sheffield and G. Till (eds), *Challenges of High Command in the Twentieth Century* (Camberley, 1999), pp. 120–21.

25 R.C. Nation, *War in the Balkans, 1991–2002* (Carlisle, Pennsylvania, 2003); R.C. Phillips, *Bosnia-Herzegovina: The U.S. Army's Role in Peace Enforcement Operations, 1995–2004* (Washington, no date).

26 I.H. Daalder and M.E. O'Hanlon, *Winning Ugly: NATO's War to Save Kosovo* (Washington, 2000); T. Judah, *Kosovo: War and Revenge* (New Haven, Connecticut, 2000); L. Freedman, 'Victims and Victors: Reflections on the Kosovo War', *Review of International Studies*, 26 (2000), pp. 335–58; S.T. Hosmer, *The Conflict over Kosovo: Why Milosevic Decided to Settle When He Did* (Santa Monica, California, 2001); B.S. Lambeth, *NATO's Air War for Kosovo: A Strategic and Operational Assessment* (Santa Monica, California, 2001); A.J. Bacevich and E.A. Cohen (eds), *War over Kosovo: Politics and Strategy in a Global Age* (New York, 2002).

27 P. Ashdown, *Swords and Ploughshares: Bringing Peace in the 21st Century* (London, 2001).

28 M. Laity, *Preventing War in Macedonia: Pre-Emptive Diplomacy for the 21st Century* (London, 2008), quote p. 9, Aracinovo, p. 24.

29 P. Kennedy, *The Rise and Fall of the Great Powers: Economic Change and Military Conflict from 1500 to 2000* (London, 1988).

30 O. Coté, 'The Trident and the Triad: Collecting the D-5 Dividend', *International Security*, 16 (1991), pp. 117–45.

31 R. Kamphausen, A. Scobell and T. Tanner (eds), *The 'People' in the PLA: Recruitment, Training, and Education in China's Military* (Carlisle, Pennsylvania, 2008); A. Scobell, D. Lai and R. Kamphausen (eds), *Chinese Lessons from Other Peoples' Wars* (Carlisle, Pennsylvania, 2011).

32 *Times*, 15 Ap. 1996, p. 10.

33 W.M. Donnelly, *Transforming an Army at War: Designing the Modular Force, 1991–2005* (Washington, 2007), pp. 19–25.

34 R.J. Reardon and J.A. Charlston, *From Transformation to Combat: The First Stryker Brigade at War* (Washington, 2007), p. 70.

35 T. Weiner, *Legacy of Ashes: The History of the CIA* (London, 2007).

36 *Strategic Assessment 1999* (Washington, 1999), pp. 9, 13.

37 P.J. Scheips, *The Role of Federal Military Forces in Domestic Disorders, 1945–1992* (Washington, 2005), pp. 441–49.

4

SIGNS OF DIFFERENCE, 1990–2000

As with the situation prior to 1990, for example with the large-scale Iran–Iraq War of 1980–88, it would be misleading for the 1990s to ignore the number of conflicts between 'Third World' forces. Some of these, as in Somalia and Afghanistan, provided the background for Western intervention, but these conflicts are of significance for more than that. Furthermore, these conflicts looked towards the situation in the early twenty-first century. Thus, the process by which the Taliban seized power in most of Afghanistan in 1996 is rather more indicative of post-1990 conflict than the American intervention in that country from 2001, and was also significant in causing that intervention and in affecting its subsequent success. Conflict between Third World forces took a number of forms, ranging from regular warfare across front lines, to insurrections, ethnic conflict, terrorism and coups. Most of this conflict occurred in Africa, but there were also important instances in Latin America, Asia and Oceania.

Continuing Cold War conflicts

It is only in hindsight and, even then, only with a European focus, that the Cold War ended abruptly. Indeed, some of the post-1990 conflicts around the world were continuations, at least to a degree, of Cold War conflicts. This was particularly true for Angola and El Salvador. Although the 1988 ceasefire in Angola was followed by the prompt departure of South African forces and, in 1991, by that of the Cubans who had fought on behalf of the Soviet-backed *Movimento Popular de Libertação de Angola* (MPLA) government, the 1989 ceasefire between the Angola government and the American-supported *União Nacional para a Independência Total de Angola* (UNITA) movement speedily collapsed. This collapse led to an upsurge in conflict, a fresh bout of diplomacy and a peace in 1991 that only lasted until UNITA rejected the results of the 1992 election.

In El Salvador, in Central America, the Americans backed the government against the Farabundo/Marti National Liberation Front (FMLN). While the Cold War was fading in Europe, it continued in El Salvador, with a large-scale

FMLN offensive in November 1989. This offensive took over part of the capital, San Salvador, for a week, but could not touch off a popular uprising. Equally, the failure of the government of El Salvador to prevent the offensive led its American sponsors to press for negotiations which eventually, in 1992, bore fruit with a settlement under which the FMLN translated its activism to civilian politics. Its guerrillas were disbanded, and, in the elections of 1994, the FMLN became the largest opposition party, following this up, as a result of the 2000 elections, by becoming the largest parliamentary party. Similarly, in Nicaragua, where the long-standing civil war was brought to an end in 1990–94, the Sandinistas won power as a result of the 2006 elections.

Horn of Africa

These and other conflicts had origins and a course that were heavily influenced by the Cold War, which helped lead to foreign sponsorship and the supply of weaponry, even if the conflicts were not defined by the Cold War.[1] The extent to which the Cold War was only part of the equation in terms of the cause and course of conflict was seen in Africa. Thus, in the Horn of Africa, there was a centuries-old rivalry between the Ethiopians, who lived in the mountainous interior, and the Eritreans and Somalis, who lived on the coast. This rivalry, readily apparent from the sixteenth century, was fuelled by contrasting religious and ethnic constructions, for example Muslim Somalis against Christian Ethiopians, and Cold War alignments adapted to them. There was a similar pattern elsewhere, for example in Sudan.

In 1993, Ethiopia eventually conceded independence to Eritrea after a long secessionist struggle in which the Ethiopian position had finally collapsed in 1991. This collapse was in part because of the fall of the brutal left-wing Mengistu regime in Ethiopia in the face of successful opposition by the Ethiopian People's Revolutionary Democratic Front and the Tigré People's Liberation Front and as a result of the end of Soviet military assistance in 1989. The Tigréan leader, Meles Zenawi, became President of Ethiopia. War between Ethiopia and Eritrea resumed in 1998–2000.

South Asia

Similarly, the Cold War and, more particularly, its international alignments and arms supplies, had played a significant role in the confrontation and conflicts in South Asia between India and Pakistan, but the Cold War was not the root cause of them and they continued after its end. Pakistani opposition to India's position in divided Kashmir was a key cause of tension, as the Pakistani government supported Muslim insurgents there, while also using this issue in order to bolster domestic support for operations both governmental and military. The extent to which insurgency operations could lead to fighting between regular forces was shown in 1999 when the Pakistani military, having moved its troops onto the Indian side of the Line of Control, disguised them as local guerrillas.

The subsequent Kargil conflict reflected the Pakistani attempt to sever the principal Indian road link to Ladakh and Siachen. At the cost of 474 deaths, India won the conflict. It displayed determination and firepower at the tactical level, combined action at the operational level, and political will and skill at the strategic level. In the first, there was a willingness on the part of the Indians to attack in the face of well-defended positions, but also to use artillery to destroy these positions. As so often with the warfare of the period covered by this book, it is a serious mistake to underrate the potential and use of artillery, not least by underplaying it at the tactical level, in a contrast to air power. In operational terms, air power played a valuable role in the Kargil conflict, notably by hitting Pakistani logistics. At the strategic level, a well-conceived but also limited Indian plan, for clearing the Indian zone, but not escalating the conflict by crossing the Line of Control, helped maintain domestic support for operations and win that of the USA. The Indians did so without enabling the defeated Pakistani military to stoke up backs-to-the-wall domestic support in Pakistan.[2]

A range of conflicts

At a very different level of scale, there was also continuity in tension within states such as the sectarian riots in the Ferghana Valley in Turkmenistan in 1988 which became more serious once the Cold War came to an end. As another instance of a conflict that, like those in Angola and El Salvador, was part of the Cold War, but not defined by it, there was a long-standing civil war in Sudan which had been waged from 1963 until 1972, and then again from 1983. Successive governments based in the Arabic-speaking, Muslim north of Sudan, notably the Islamic military junta that gained power in a coup in 1989, thwarted separatism in the non-Arab, non-Muslim south. However, the northern forces were unable to subjugate the vast region of the south. The southern separatists of the Southern Sudan Independence Army and the Sudan People's Liberation Army had initially lacked modern weapons, many relying on spears, but their use of guerrilla tactics gravely weakened the Sudanese army's position in the south. The great size of Sudan also told against the army which, on the other hand, was more successful in its policy of turning for support in the south to the Nuer tribe, rivals of the Dinka tribe that was prominent in the resistance. The resistance, however, increasingly benefited from international support, including military supplies. Thus, the ground-to-air missiles of the Sudan People's Liberation Army made the aerial resupply of government garrisons hazardous, while the attack on the government's oil pipeline at Atbara in 1999 demonstrated the state's vulnerability. It was greatly dependent on its ability to earn foreign currency, and indeed interest, through oil exports, a situation also seen with Angola.

Ethnic and regional issues were not only intertwined in Sudan. For example, at a smaller scale, they were seen in a conflict in the Caprivi Strip of Namibia that began to receive international attention in 1999. Like many Third World conflicts, one side sought to overturn imperial territorial settlements, and the warfare reflected the failure of the state to incorporate minorities. The Caprivi Strip is an acute case of the artificiality of colonial boundaries, and the area is very remote from the centre of government in Namibia. A secession attempt was mounted by the Lozi-speaking people of Caprivi, who are dominated by the Ovambo majority of Namibia. In 1999, about 200 fighters of the Caprivi Liberation Army attacked key points in the provincial capital, Katima Mulilo, but the ill-planned attack was swiftly defeated. Paramilitaries from the Special Field Force and members of the Central Intelligence Service then seized large numbers of suspects and treated them brutally.

This is a small-scale conflict that was widely ignored and can be readily omitted from books in which space is at a premium, but this fighting in the Caprivi Strip is instructive for throwing light on a type and degree of tension and violence that is widespread around much of the world. In considering ethnicity as a key element in conflict, it is also necessary to note the extent to which ethnicity involves elements of construction, with cultural and political beliefs and practices serving to entrench differences and a sense of ethnic consciousness. Conflict and the recollection of conflict could play a major role in this process, and still do so.

Indonesia

At a very different level of scale to the Caprivi Strip, Indonesia, an effective non-Western imperial power, had successfully annexed western New Guinea (as West Irian or Irian Jaya) from the Dutch in 1963 and East Timor as the Portuguese empire collapsed in 1975. Demands for independence, by the Free Papua Movement in West Irian and the Fretilin movement in East Timor, were brutally resisted. The reliance on force in East Timor proved seriously counter-productive, as it failed to assuage local separatism and also led to international condemnation, especially after the shooting of unarmed demonstrators at a cemetery in Dili on 12 November 1991 resulted in hundreds of deaths or injuries and was filmed by Western journalists.

In 1999, the Indonesians responded to continued separatism and to international pressure by giving East Timor the choice of independence or regional autonomy. The people overwhelmingly chose independence, despite serious pressure from militias supported by the army. After the election, the coercion was stepped up, but international attention and anger mounted and finally led the Indonesians to accept the popular verdict. Australian forces under UN auspices secured the new situation, while, in Indonesia, failure helped discredit the army-backed government of Bacharuddin Habibie, who was forced to resign in 2001, although that resignation owed much to corruption scandals.

As an indication of the extent of rival internationalisms, Osama bin Laden chose to see East Timor's independence as a blow to the Muslim world (Indonesia is preponderantly Muslim), and first criticised Australia as a result of its intervention there.

The Indonesian government was more successful in resisting separatism in West Irian, and in Aceh in Sumatra. In part, this success reflected the lack of international attention and intervention, but there was also a stronger drive for independence in East Timor, which had been a Portuguese, rather than (like the rest of Indonesia) Dutch, colony prior to Indonesian control. In Aceh, the government eventually made concessions to demands for a more Islamic system of law, and, therefore, social regulation.

Separatism was not the sole cause of conflict across the Indonesian archipelago. More generally, the 1990s brought a strengthening of ethnic tension and regional consciousness, with widespread violence. Thus, in Kalimantan (Indonesian Borneo), from 1997, native Dayaks fought Madurans who had immigrated since the 1950s in part with government encouragement: thinking of Indonesia as a unit, the government sought to move people from areas of overcrowding without the consent of the population in the receiving area. Beheading played a major role in the violence: it was important in traditional Dayak culture as it was seen as the way to win favourable magic. Similarly, in Assam in north-east India, the separatist United Liberation Front of Asom [Assam] directed much of its violence against migrant workers from elsewhere in India, for example in 2007.

Africa

The numbers involved in conflict between Third World states and opposing movements could be considerable. In 1999, it was estimated that Indian security forces resisting insurgency in Kashmir, forces which included not only the army but also the Central Reserve Police Force and the Border Security Force, numbered 400,000. As an instance of the potential scale of conventional conflict in the Third World, in 2000 Ethiopia invaded Eritrea during a war that had broken out in 1998 and was a frontier struggle that was also a conflict over hegemony. As with many Third World conflicts, it is difficult to be precise about numbers and events, but the Ethiopians benefited from superior air power, better armour (Russian T-72 tanks) and greater numbers, only to find that the Eritreans fought well, taking advantage of the terrain. A settlement was arranged by the UN that year, but not before about a fifth of the Eritrean population had been displaced. Clashes between the two states continued and also affected Somalia, with Eritrea, from 2007, aligning with the Islamic Courts groups against Ethiopia which had intervened in Somalia.

In contrast, in Liberia from 1989 and Sierra Leone from 1991, the chaos that accompanied what was referred to as 'failed states' saw conflict that lacked much central direction. In both, drugged teenagers (many of them orphans) and outright looters had little, if any, idea of the cause they were fighting for, except for their own personal gain. The use of child soldiers, also seen with insurrectionary movements in Nepal and Uganda, can be regarded as an aspect of the totality of these struggles. Looked at differently, this use was also a reflection of the extent to which Western norms were not followed. As a result, Western commentators could treat such conflicts as 'total'.

Political objectives, beyond the capture of power, were certainly hazy, and 'wars' benefited from the large-scale availability of small arms and were financed primarily by criminal operations and forced extortions. As a reminder of the range of circumstances subsumed within 'war and society' there were, in Liberia and Sierra Leone, no chains of command or (often) even uniforms that distinguished 'troops' from each other, or from other fighters. Politically, these countries offered an instance of a more widespread process in which warlords moved from being rebels to presidents or vice versa, while ethnicity helped exacerbate conflict.[3] In Liberia and Sierra Leone, drug-taking adolescent fighters, operating on behalf of factions, reduced both countries to a form of gangland chaos, and this situation made it difficult for regulars to identify opponents who could be defeated. In Sierra Leone, where a private military company, Executive Outcomes, had proved a crucial support to the government, the civil war was declared over in January 2002, and an international peacekeeping force began to disarm combatants.

In Liberia, a coup in 1980 was followed by a rebellion by Charles Taylor started in 1989. Having become the most powerful warlord in Liberia, he became its President in 1997, but a rebellion against him, which began in 1999, led to his opponents advancing into the capital, Monrovia, in 2003. Taylor resigned in the subsequent chaos, and Nigerian peacekeepers took over Monrovia. In response to these crises of ungovernability and large-scale violence, the Nigerian army played a role in peacekeeping in Liberia and Sierra Leone, although this also reflected Nigeria's own regional agenda as the dominant power. Poorly trained for the task, the Nigerians tended to use firepower as a substitute for policing. The civil war in Liberia claimed about 120,000 lives and created an estimated 400,000 amputees. Taylor's forces in particular made a practice of amputating limbs from those they wished to terrorise, as a visual deterrent and as a form of sadism.

West Africa had areas of relative stability, such as Ghana. However, in the 2000s, as Sierra Leone and Liberia became more peaceful, Ivory Coast slid into civil war. In the early 2010s, the Nigerian army, moreover, was to find it very difficult to deal with the terrorist violence of Boko Haram, an Islamicist movement in northern Nigeria.

Rwanda

In Rwanda, in Central Africa, civil war was not as disorganised as in Sierra Leone and Liberia, but it was even more bloody. In 1990, the Tutsi émigrés of the Rwanda Patriotic Front (RPF) invaded Hutu-dominated Rwanda from neighbouring Uganda. There, in an example of the interrelationship of struggles in different states, the RPF and its army, the Rwanda Patriotic Army (RPA), had fought with Ugandans under Yoweri Museveni against the dictators Idi Amin and Milton Obote, deposing Obote in 1985. After Museveni won, the RPA had his support when they invaded Rwanda in 1990. The initial invasion failed, and led to the RPA taking shelter in the mountainous Virunga region. In 1991, a more wide-ranging offensive by the well-led RPA kept the initiative away from the government forces. By 1993, the capital, Kigali, was under threat by the RPA. As a result, the Hutu government was willing to accept a peace agreement in August 1993, which was monitored by a small, largely Belgian, UN peacekeeping force.

In 1993, however, a Tutsi coup in neighbouring Burundi against the Hutu government led to the killing there of over 100,000 Hutus, increasing tension in Rwanda. In April the following year, an extremist group of Hutus, determined to prevent Hutu–Tutsi power-sharing in Rwanda, a method that might well have lessened ethnic strife, seized power. They rapidly began a mass slaughter which left about 937,000 Tutsi and moderate Hutus dead: the figure may have been over a million, one in seven of the population. Rather than seeing the violence simply in terms of ethnic division, each ethnic group was divided between moderates and extremists. Nevertheless, Hutu extremists, notably the Interahamwe militia, were responsible for the 1994 slaughter. They established road blocks, killing large numbers of those they stopped there, and also attacked Tutsi settlements. Those taking refuge in churches were killed. Many were hacked to death with machetes.

The failure of the international community to prevent genocide, not least to send reinforcements or instructions to the UN Assistance Mission for Rwanda, raised a question mark against both the UN's ability to enforce norms and the willingness of the world's leading power, the USA, to act. France itself was partly responsible for the crisis. Drawing on a long-standing tradition, which President Mitterrand had expressed while a minister in the 1950s, the French government saw an Anglo-Saxon threat to *Françafrique*, a zone including not only former French colonies but also the ex-Belgian colonies of Rwanda, Burundi and Congo. France regarded continued control of this vast region as important not only economically but also to its international power and prestige. This view was taken by the Africa Unit, a group of officials, particularly in the secret services, that was influential under the governments of the Fifth Republic, both left- and right-wing, notably the Mitterrand government. Corruption played a major role, as money provided by companies involved in Africa, such as the state-run oil giant Elf-Aquitaine, helped lubricate political campaigns.

Regarding the RPA as an Anglo-Saxon-backed Ugandan army, the French government had dispatched troops to help the Hutu regime in the civil war of 1990–93. Large amounts of arms, moreover, were sent to the Rwandan army, which was put under effective French control. The French proved willing to encourage the Hutu extremists to slaughter the Tutsis, including providing direct assistance in the genocide launched in April 1994, as well as in earlier killings.

Congo

After the Hutu regime was overthrown in July 1994 by the ably commanded and well-disciplined RPA, the French government sent their military to assist their Hutu allies in taking refuge in camps at Goma in the neighbouring eastern Congo, where the presence of the Hutus helped accelerate the crisis in Congo to one of large-scale instability and the interaction of politics with civil strife. Yet again, it proved impossible to isolate conflict, and Rwandan and Ugandan forces intervened against the Hutus in Congo from November 1996. Rwanda claimed, accurately, that President Mobutu Sese Soko, the dictator of Congo, a long-term ally of France, was not restraining the Hutu extremists in Congo.

Initially the Rwandan forces had operated only against the Hutu camps, but the reinforcement of the Hutu *genocidaires* by Mobutu, and their movement into the interior, led the RPA, in turn, to advance. Mobutu's demoralised and poorly commanded army disintegrated as they did so. RPA forces walked west to Kinshasa, the Congo capital, and to the Atlantic, a distance of over 2,000 kilometres. This advance led to the overthrow of the Mobutu government in May 1997, again much to the irritation of the French government which, on earlier occasions, had intervened to help prop up his regime, including by the dispatch of troops.[4]

Laurent Kabila, the corrupt President of Congo, who replaced Mobutu, turned, however, against his recent Rwandan and Ugandan allies, leading to a new war in 1998, with Rwandan units again invading eastern Congo. They had less success than in 1997 when they tried to move on to capture Kinshasa again, being beaten by more strongly armed forces from Angola and Zimbabwe which had intervened in support of Kabila. So also did Namibia. The Angolan forces, like their Rwandan counterparts, had the benefits of experience and cohesion as a result of lengthy recent conflict. The war in Congo continued until 2002. Yet further confusing the situation, and indicating the range of competing interests, Rwandan and Ugandan forces themselves clashed in 1999–2000.

State borders inherited from old imperial boundaries that cut across perceived ethnic and tribal configurations contributed significantly to such interventions. This interventionism also reflected an overlap between international and domestic conflict. In some cases, this overlap can be seen as an aspect of warfare; in others, of large-scale feuding; and in some, of politics. Disputes between local peoples and states had often interacted with, first, the spread of Western imperialism and, subsequently, the Cold War, as the protagonists in the latter sought local allies. This pattern continued after the Cold War ended, with parties to disputes seeking powerful outside supporters that could offer international backing and provide arms.

In Burundi, the civil war, which started in 1993, continued into the 2000s despite efforts to stop it. Over 150,000 people were killed and at least three-quarters of a million became refugees. The Tutsi-dominated army there was opposed by Hutu militia. Ethnic violence was also common elsewhere in Africa, for example in Mauritania, where clashes between Black Africans and the dominant Arabs led to violence in 1989–90, and in Nigeria, where, it has been claimed, over 50,000 people were killed in such violence between 2001 and 2004 alone.

Such conflicts were a modern demonstration of the argument that a general tendency of 'primitive' warfare is to cause higher casualty rates than the majority of conflicts involving regular forces.[5] The number of combatants in such 'primitive' warfare is also higher as it is not restricted to regular forces. In turn, the greater number of casualties reflects the anti-societal character of much of such warfare, a character summed up in the term 'ethnic cleansing'. This pattern continues to the present, notably in the Central African Republic, with Muslim and Christian militias attacking civilians there in 2013–14.

Coups and military regimes

At a very different scale, force was also displayed as an integral part of the political process, although any listing of coups and related military moves has to note the very different levels of violence seen in coups, which, in large part, reflected their contrasting causes. Coups were certainly an important part of the military history of the period. The politicisation of the military by civilian governments keen to use its strength to achieve their goals also helped encourage the military to overcome inhibitions to the use of force.[6] Other coups were the product of inter-military divisions, and some involved rivalry with paramilitary forces. Coups in Africa included those in Mali (1991), the highly unstable Comoros archipelago in the Pacific (1995 and 1999), as well as in Niger (1996 and 1999), Sierra Leone (1997), Ivory Coast (1999), Mauritania (2005 and 2008), Togo (2005 and 2008) and the Central African Republic (2013).

Coups reflected both the ambitions of the military and also the willingness to turn to foreign support. Thus, in Congo-Brazzaville, Denis Sassou-Nguesso, an army officer active in coups and coup attempts in the 1960s and 1970s, and President from 1979, did not accept his loss of power in the election of 1992, and, instead, turned to civil war, drawing on support from French oil interests, which were/are closely linked to the French government, and on militias from Congo. He finally regained power in 1997. In Asia, a military regime was created in Pakistan in 1999, although it was to accept electoral defeat and replacement by civilians in 2007.

Coups in the New World included those in Haiti in 1991 and 2004, and in Ecuador in 2000. Moreover, the use of force both played a role in changes in civilian government, such as those in Peru and Colombia in the 1980s and 1990s, and also led to the creation of military governments, reflecting the widespread conviction among Latin American militaries that their function included the suppression of internal enemies. In 1992, the Peruvian President, Alberto Fujimori, used the army to shut down Congress and the courts.

Control over the military was even more important to the Castro regime in Cuba. A key player, Fidel Castro's brother, Raoul, was First Vice-President and Defence Minister. The latter ministry controlled the 50,000 regulars of the Cuban Revolutionary Armed Forces (FAR: *Fuerzas Armadas Revolucionarias*), as well as the million-plus reservists and territorial militia. In 1989, the Ministry of the Interior was subordinated to the FAR, which gave Raoul Castro authority over the 15,000 police.

Some military regimes were short term, such as that created in Niger in 1999, when Ibrahim Bara Mainassara, the President, who had himself led a coup in 1996, was shot dead by the head of his bodyguard, who then briefly seized power. More impressively, Colonel Ely Vall, the head of the secret service, who seized power in Mauritania in 2005 in a bloodless coup, overthrowing Maaonya Taya, President from 1984, promised elections within two years in which no coup leader would compete. Free elections were indeed held in 2007, but a fresh coup occurred in 2008.

A few military regimes were long lasting. In Myanmar (Burma), where the military ruled as the State Peace and Development Council, the elections held in 1990 were annulled when a pro-democracy movement won, and the military held on to power for two decades. The political reforms there in 2011 still left the military and linked politicians dominant. More commonly, military rule both reflected and created crisis and proved unstable.

In Nigeria, after a coup on 31 December 1983, rule by the Supreme Military Council (1984–85) saw the use of troops to suppress strikes and demonstrations. This corrupt regime was followed by a coup in August 1985 by the Chief of Staff, General Babangida. Losing the presidential election in June 1993 to Moshood Abiola, who was not from the military, he annulled the election, but the ensuing instability and violence led Babangida to hand over power to an Interim Governing Council (IGC) led by his ally Ernest Shonehan. In turn, the IGC was overthrown that November in a coup by General Sani Abacha, the Minister of Defence, who declared himself commander in chief and head of state. As with many coups, this was as much a coup against other groups in the military, as against civil society. Babangida's allies in the military were forcibly retired, while Abiola was imprisoned until his death in 1998. The military joined the police in violently repressing opposition activities, including demonstrations. Force was also used to suppress the Ogoni of the oil-rich Niger delta who demanded autonomy. Abacha remained dictator until he died of a heart attack in June 1998. Another general, Abdulsalami Abubakar, came to power as a result of action by his colleagues, but he decided on democracy, and free elections were held in 1999. Nigeria has remained a democracy since.

In the short term, authoritarian regimes reliant on force were less powerful or rigid in practice than they appeared, and they operated by accepting the circumvention of their nostrums and structures by their own members, as well as by vested interests and by the public itself. In the long term, these regimes found it difficult to contain political problems and to satisfy popular demands. Thus, the military lost power in Bangladesh and Chile in 1990, the first as a result of popular demonstrations, and in Thailand in 1992, while in Indonesia, General Suharto, the army chief of staff, who had taken over power in 1967, was forced to surrender power in 1998: he had been discredited as corrupt and was put under considerable political and popular pressure. The *Tentera Nasional Indonesia* (Indonesian National Military), however, remained important in Indonesian politics and, far more, to the Indonesian state.[7] The Thai army staged another coup in 2006, although it swiftly accepted a return to democracy, and another in 2014. In Bangladesh, the army seized power in 2007, failed to bring stability, and returned to the barracks in 2008. However, another coup was feared in 2014. Pervez Musharraf, the Pakistani army chief, who seized power in 1999, ruling for eight years, was put under house arrest in 2013 and then tried for suspending the constitution in 2007. The arrest and trial were seen as a way to assert civilian supremacy over the armed forces.

At the same time, the major role of the military in the economy increased their impact in many states, for example Indonesia, Pakistan, North Korea, Egypt and China. Aside from economic distortions, distortions that the military concealed, and the resulting major effect on public finances, this role also influenced the political process. The impact of the military in this fashion indicated the extent to which they could serve as a costly protection system that constrained the possibilities for government. The subsidies the military's uneconomic companies received were as pernicious as unnecessary procurement policies.[8]

Unsuccessful coups, and indeed plans for coups, were also an important and instructive aspect of military history. Failed coups included those in Mauritania and Nigeria in 1990, Russia in 1991, Equatorial Guinea in 1997 and 2004 and Congo in 2004. The significance of attempted coups helped ensure that governments had to see coup avoidance and suppression as one of the most important tasks of their military policy.

Careful attempts were made to woo the military and, at the same time, to lessen their power by building up rival paramilitary services. The attempt to create links with the military led rulers to foster personal and symbolic relations, with Hafez Assad, the President of Syria, having his son and intended successor join the army in 1994: he became President in 2000 and used brutal force to hold onto power in the face of a large-scale rebellion in the early 2010s. Rival paramilitary services were important to governmental control in a number of states, for example Saudi Arabia, Iraq and Yemen, leading to the counterpointing of the army with the National Guard in Saudi Arabia, the Central Security Forces in Egypt, the Defence Regiments in Syria, the Republican Guard in Iraq and the Revolutionary Guard in Iran.

A stress on coup avoidance represents a way to approach military history that is totally different to the established one. This stress reflects the significance of force in the politics of the modern world. The use of force did not necessarily involve what can be seen as fully fledged war, but the conflict could be violent. Thus, in February 2014, the use of riot police, notably the 'golden eagles', against thousands of protestors in Kiev and elsewhere in Ukraine saw the deployment of armoured vehicles, water cannon and snipers firing stun grenades, rubber bullets and more lethal firearms. There were fatalities on both sides before the government fell. Similarly, in Thailand, there were deaths in riots and the deployment of large numbers, notably 15,000 police in the Peace for Bangkok police operation, before the army seized power.

The distinction between armed police, paramilitaries and the military is often limited, and sometimes that of name rather than function. Alongside the police and the paramilitaries, the military was (and is) the prime source of readily deployable force for governments. The role of the military in the politics of individual states varied greatly as circumstances altered, but they were frequently an important element in responding to potential rebellions and in maintaining cohesion, or, at least, control. That the military themselves played a central role as the most likely source of coups, and the most probable basis for resistance to them, further complicated the situation.

Notes

1 E. Karsh, 'Cold War, Post-Cold War: Does it Make a Difference for the Middle East?' *Review of International Studies*, 23 (1997), pp. 271–91; M. Connelly, 'Taking Off the Cold War Lens: Visions of North-South Conflict during the Algerian War of Independence', *American Historical Review*, 105 (2000), pp. 739–69.

2 V.P. Malik, *Kargil: From Surprise to Victory* (London, 2006).

3 A. Clayton, *Factions, Foreigners and Fantasies: The Civil War in Liberia* (Sandhurst, 1995) and *Frontiersmen: Warfare in Africa since 1950* (London, 1999); T.M. Ali and R.O. Matthews, *Civil Wars in Africa: Roots and Resolution* (Montréal, 1999).

4 R. Dallaire, *Shake Hands with the Devil: The Failure of Humanity in Rwanda* (New York, 2005).

5 L.H. Keeley, *War before Civilization: The Myth of the Peaceful Savage* (Cambridge, Massachusetts, 1995).

6 J.S. Ikpuk, *Militarisation of Politics and Neo-Colonialism: The Nigerian Experience* (London, 1995); J. Peters, *The Nigerian Military and the State* (London, 1997).

7 L.C. Sebastian, *Realpolitik Ideology: Indonesia's Use of Military Force* (Singapore, 2006).

8 A. Siddiqa, *Military Inc.: Inside Pakistan's Military Economy* (London, 2007).

5

THE WAR ON TERROR

Writing about a period that is in progress poses many problems, not least those of significance and sympathy. More particularly, the future becomes present and can readily upset the analysis. Will the American-led clash with radical Muslim fundamentalism, for example, however serious, be any more than an interlude before, largely as a consequence of the rise of China, great power confrontation revives and poses new challenges for the American military?

Al-Qaeda and terrorism

The surprise attacks launched by Osama bin Laden's al-Qaeda (The Base) terrorist movement on New York and Washington on 11 September 2001 led to about 3,220 fatalities, the majority in the Twin Towers in New York.[1] This terrorist employment of Weapons of Mass Effect in the centres of American life transformed American attitudes, focused American concerns and ensured that the American government took a more determined position in warfare in the early 2000s than had been the case in the Balkans in the late 1990s.

The replacement of Bill Clinton by George W. Bush as President in January 2001 was also significant, in that Bush was more prone to adopt a militarised response. Moreover, at least initially after 11 September, the Americans benefited from widespread international support in their self-proclaimed 'War on Terror'. Concerned to 'dry up the swamp', the American government found it essential, in resisting terrorism, and in particular the alarming challenge posed by suicide terrorism, to strike back and to be seen to regain the initiative. This response led to attacks, overt and covert, on what were identified as terrorist bases and supporters. These attacks represented another stage in the movement towards action that had followed the end of the Cold War. There was parallel activity directed against terrorist financial networks and arms supplies.

Before plunging on with the narrative of American action, and the consideration of how far it matched notions of an RMA, it is pertinent to offer a context by considering how far other attempted 'revolutions in military affairs' require discussion, in particular those sought by terrorist groups and by so-called rogue states, each the target for American action. The focus, for the 2000s, is generally on the failure of Western interventionism and of the RMA to achieve goals and fulfil hopes. However, it is necessary to consider other failures as well. In the case of terrorist groups, the attempt in 2001 by al-Qaeda to use terrorist methods to a strategic end by crippling, or at least symbolically dethroning, American financial and political power failed. The attempt apparently rested on a greatly flawed assumption about the concentrated and top-down nature of American power. There was also a misplaced assumption that it would prove possible to crack American morale, although, as another view, it has been argued that al-Qaeda was surprised by the very impact of its attack.

The 11 September attacks also indicated the extent to which the terrorist repertoire was far from fixed. Although it is true that al-Qaeda did not deploy weapons of mass destruction, such as atomic devices, in 2001, its ability to make use of Western technology, in this case civilian aircraft, indicated the challenge it posed. So also did the determination it shared with many other terrorist movements to ignore any boundaries between military and civilian. Similarly, in 2004, dependence on public transport was exploited in the deadly al-Qaeda attacks on commuter trains in Madrid, while, in 2005, British Islamic terrorists acting on behalf of al-Qaeda had the same effect in London. Attacks in Mumbai followed in 2008.

Al-Qaeda's apocalyptic and millenarian aspirations and tendencies, and those of related groups, also make them particularly serious as it is difficult to see how the threat they pose can be lessened through negotiation. Moreover, the extent to which al-Qaeda appears in part to function by supporters seeking to work towards the leader's declared aspirations increases its deadliness, as dislocating the structure of the formal organisation will not therefore end the threat. This point underlines the extent to which, although al-Qaeda also draws on classic works on guerrilla warfare,[2] it poses a cultural challenge, rather than one from a network that can be defeated by such conventional means as destroying the leadership.

This terrorism is a more serious problem for international relations than that posed by particular aggressive states because the nature of a stateless entity is that it does not need to respond to the constraints that arise from claims to sovereign power, although such stateless groups are also in a competition for legitimacy. The military equivalent to the lack of constraints is that these stateless entities may not have a territorial space that can be attacked or occupied. As a result of this lack of constraint, the challenge posed by terrorist movements can seem greater than that from terrorist states, especially as the movements can seek to base themselves in failed states, such as Afghanistan, Somalia and Yemen, where it has been difficult to take action short of full-scale military intervention against them. The latter point underlines the significance of the capability brought by the drone and its use for selective assassination.[3]

Moreover, terrorist movements, and those of guerrilla organisations, can take place in war by proxy, such as Iran's use of Hizbullah both in Syria and as a threat against Israel. Most terrorism is in fact aimed at states in the Third World, where the number of victims is also far higher than in the First World. Moreover, a large number of them are Muslims killed by other Muslims. However, the challenge from terrorism is particularly notable for strong powers, especially the strongest, the USA, as they have less practicable need to fear attack from other states than weaker states do: were the forces of these states to attack the USA, they would be defeated, and their territory could certainly be attacked. This demonstrates a key element of asymmetry.

This distinction in vulnerability, however, is challenged by the attempts by rogue states to acquire weapons of mass destruction and related delivery systems. In the early 1990s, it was discovered that North Korea was developing plutonium, which could be used to make nuclear warheads, and, in 2002, it admitted it was trying to enrich uranium. In 1998, moreover, North Korea tested a medium-range Taepodong missile, firing it over Japan into the Pacific. North Korea was not alone: concern over Iran's nuclear ambitions and developments became more pronounced in the mid-2000s and led Israel and the USA in the early 2010s to consider pre-emptive attacks.

The overthrow of the Saddam regime in Iraq in 2003 encouraged the governments of North Korea and Iran to press ahead with such schemes as they thought the presence of weapons of mass destruction was likely to deter American attack, and thus both increase their own ability to intimidate and coerce regional powers and preserve their own regimes. Although the regular forces of states such as North Korea and Iran probably lack the capability and ability in defence to defeat the conventional forces of stronger powers in a sustained attack, and certainly could not stage an effective offensive war, such weapons of mass destruction would enable them to threaten these forces and, perhaps even eventually, home territory; while the real or potential availability of such weapons would also challenge the aspect of international aspirations and force projection represented by interventionist policies and alliance systems.

Afghanistan

The challenge from terrorism appeared to mark a key stage in the ending of the Cold War. In 2001, Russia lent diplomatic support to the American air offensive against the Taliban regime in Afghanistan, which had provided sanctuary for al-Qaeda. This support was despite the fact that this American campaign, launched on 7 October, entailed the establishment of American bases in Central Asian republics that had until 1991 been part of the Soviet Union, such as Uzbekistan. Although willing to see action against al-Qaeda, Russia was particularly sensitive to the establishment of bases in former parts of the Soviet Union: aside from the military potential the bases offered, they were a clear demonstration of the extent to which the end of the Soviet

Union had brought a geopolitical transformation. With time, Russia became more opposed to these bases.

The Taliban emerged from the chaos that was Afghanistan in the early 1990s. Mohammad Najibullah had been put in power by the Soviets in 1987 as a more conciliatory replacement to Babrak Kemal, the President from 1979, and as part of the Soviet search for a new solution to the Afghan problem, an unsuccessful search that had led them into Afghanistan in the first place. Najibullah's regime finally fell in April 1992 when the guerrillas entered the capital, Kabul: the government had been greatly weakened by the defection of its northern strongman, Abdul Rashid Dostum.

Victory, however, for the guerrillas was followed by an upsurge in already strong ethnic regional tensions within Afghanistan. In particular, the northerners, who had seized the capital in 1992, were opposed by Gulbuddin Hekmatyar, a Pushtun and the leader of the Afghanistan Islamic Party, who attacked Kabul. As the country was divided by warlords and the economy collapsed, feeding the flight of refugees, looting became the best way to supply warring forces. The war of the 1980s had left plentiful modern weapons.

This situation was challenged by the Kandahar-based and Pakistan-backed Taliban movement, which sought control over the entire country and wanted to impose a fervent religious orthodoxy. Benefiting from Pushtun support (the numerous Pushtuns span the frontier between Afghanistan and Pakistan), as well as from the ample profits of opium-dealing, and from a strong conviction of divine mission, the Taliban overran much of the country in 1996, seizing Kabul that year. Najibullah, who had taken refuge in a UN compound, was executed.

Pakistan provided help because victory for a Pushtun protégé movement was seen as a way to limit Indian regional influence and to give Pakistan strategic depth in any conflict with India. Indeed, this Pakistani policy provided a key instance of the degree to which the War on Terror was mediated through pre-existing rivalries and geopolitical structures. This process was scarcely new, having been seen in their region, as well as others, during the Cold War, but it helped explain the problems faced by the USA in dealing with its allies, notably, but not only, in Pakistan.

In 1996, bribes played a role in dissolving much of the opposition to the Taliban. Accepting such bribes reflected a sense that the situation could or might change, or was changing, and that it was necessary to be on the right side of any change. However, in the non-Pushtun areas, particularly in the north, the Taliban encountered serious resistance, which stopped their advance. This resistance helped provide the Americans with allies when they attacked the Taliban regime in 2001, in the aftermath of the 11 September attacks on New York and Washington. Nevertheless, from 1996, the Taliban controlled most of the country. The Taliban, in practice, had little to offer in Afghanistan bar ceaseless struggle against heretics and infidels, and this was central to their brutality towards those with whom they disagreed. Ethnic violence played a role, as with the driving of large numbers of Tajiks from their land in 1999.

In 2001, the Taliban regime refused to hand over Osama bin Laden and other al-Qaeda members for trial, seeing them, instead, as defenders of Islam and as protected by conventions of hospitality. In addition, al-Qaeda provided the Taliban with money. Mistakenly confident as a result of the failure of Soviet occupation of Afghanistan in the 1980s, and because it saw the situation in its own terms, the Taliban did not appreciate that the Americans posed a more formidable threat than the Soviets. As a result of the failure to hand over al-Qaeda leaders, Afghanistan became the target for American action, and with the full support of the UN.

This action was rapidly effective, with American Special Operations Forces teams infiltrated from 19 October 2001. They played a key role not only in winning local backing, but also in calling down and guiding large-scale American close air support. Unused to protecting themselves from such attack, and in terrain much of which provided only limited cover, Taliban forces in the north were heavily battered. The regime's fall indeed was seen as a success for American air power, which included long-range B-52 and B-1 'stealth' bombers, extensive aerial refuelling, enabling planes to fly very long missions, Tomahawk cruise missiles from warships in the Arabian Sea, AC-130 gunships, unpiloted drones providing reconnaissance or firing missiles, and CBU-130 'Combined-Effects Munitions' which spread cluster bombs. The availability of dual-mode, laser and Global Positioning Systems (GPS) guidance for bombs increased the range of precision available, while the air assault benefited from the effective and, crucially, rapid management of information from a number of sources, including forward air controllers and ground-based GPS devices. In addition, the absence of hostile air power and of effective anti-aircraft fire was important.

The Taliban, however, ultimately had to be overcome on the ground by rival Afghan forces, particularly the United Front, the so-called Northern Alliance. In doing so, the lack of coherence of the Taliban regime and the porosity and changeable nature of alignments in Afghanistan were both important to the war's outcome, and far more so than those who focused on American action and air power enthusiasts were to accept. Warlords switched allegiance, in large part as a result of American bribes, and the Taliban position collapsed on 9–13 November 2001 with the fall of the cities of Mazar-e Sharif, Herat and Kabul. The Taliban were unable to regroup after the fall of Mazar-e Sharif, in the north, not least because defections that stemmed from the Taliban's divisions accentuated a failure of command and control. American air power and Afghan ground attack combined to ensure the fall of the more firmly defended city of Kunduz on 23 November. Taliban forces tried to regroup at the city of Kandahar, their centre; but, as their regime unravelled, abandoned it on 7 December. Many of the leaders fled into Pakistan.

The Taliban position had been broken by the combination of American and Afghan assault, the latter an instance of the proxy warfare seen throughout the Cold War. The American air attack helped switch the local political balance within Afghanistan.[4] Some of the fighting was traditional, with Northern Alliance forces using cavalry charges. At the same time, for example on 9 November on the approach to Mazar-e Sharif from the south, B-52s were needed to overcome Taliban defences which included multiple rocket launchers. Moreover, the willingness, under heavy American pressure, of President Pervez Musharraf of neighbouring Pakistan to cut, at least ostensibly, links with the Taliban and to provide assistance, including permitting American overflying and moving Pakistani troops into border areas, was important.

Nevertheless, the victorious campaign did not lead to the clear-cut, pro-American triumph that had been hoped for. Instead, it became readily apparent that the war had provoked a regrouping and realignment of factions, uneasily presided over by the weak, new pro-Western President, Hamid Karzai, whose effective power extended little further than the capital, Kabul. Far better than nothing, but not forcing opponents to accept the will of the victor, let alone the legitimacy of this government.

Furthermore, analysis of the impact of the air attack revealed that, while it had been considerable in the initial attacks in northern Afghanistan, it subsequently became less so in the ground operations launched by Afghanistan and allied forces against Taliban and al-Qaeda survivors in Tora Bora (December 2001), and in Operation Anaconda, south of Gardiz (March 2002). This decline in effectiveness, which underlined the already known limitations of air power for suppressing insurgents,[5] was attributed to poor American command as well as to the Taliban's ability to respond by taking advantage of extremely difficult terrain features, such as caves, for camouflage and cover.[6] This decline in the effectiveness of air attack matched the British experience in the 1920s and 1930s.

In the absence of adequate American air cover during stages of Operation Anaconda, Taliban mortars inflicted damage.[7] Helicopters provided important fire support and lift for the Afghan forces, but they also took damage from ground fire to which they are very vulnerable. Al-Qaeda and the Taliban stood and fought, thwarting the initial American-led Afghan ground attack. Eventually, however, al-Qaeda and Taliban forces were overcome after more Afghan and American support was provided.

More generally, there was also the key problem posed by a reliance on local allies who, understandably, had their own agenda. This is a problem that has affected alliances and imperial powers across the centuries. The Americans had found the Northern Alliance a beneficial partner, but that was because their goals were shared. This situation no longer proved the case in operations in Tora Bora, and the lack of effective American ground forces to act as a substitute was crucial in that operation. This lack helped bin Laden to escape. The failure to capture bin Laden represented a major failure as, whatever his particular command significance, this inability led to a sense of impotence. Moreover, Pakistani support for the Taliban, especially from the influential Inter-Services Intelligence Agency, helped Taliban and al-Qaeda forces to retreat into Pakistan from Tora Bora. Having taken refuge in Pakistan, bin Laden was to be killed there by American special forces in 2012.

The problem, for both sides, of partnership between the USA and local allies[8] was to recur in the American aftermath of the invasion of Iraq in 2003, with the assumption that the tempo of local politics could be directed to produce political co-operation, as well as allied forces willing to act on American terms, again proving mistaken. Indeed, a careful reading of the Afghan conflict, not least of the aftermath to the collapse of the Taliban regime, should have encouraged greater caution in planning for Iraq. There are few signs, however, that such a reading affected the decision-makers, in part because wish-fulfilment played a key role in their attitudes and ambience.

Operations by the International Security Assistance Force against al-Qaeda supporters in Afghanistan were the most prominent aspect of the American and American-allied War on Terror that followed the attacks of 11 September 2001. Not only Americans and Afghans were involved. Thus, the British government under Tony Blair proved eager to send not only special forces, but also ground forces into Afghanistan. The latter took over the key air base at Bagram, near Kabul, in November 2001 as a move intended to help nation-building.

The War on Terror outside Afghanistan

Operations in Afghanistan were far from the only moves in the War on Terror prior to the Iraq invasion of 2003. Instead, American Special Operations Forces units were deployed against Muslim terrorist movements linked to al-Qaeda. This process was particularly so on and near the Philippine island of Mindanao where, from 2003, the Americans provided military support to the army against the Abu Sayyaf group in a long-standing confrontation that, in part, looked back to opposition to American conquest after the American–Spanish War of 1898. Also in 2003, the pro-Western republic of Georgia was provided with help against an al-Qaeda force in the region of the Pankisi Gorge, which was also a base for Chechen rebels opposing neighbouring Russia.

Terrorism linked to al-Qaeda affected a number of countries, not only in the West, but also in such Asian centres as Bali and Mumbai (2008). Attacks in the Muslim world were frequent. For example, Turkey was hit by suicide bombings in 2003, Saudi Arabia in 2003–4, Jordan in 2005 and Algeria in 2007. Terrorist links were not always easy to unravel. The suicide bombers who, in 2004, struck Tashkent, the capital of Uzbekistan, then an American ally and also a Muslim state, may have been linked to al-Qaeda via the Islamic Movement of Uzbekistan, members of which served as jihadists in Afghanistan and Pakistan. Abortive terrorist attacks included those in Singapore in 2001 and Jordan in 2004.

There was an (understandable) tendency to treat all militant Islamic groups as closely linked, even though the key element was often as much indigenous causes. Thus, Algerian terrorists were linked to al-Qaeda, with which they formally merged in 2006, but the root cause of the violence by Muslim militants within Algeria was the decision in 1992 by the State Council to ban the Islamic Salvation Front and proclaim a state of emergency, a measure taken in order to preserve power in the face of the electoral appeal of the Front. This action led to a civil war that remained at a high level until 1999 and that resulted in over 100,000 deaths and, maybe, over 150,000. In turn, this conflict helped make violence normative in Algeria. It also became a base for terrorist attacks elsewhere, a process helped by the Algerian diaspora, both in France and Britain.

Al-Qaeda was keen to assert links between such struggles, as they were seen as ways to aid recruitment and fund-raising: al-Qaeda portrays Islam as under consistent attack from without and within, an attack requiring a violent defence. Yet, the links, for example with the militants responsible for suicide bombers in Morocco in 2003 and 2007, could be tenuous. Frequently, it was rather the case of a similar method and rhetoric, as with Ansar Bayt al-Maqdas (Companions of Jerusalem), a jihadist group in the Sinai that attacked Egyptian police and army positions in the early 2010s. Like Pakistan's North-West Frontier and the desert hinterlands of Libya and Mali, Sinai was an area under limited governmental control.

There were rivalries within the fundamentalist camp, for example between Waziris and (foreign) Uzbeks in Pakistan in 2007. Indeed, the Waziris were able to draw on support from the army in this fighting. These rivalries were part of a more general process in which local fundamentalists often resent foreign jihadists, a situation seen in Iraq and Syria. This tension is a reflection of the multiple differences within Islam, the strong sense of ethnic distinction, competition over resources, and disagreements over leadership and tactics. All are underplayed by broad-brush talk of the War on Terror. This tension is readily apparent with the divisions within the Boko Haram movement in Nigeria and with the tension between the Islamic Courts groups and the *Shabab* groups in Somalia.[9]

Counter-terrorism

For states confronting terrorism, counter-terrorist operations posed serious difficulties, not least the identification of opponents and the brevity of the period in which it is possible to engage with them; problems which were greatly exacerbated by the terrorists' use of suicide as a method. Under the guise of 'martyrdom', this indeed is al-Qaeda's trademark, one designed to cause massive casualties, to exploit unpredictability and to instil fear, as well as to demonstrate commitment and devotion.

There are also conceptual problems in such conflict that are linked to the question of policy. The terminology used towards opponents delegitimates them: instead of 'freedom fighters' and 'war', we have 'terrorists' and 'terrorism', but this terminology can make it more difficult to conceive of a strategy that matches political with military methods and goals. As a result, this approach may make it harder to probe the possibilities for an exit strategy. On the other hand, the extreme anti-Western position and millenarian goals of al-Qaeda and its allies, and their apparent relish for extraordinary violence, do not make negotiations an easy option, as was revealed in 2014 in negotiations between the government of Pakistan and the Pakistani Taliban.

Aside from the specific need to respond to al-Qaeda, not least to lessen the chance of fresh attacks, it is not surprising, in light of its strategic culture and governmental assumptions, that the USA sought a military solution for what appeared to be its more general strategic crisis. The National Security Strategy issued in September 2002 was strategically and operationally ambitious. Pressing the need for pre-emptive strikes, in response to what were seen as the dual threats of terrorist regimes and 'rogue states' possessing or developing weapons of mass destruction, the strategy sought to transform the global political order to lessen the chance of these threats developing. To that end, the first paragraph proposed a universalist message that linked the end of the Cold War to the new challenge:

> The great struggles of the twentieth century between liberty and totalitarianism ended with a decisive victory for the forces of freedom ... These values of freedom are right and true for every person, in every society – and the duty of these values against their enemies is the common calling of freedom-loving people across the globe and across the ages ... We will extend the peace by encouraging free and open societies on every continent.

In an interesting echo, General Yuri Baluevsky, the Chief of the Russian General Staff, declared on 8 September 2004 that Russia could deliver pre-emptive strikes on terrorist bases anywhere in the world. In the hands of some excitable writers, the notion of pre-emption was pushed very far indeed. John Keegan, a British military historian and newspaper defence correspondent, wrote:

> The World Trade Centre outrage was coordinated on the internet ... If Washington is serious in its determination to eliminate terrorism, it will have to forbid internet providers to allow the transmission of encrypted messages ... Uncompliant providers on foreign territory should expect their buildings to be destroyed by cruise missiles.[10]

Iraq

Striking against terrorist bases, as in Afghanistan, became part of an American doctrine, named the Bush Doctrine, of pre-emptive attack against hostile states. As a result, conflict returned to the Gulf in early 2003 when Iraq was attacked by a preponderantly American force, with the participation of a large section of the British military and of small Australian, Polish, Czech and Slovak contingents. The key element was the 125,000 US combat troops on the ground, although Britain supplied 45,000 troops and Australia 2,000. However, the Coalition involved was far smaller than that in 1991, not least with the absence of Arab and French participation. Moreover, King Abdullah would not allow the USA to advance into Iraq from Saudi Arabia; and Turkey also refused transit, a key development as such consent had initially been anticipated. These refusals affected not only the military options for intervention but also the political possibilities, and thus altered the strategy in both respects.

The campaign, and the preparations for it, was conducted in the glare of media attention and pundit discussion, and there was considerable speculation as to how far it corresponded with current notions about an RMA, as well as related debates about the character of modern Western military capability and development. Iraq provided the USA with a definite (and defiant) target with regular armed forces; rather than the more intangible struggle with terrorism, which challenged Western conventions of warmaking. The attack was presented in terms of 'drying up the swamp' – eliminating a state allegedly supporting terrorism, for example against Israel (although not in fact, despite claims by American politicians and officials, backing al-Qaeda) – as well as, more specifically, destroying Iraq's supposed capability in weapons of mass destruction and ending Iraq's breaching of UN resolutions. There were particular concerns about Iraqi chemical and bacteriological warheads, and indeed the conviction that they existed affected the military planning and also encouraged an early attack. However, the claims about Iraqi weapons of mass destruction were subsequently to be discredited.

Operation Iraqi Freedom, the American-led and dominated campaign in Iraq in 2003, with its rapid and successful advance up the Euphrates valley on Baghdad, was widely praised for its manoeuvrist character and for its ability to gain and seize the initiative, disorientating the Iraqi military and government, and hitting their capacity to respond. Echoing mistaken assumptions in 1991 about the strength of the Iraqi defence, predictions that the Iraqis would use chemical weapons and blow up bridges and dams, or that it would be hard to overrun the Iraqi cities and that they would pose problems like those faced by the Germans in Stalingrad in 1942, with the American military being chewed up in the course of their capture, were all totally disproved.

These predictions had rested on the assumption that the Iraqis had responded to their defeat in 1991 by deciding not to contest the Americans in manoeuvrist warfare (the technology of which would give the Americans an advantage), and, instead, to abandon the desert and focus on the cities, hoping to repeat the success of Mohamed Aideed in Mogadishu in 1993. Indeed, both in 1991 and in 2003, Saddam Hussein appears to have counted on the Americans suffering if they could be forced to abandon the distant use of firepower for close combat. He appears to have anticipated that the problems of urban warfare would lessen American technological advantages and lead to casualties that obliged the American government to change policy.[11]

If so, Saddam's analysis was certainly mistaken in the short term, and anyway could not prevent conquest by a well-organised and high-tempo, American-dominated invasion force. This rapid conquest was a result that suggested that America's opponents elsewhere would need to turn to other methods of deterrence and opposition, most obviously nuclear arms. The coherence of the Iraqi regime, its ability to intimidate the population, and the possibility of exploiting American vulnerability along their long lines of advance were all overcome by the high tempo of American attacks and the ability to sustain the advance at this rate. This tempo accentuated weaknesses in the regime, including its long-standing fear of the Iraqi military and concern about the possibility of coups. The Iraqi attacks on American supply lines, for example at the Euphrates bridge-town of Nasiriya, attracted considerable media attention, but the forces available for such attacks were a local irritant that could be bypassed on the drive on Baghdad, rather than operationally significant. Despite short-term problems, which were understandable given the fast tempo of the advance, American logistics proved able to support the offensive. Saddam's use of Fedayeen irregulars, some of whom fought vigorously, did, however, lead to somewhat naïve American complaints about such Iraqi tactics as disguise and fake surrender.

Much of the Republican Guard ran away in the face of American firepower. Units that redeployed or stood and fought were pulverized, with particular effort being devoted to destroying Iraqi artillery and armour. This effort represented the tactical and operational value of American air power. These tactical attacks accomplished more than the 'Shock and Awe' assault on Baghdad from the night of 19 March 2003 at the outset of the struggle, although the latter's impact on Iraqi command and control was significant. Moreover, had it occurred, the killing or wounding of Saddam Hussein in an air strike would have reflected the strategic value of air power in disrupting opposing leadership. Air power also brought a valuable dominance of reconnaissance. Thus, Coalition units were informed of the location of opposing Iraqi units, while it was difficult for the Iraqis to find targets, most obviously for their artillery, until they were engaged by them.

In their campaign, the Americans made particular use of Joint Direct Attack Munitions (JDAMS) which employed GPS to make conventional bombs act as satellite-guided weapons. This capability was an important addition to the improvement in American air power capability that characterised post-Vietnam developments. Although there were differences of opinion between Britain and the USA over targeting, a pattern already seen in the Bosnian and Kosovo crises, the air assault did not face the constraints that had affected the attack on the Serbs in Operation Allied Force in 1999. Instead, with a clear target, it was possible to use air power effectively, and, in turn, to contribute to its reputation for effectiveness. About 70 per cent of the aerial munitions employed were 'smart' or guided, rather than 'dumb' or unguided, in contrast to 10 per cent against Iraq in 1991.

The Americans also benefited from the use of helicopter gunships, especially the impressive AH-60 Apache, from Predator and Global Hawk UAVs and from improvements in the accuracy of artillery fire. The Iraqi Russian-built T-55s, T-62s and, even, T-72s that were not destroyed by air attack, as many were, could not prevail against the American Abrams and the British Challenger II tanks (which were also able to resist rocket-propelled grenades). Moreover, the American use of night-vision goggles enabled them to maintain the pace of the assault, and thus to prevent the Iraqis from resupplying and regrouping. The Coalition's armoured personnel carriers were also better than the Iraqi counterparts. More generally, the Americans benefited from intensive realistic training from the 1980s, while the British forces also proved well trained.

In turn, the Iraqis had good artillery and made effective use of rocket-propelled grenades, a dangerous enhancement to infantry firepower. However, although there had been improvements in Iraqi quality, as a honed-down force was sought, their military was far weaker than in 1991, in large part because the impact of international sanctions since then had limited the build-up of modern weaponry. Much of the Iraqi weaponry was obsolete, a result of arms embargoes after the 1991 Gulf War; but, more significant, was a lack of morale and cohesion on the part of much of the regular army. Conscripted through intimidation, much of this army were disaffected Shias who were ready to desert. The destruction of the regime's grip proved a key element in encouraging mass desertion, with the troops melting into the population, a process aided by the degree to which much of the conflict occurred in the south, where the Shias were in a majority. In addition, the officer corps was demoralised. Some had plotted against the regime, relatively few had much time for it, and the collapse of the regime's grip increased the tendency towards disaffection and the disintegration of units.

The morale of the regulars had been lessened by the favour shown to the rival Republican Guard, a force of 50,000–60,000 troops that received better pay, food and equipment. Nevertheless, the Republican Guard also had varied loyalty and limited training, while their equipment had deteriorated in the 1990s due to an absence of upgrading and of adequate maintenance. The lack of training proved particularly serious, and helped ensure that troops that were willing to die caused relatively few casualties among the Coalition forces. This situation was also true of the irregulars who had been built up into a force by Saddam's eldest son, Uday.

Once they had closed on Baghdad, the Americans, from 5 April 2003, launched 'thunder runs', armoured thrusts into the city demonstrating that their opponents could not prevent these advances, and therefore greatly undermining their position there. In at least this case, manoeuvre warfare was thus shown to work in an urban context, and tanks proved able to destroy those who fought back. The lack of any real Iraqi attempt to use the very extensive urban cover offered by Baghdad helped the Americans. Having captured Baghdad, where organised resistance collapsed on 9 April, the Americans pressed on to overrun the rest of Iraq without encouraging the large-scale opposition that was feared, especially in Saddam Hussein's hometown of Tikrit, which fell on 14 April.

The British meanwhile had taken Basra, Iraq's second most populous city, which finally fell on 6–7 April. However, they were too heavily committed thereabouts to offer effective assistance further north. This success proved a striking contrast with the failures of repeated Iranian attacks on Basra, their key goal, during the war of 1980–88.

A prime element of debate before the campaign, which was revived during it when American supply lines came under serious attack, had related to the number of troops required for a successful invasion. The Secretary of Defense, Donald Rumsfeld, and other non-military commentators had been encouraged by the rapid overthrow of the Taliban regime in Afghanistan in 2001 to argue that air power and special forces were the prime requirements for successful operations, and that the large number of troops pressed for by the army leadership, both for the Iraq invasion and for the subsequent occupation of Iraq, was excessive. In the event, military pressure led to the allocation of sizeable numbers for the invasion of Iraq, but these were less numerous than those deployed in 1991.

Moreover, the 2003 campaign did not see the full committal of forces originally envisaged because the Turkish refusal to allow an invasion across their frontier with Iraq ensured that troops from the American Fourth Infantry Division prepared for that invasion could not be used at the outset of the war. However, American special forces, landed by air from the night of 22–23 March, helped direct Kurdish pressure (and American bombing) on government forces in northern Iraq. Kurdish and American forces captured the city of Kirkuk on 10 April, and, the next day, Mosul, the most important city in the north, surrendered. Concern that Turkey would complicate the situation by invading northern Iraq and clashing with the Kurds proved unfounded, while Iran also did not intervene. The failure of Iraq to fire their Saud missiles against Israel also ensured that the internationalisation of the conflict was limited.[12]

The consequences of the rapid fall of Iraq did, however, expose one of the problems with having insufficient troops in that it proved difficult to restore order and the workings of government. Too few troops had been dispatched, in part because of a conviction that American capability was such that only three divisions would be required and, in part, due to an underrating of the difficulty of securing internal support. The mass welcome in Iraq that had been anticipated, in large part as a result of a willingness to accept the promises of exiles, did not materialise. Rumsfeld indeed planned to redeploy much of the invasion force out of Iraq as soon as the invasion was over. There was also inadequate preparation for post-war disorder and division, not least widespread looting; a failure that was largely due to Rumsfeld and to misplaced confidence by him and his advisers.[13] They made frequent reference to the ease of maintaining control in Austria, Germany and Japan in the late 1940s. In building up a new government, support was given to Ahmed Chalabi, although it turned out that he was far less popular than he had led the Americans to assume.

The collapse of the Saddam regime led to American talk of pressing on to attack other states that harboured terrorism and were developing weapons of mass destruction, particularly Iran and Syria. Yet, the failure to restore order in Iraq and the costs of that commitment, in turn, swiftly fostered caution, and led to a reaction against interventionism in this form. The situation in Iraq swiftly proved intractable, with American forces unable to fill the security vacuum left by the rapid and total collapse of the Baathist regime. Nor were they able to enforce a monopoly of force. The American decision to disband the Iraqi army and to push through a policy of de-Baathification helped rally support for a Sunni insurrection, and both supporters of the regime and unemployed former soldiers played key roles in the insurgency. The capture of Saddam Hussein on 13 December 2003, and his subsequent trial and execution, made no difference. Part of the violence was directed against American forces, in what can be termed an insurgency, although it was in practice less coherent and more disorganised than such a term might suggest.

The insurgency developed just after the overthrow of the Saddam regime. It was related to greatly increased sectarian violence, verging at times on civil war, with Sunni–Shia differences intertwined with disputes over autonomy and oil revenues. In particular, many of the Sunnis were at best ambivalent about a democratic Iraq governing the entire country, which they saw in terms of rule by the majority Shia, whose backlash they feared. There was also a pronounced overlap between Sunni insurgent activity and straightforward criminality, not least in the propensity to resort to kidnapping. This overlap also made suppression of the insurgency particularly difficult. Saddam Hussein's freeing of criminals from the prisons compounded the problem.

In turn, the numerous Shia militias provided the Shia population with a degree of protection against the suicide bombings of Sunni extremists. There were also major differences within the Shia and Sunni communities. In part, these rivalries could be subsumed into wider themes by presenting them in terms of a clash between fundamentalism and moderation, but the situation was more complex. Clan, factional and personal ambitions all played a role, not least with the struggles between Shia militias to control branches of the Iraqi state.

In response, the American military adopted a big-unit approach, with an emphasis on conventional tactics, rather than on those appropriate for counter-insurgency. The stress on armour and air support provided firepower, and it proved possible to detain thousands of Iraqis, but such detention exacerbated resentment without winning support. Although they faced serious problems in and around Bosnia, British military observers felt the American response inappropriate and unlikely to win 'hearts and minds', as also, with time, did a growing number of American commentators.[14] In terms of a response reliant on force, there were insufficient troops as well as inappropriate tactics.

Problems were also created by shifts in American policy. The priorities rapidly moved from that of removing Saddam Hussein to establishing a liberal democracy that would bring stability and create a model for the Muslim world; indeed for a transformation of values and practices that would help anchor the international order. This highly ambitious plan was not only seriously unrealistic but also required a degree of peacefulness that made disorder a particular challenge and threat. In time, the Americans moved from this goal to that of extrication. However, political exigencies within the USA were a powerful constraint, not least George W. Bush's determination to win re-election in November 2004. He felt that he needed to be seen to have succeeded in Iraq. Re-election was particularly challenging due to the precarious nature of Bush's election in 2000. After re-election, there was the matter of his concern with 'legacy' issues.

Post-war disorder did not cease when the Americans handed over power to an Iraqi government in June 2004. Most resistance was faction-based. Sunni insurgents took over control of towns and were able to resist American and Iraqi attempts to drive them out. The insurgency drew on foreign volunteers, but also on members of Saddam Hussein's forces who regrouped during the American occupation.

A major challenge also came from Shia activists, especially the large 'Mahdi Army' militia of the firebrand cleric Moqtada al-Sadr. This militia rebelled in April 2004,[15] and took over the town of Najaf and held it against attack in August 2004. Looking to Iran for support, Shia militias were able to resist the new Iraqi army. The Shia-dominated al-Maliki government of Prime Minister Nuri al-Maliki, which took office in May 2006, was readier to accommodate itself to power within the Shia community than to confront it. The extent to which the Iraqi police was riddled with factions was also a major problem.

The situation on the ground in 2006 undermined the American attempt to transfer control to Iraqi security forces. Terrorist attacks that caused large numbers of civilian and military casualties undermined any sense of stability. The replacement of General George Casey by General David Petraeus in the winter of 2006–7, however, led to a new engagement with counter-insurgency. A 'surge' in American numbers in 2007, with the addition of 30,000 more combat troops, considerably eased the security situation, while also responding to the debate within the USA over the goals, implementation and timing of policy. This 'surge' was designed to provide the opportunity to create an effective relationship between the Iraqi public and government, bypassing, in the process, both insurgents and independent militia.

The US forces were successful in sponsoring the formation of 'concerned local citizen', later called 'Sons of Iraq', groups: neighbourhood militias that would contribute to stability. Whereas, earlier, Iraqi support for the US-backed government had been from some sections of the Shia community, many of these groups were Sunnis and their action represented a choice against the chaos and brutality of al-Qaeda-linked terrorists. The US also negotiated with former insurgent groups such as the 1920 Revolution Brigades. Al-Qaeda brutality, for example the killing of tribal leaders and the forcible recruitment of suicide bombers, had alienated much Sunni support for al-Qaeda, and this had strategic consequences. The *Sahwa* (awakening), the co-operation of Sunni tribesmen with the Americans against al-Qaeda in 2008, helped turn the tide politically.

Al-Qaeda brutality received far less attention in the West than occasional and unauthorised brutalities by Coalition forces, as in the Abu Ghraib prison. The respective degree of attention devoted to the two types of brutality is highly instructive, for Western self-criticism, while praiseworthy, also leads to a marked failure to appreciate typicality and proportionality. At the same time, an understanding of failures on the part of Coalition forces, however atypical these failures may be, is important when considering popular attitudes in Iraq and Afghanistan. The treatment of civilians during policing operations aroused a lot of local anger, notably the extent to which the privacy of women was not respected when homes were raided.

The sponsoring of allied forces by the USA in Iraq was an aspect of 'the surge' which was successful, as was the negative goal of thwarting civil war. The USA understood that it had to operate in response to Iraq's sectarian divides. By creating a shared constituency with the Sunni, the Americans reduced their own dependence on the Shia and gave the latter more reason to compromise, and thus to accommodate Sunni interests. In turn, the Sunni were provided with a way to abandon the insurgency. There were parallels here with British policy in Northern Ireland in the 1990s. The key goal was to try to differentiate among opponents, and to create the basis for compromise with some of them.

As a military correlate, there was an emphasis on information-driven operations, especially raids, rather than on the larger-scale application of force. In particular, there was an attempt to regain the initiative from the insurgents, especially by killing their leaders and attacking their safe havens and logistical bases. In place of raid-and-return, a method that aroused popular anger as well as fear, the emphasis for the Coalition forces was on moving troops among the people, to heighten confidence and to create a sense of security. This emphasis reflected a more appropriate doctrine, as well as improved training and tactics. Thus, a more pragmatic politics was accompanied by more pertinent tactics. Four years too late, of course, but better than nothing and also showing the capacity of the military to change and develop. This capacity places a question mark against the commonplace comments about inherent national cultural military styles, although, looked at differently, the degree of such a capacity can be an aspect of military style and culture.

More specifically, the challenge of operations in Iraq affected the balance between and within American arms. There was a stronger emphasis, as a result of these operations, on current and likely future roles for infantry and special forces, and a decline in that allocated for armour and artillery. Instead, armour and artillery units were sent to Iraq without their equipment and were expected to act as infantry there: the case for three-quarters of the American armoured units sent. This practice hit training and familiarisation with weaponry and aroused concern among commanders about the loss of skills. Ironically, the increased use by insurgents of improvised roadside bombs and the serious damage they inflicted on infantry ensured that it became necessary to increase the armoured protection of ordinary troop transports and armoured personnel carriers. While not tanks, the results were a reminder of the need to combine protection with mobility.

Aside from problems in Iraq, the wider political and geopolitical equations moved against the USA as it found itself entangled in a crisis that lessened its options elsewhere, both in the Arab world and more widely. The issue was played out in American politics, with the Bush administration emphasising the need to stay the course, but this was as part of an increasingly pessimistic prospectus in which the stress was on extrication and on leaving Iraq to the Iraqis. Compared with hopes in 2003, this stress represented a more limited definition of success which, indeed, may be an aspect of modern warfare. In addition, the American ability to act elsewhere had been lessened, politically, financially and in terms of the armed force available. Thus, there was no military intervention to stop genocide in the Darfur region of Sudan.

The Iraq War led the Americans to devote renewed effort to their already vigorous debate about force structure and tasking. At the risk of considerable simplification, this debate located discussion about weaponry within consideration of the continued validity of a military centred on separate services. Rumsfeld was particularly keen on breaking with what he perceived as a conservative inheritance advocated strongly by the army out of line with what he saw as the need for rapidly delivered force. Interest in new weaponry focused on AirLand combinations, but included research into space weapons systems as well as on low-yield nuclear weaponry that was regarded as an important way to upgrade America's nuclear capability. The Iraq commitment helped to drive change. COIN strategy, doctrine, training and equipment became far more significant than in the 1990s. The public endorsement of COIN was seen with the doctrine presented by the Army and Marines in Field Manual 3–24 *Counter-Insurgency* (2006).

Meanwhile, due in large part to the War on Terror and the Iraq commitment, American defence expenditure rose. It had risen from $276 billion in 1998 to $310 billion in 2001. As an instance of the less threatening atmosphere prior to the War on Terror, William Cohen, Secretary of Defense under Clinton, had called in February 1999 for spending to reach $318.9 billion by 2005. In the event, by 2010, the USA was spending about $693 billion a year.

Moreover, America's share of world military expenditure was very high. In 2000, the USA already spent $295 billion, compared to a figure for Russia and China combined of $100 billion. The 2001 figure was more than the next nine largest national military budgets combined, while, for 2002, the sum was about 40 per cent of the world's total military spending, although expectations of, and costs for, items such as pay, food and social benefits varied greatly across the world. This expenditure on military social welfare, however, does not necessarily translate into lower effectiveness for the high spenders, as attractive conditions and high morale help with recruitment and the crucial issue of retention.

The total cost of the Iraq War and subsequent occupation is a matter of controversy, and much of it does not appear in the military budget, not least as a result of the outsourcing represented by the large-scale use of contractors. Controversy surrounded the conduct of the most prominent, Blackwater, which was criticised for exacerbating relations with Iraqi civilians. By 2007, there were about 100,000 contractors in Iraq, including 35,000 with explicit private security commitments. Contractors suffered the second-largest number of Coalition casualties in Iraq: after the American military, but more than its British counterpart. There were claims that the large-scale use of contractors represented a privitisation of the military; it was certainly an application of outsourcing in a sphere in which it had been relatively uncommon in recent centuries.

A 2008 study suggested that the costs, for the USA, of the Iraq and Afghanistan conflicts, by then ranged between $2.2 trillion and $5 trillion.[16] This expenditure put a heavy burden on American public expenditure, which, in turn, exacerbated the divisions in American politics. Moreover, popular views that the war was not worth fighting contributed to a broader pattern of damage in the 2000s to the political fabric of American society.[17] These views also affected the international effectiveness of America by lessening support for a future conflict.

More specifically, the wars posed serious issues for the structure of the military. Manpower strains were acute. Possibly the attacks in 2001 represented an opportunity for a mobilisation of opinion within the USA behind a new commitment to public service, notably in the National Guard, and even a degree of conscription, or the far easier alternative of the expansion of army strength through improved pay funded by taxation. That, however, was not the route taken by the Bush government, not least due to its commitment to Transformation and emphasising new weaponry. This situation helped ensure that the manpower available was put under enormous pressure by the addition of the long-term commitments in Afghanistan and Iraq to existing obligations. For example, in March 2006 there were 138,000 American troops in Iraq.

Lengthened tours of service greatly affected morale and, thus, retention in both the army and the National Guard, and, breaching Pentagon guidelines, reduced the time available for training. Nevertheless, the determination of the military remained apparent. Polls indicated declining support for the war within the army, but, while this probably contributed to a rise in suicide rates and certainly influenced retention, it was not pushed towards public disaffection. For example, in 2006, Lieutenant Ehren Watada refused to serve in Iraq on the grounds that the war was 'not only morally wrong but a horrible breach of American law', but this was very much an isolated stance. Similar manpower issues affected Britain and Canada, both of which sent troops to Afghanistan.

Repeated tours did not bring much of an understanding of local culture,[18] but certainly increased experience of counter-insurgency warfare. For example, American troops gained experience in how to counter improvised explosive devices (IEDs). They developed relevant technology, such as jammers designed to thwart remote triggers for IEDs, as well as relevant tactics. These tactics were not only defensive but also offensive, for example the deployment of snipers near likely ambush spots. In turn, the insurgents used larger bombs as well as their own snipers, creating a new front line around the use of IEDs. IEDs became a major problem for soldiers and civilians, not only in Iraq but also in Afghanistan. Suicide car bombs were also employed in both, against Western forces and their local allies.

In Iraq, the Americans were able, not least thanks to their 'surge' in troop numbers in 2007 (by when they were spending $54 billion annually to support their military operations in Iraq), as well as their building up of a new Iraqi army and police, to improve the security situation considerably. Much also depended on the willingness of hostile Iranian-linked Shia militias to draw back from confronting the Americans. Instead, in pursuit of influence, these militias focused on conflict with each other. The American-backed government enjoyed only limited authority. It increasingly looked to Iran and the Iranian ability to influence the militias. In contrast, concerned about Afghanistan, the Americans sought disengagement. At the end of 2011, in response to demands from the Iraqi government, the Americans withdrew their last combat troops from Iraq.[19] There was no sense of triumph and only a limited sense of a mission fulfilled.

Sectarian conflict in Iraq resumed after the departure of American forces. The Shia-led government of Prime Minister Nuri al-Maliki was unwelcome to most Sunnis, who complained about what they saw as their marginalisation. At the close of 2013, conflict broke out in the Sunni-dominated province of Anbar, with anti-government tribal fighters taking over government buildings in the two main cities: Fallujah, long a centre of opposition, and Ramadi. Fighting the national army, the Sunni tribal fighters treated it as a Shia militia force loyal to al-Maliki. As a separate issue, Islamist militants linked to al-Qaeda stormed police stations in Anbar, freeing prisoners and seizing weapons. In 2014, they overran most of the Sunni areas of Iraq.

With the example of Iraq, Shia–Sunni conflict had also become more common and bitter from 2003 across the Islamic world. It led to violence against minorities, for example in Pakistan. International alignments were also affected. The influence of Iran in Afghanistan was limited, because Iran is a Shia state and most Afghans are Sunnis. This encouraged the Afghans to look to Pakistan, both to the Taliban and to the Pakistani government. Sectarian violence interacted with other tensions, for example ethnic, regional and economic. Thus, in northern Yemen in late 2013, Houthis, followers of the Zaidi school of Shia Islam, fought Sunni tribesmen.

As with the different political and military case of Afghanistan, Iraq, from the Western perspective, can be viewed as an instance of an inability to create effective peacemaking that contrasted with the initial military victory. This is a common issue. However, as with Afghanistan, Iraq can also be seen in terms of a more continual process of conflict between groups within the society, with a measure of external intervention as well. In this process, peacekeeping can be understood as an attempt to contain counter-attacks between the local warring groups as well as from them against the peacekeepers. This situation thus brings together two very different military narratives, with current equations of Western power, such as kill-ratios or troop density, only being of limited value.

New weaponry

Although no other power could match American expenditure, the impact of American weaponry in Iraq in 2003, and the claims that it ushered in a new age of warfare, encouraged interest elsewhere in procuring similar weapons. This situation was true, for example, of Britain and Israel, in each of which the development of drones was stepped up, and also of Japan, which felt increasingly threatened by North Korean rocketry. This fear led to Japanese interest in anti-missile defences and in satellite surveillance. Japan launched its own spy satellites in 2003.

Article Nine of the Japanese Constitution, which the USA imposed on Japan after World War Two, states that 'land, sea, and air forces, as well as other war potential, will never be maintained'. As a result, Japan has 'Self-Defence Forces' (SDF). However, these are very numerous, 258,000 strong in 2003, and well armed, indeed one of the most powerful militaries in the world. Nevertheless, the 1992 Japanese law authorising the SDF to deploy abroad included strict restrictions on what they could do: they could only be sent to areas where a ceasefire was in place. SDF troops were sent to help UN peacekeepers in Cambodia (1992), Mozambique (1993) and East Timor (1999 and 2002); to help Rwandan refugees (1994); and to assist in peacekeeping in Iraq after the Second Gulf War.

Cruise missiles attracted greater international interest after their large-scale use in Iraq in 2003. The following year, there was speculation that a Chinese invasion of Taiwan would be countered by a Taiwanese cruise missile attack on the Three Gorges Dam in the Yangzi Valley, exploiting a key point of economic and environmental vulnerability. The same year, Australia agreed to spend up to AUS$450 million on buying air-launched cruise missiles with a range of at least 250 kilometres. The Chinese *Shang*-class nuclear attack submarines that are currently entering service will be able to deploy land attack cruise missiles as well as anti-ship cruise missiles, the latter designed to limit American access to waters near China.

A continual process of innovation was an aspect of the procurement process, and the cruise missile was far from alone in this. In 2006, for example, the American air force conducted tests in which aircraft used synthetic fuel as part of their jet fuel. Moreover, stealth technology was increasingly applied to aircraft, for example to the Joint Strike Fighter developed by the USA and other partners, including Australia.

Israel

The development of satellite capability by Japan was one response to the challenges of the 2000s by a power employing advanced military systems, while India used the threat of Islamicist terrorism to justify the Prevention of Terrorism Ordinance promulgated in October 2001.[20] Israel confronted more immediate problems. Indeed, albeit in very different contexts, developments in Afghanistan, Iraq and Israel in the mid-2000s indicated the problems facing advanced militaries using the latest technology when confronted by insurrectionary movements employing guerrilla tactics and terrorist methods.

Negotiations between Israel and the Palestinians at Camp David had broken down in 2000 over the issues, first, of Israeli settlements on the West Bank of the Jordan, secondly, Arab demands that refugees, many from 1948, be allowed to return to Israel, the so-called 'right of return', and, thirdly, the status of Jerusalem. On 27 September 2000, the visit of Ariel Sharon, a retired general, then leader of the opposition Likud party, to the Haram al-Sharif, the holiest Muslim shrine in Jerusalem, in the al-Aqsa compound on the Temple Mount, led to Palestinian demonstrations and to a forcible Israeli response in which Palestinians were killed. Violence fed more violence on both sides, with Arab attacks on Israeli civilians leading to what rapidly became a more violent rising than the first *intifada*. The combination of Arab rejectionism at Camp David and the violence of the new *intifada* encouraged Israeli public opinion to regard peace talks as a failed option.

Winning power in February 2001, in part by rejecting the idea of land cessions without peace talks, Sharon promised to increase the number of settlements in the occupied territories, and, the following month, suicide bombers were used by the Hamas movement, which was more radical than the PLO (Palestinian Liberation Organisation). Israeli operations in the West Bank and Gaza indicated the limitations of Israeli military and political options: the killing of militant leaders did not stop attacks, while Israel found it difficult to foster the creation of a Palestinian constituency for effective negotiations. Equally, the attitudes and policies of the Palestinian government of Yassir Arafat made negotiations difficult. In response to continued attacks by suicide bombers, the Israelis began the construction of a security wall designed to seal off the West Bank, except through checkpoints, and thus to block suicide attacks. Sharon also switched to the very policy he had rejected, unilateral withdrawal, the policy followed by the Labour government under Ehud Barak, a former general, when Israel evacuated its 'security zone' in southern Lebanon in 2000. In 2005, the Israelis evacuated the Gaza Strip, and the army was deployed to force obdurate Jewish settlers to leave their settlements.

The use of rockets, however, ensured that Israel's hopes of clear borders and of employing fixed defences, such as walls, to provide protection appeared limited; although, in turn, the Americans helped Israel develop an anti-rocket defensive system, while walls were largely designed to provide checkpoints that would limit vulnerability to suicide bombers. In 2004, the wall between Israel and the occupied territories appeared to reduce the rate of suicide attacks; but, nevertheless, they continued, as did Israeli reprisals. Thus, in September 2004, Israel launched a missile strike that killed fourteen Hamas activists in Gaza in response to a double suicide bombing in Beersheba that had killed sixteen Israelis. A ceasefire was agreed in 2005.

The Israeli failure to win much Arab backing, a failure underlined by Hamas' success in the Palestinian Council elections of 2006, was a more serious challenge, but one that exposed the absence, in the case of Israel, of the necessary political dimension for any counter-insurgency campaign. Neither Israel nor the Palestinians nor outside powers were able to secure politically the goal of a viable Palestinian state alongside a secure Israel. This failure provided the background to acts of violence on both sides that served little point other than underlining the absence of stability and the reliance on a politics of reprisal.

Israel suffered from its inability to determine developments among other players, especially the ability of Hamas to take over control of the Gaza Strip. Israel was not able to prevent this, and thus became far more vulnerable to short-range rocket attacks mounted by Islamic Jihad, a group Hamas did not hinder. Israeli commentators calculated that, by 2012, Hamas had fired maybe 12,000 missiles from Gaza. Israeli land and air counter-attacks on rocket squads in the Gaza Strip failed to end these attacks, and Israel developed an 'Iron Dome' anti-missile system over its major cities. A ceasefire in 2012, however, led to the number of rockets fired falling from 1,500 in 2012 to 50 in 2013, in large part because Hamas forces guarded the frontier against militants.

A parallel case operated on Israel's northern border where Hizbullah consolidated its power in southern Lebanon and mounted attacks from there on Israel. In response, and more particularly to a Hizbullah ambush on 12 July 2006 of an Israeli unit patrolling the frontier, Israel decided to destroy Hizbullah's military power and capacity, especially its leadership and its large and dangerous rocket arsenal. To that end, Israel blockaded Lebanon and launched a large-scale limited invasion that month, combined with extensive aerial attack, focused in particular on rocket sites.

This offensive, however, proved misconceived and poorly executed. Several of the Israeli heavy Merkava tanks fell victim to Hizbullah use of large roadside explosive devices, and this tactical problem was an aspect of the degree to which the Israeli desire for movement and speed had to confront the exigencies of position warfare. Moreover, the Israeli air assault failed to crush resistance and, instead, racked a degree of devastation on Lebanon's civilian population that challenged Israel's international reputation, and helped ensure that Israel lost the information war. Tony Blair found his position as head of Britain's Labour Party badly damaged as a consequence, and this contributed to his resignation as Prime Minister in 2007.

In response to the Israeli attack in 2006, Hizbullah fired about 5,000 rockets, dramatically confounding Israel's capacity for deterrence. Close to a million Israelis moved south away from exposed frontier areas or took shelter in air-raid shelters. Haifa, the key city in the north, was particularly exposed. Public criticism rose, but, on the other hand, civilian resolve was not crushed. Both sides used drones, with the Israelis making particularly marked use of them as an instance of their aerial dominance and attack capacity. Hizbullah's drones had been provided by Iran, which uses its oil wealth to fund the movement, supplying it via Syria, and thus benefiting from Syria's position as Lebanon's neighbour. In 2006, Israeli air power proved unable to end rocket attacks from Lebanon, although a large percentage of the long-range Hizbullah rocket systems were destroyed.

The difficulties encountered by Israel indicated the contrast between force projection and military output (which missiles have greatly enhanced), and, on the other hand, being able to predict and force a successful resolution of the crisis. During the crisis, Israel had about 150 fatalities (120 soldiers, 30 civilians), and Hizbullah had 500–700 dead. There was no sense of achievement in Israel, which Sharon had earlier declared a regional superpower, and the Defence Minister during the war, Amir Peretz, was defeated when he stood for leader of the Labour Party in 2007. A sense of anger in Israel was seen in media criticism during the war and in the establishment by the Government of the Winograd Commission to investigate the conduct of the conflict.

Reporting in early 2008, the Commission found poor preparation and inappropriate strategy. In part, this strategy had rested on a failure to understand the extent to which Hizbullah had become more effective, making expectations about Israeli success unrealistic. Leaving aside the misguided nature of the assumption that problems could be overcome simply by the use of force, there was a failure to understand the relative military balance at the tactical, operational and strategic levels.

The major role of the international context was abundantly demonstrated by the Lebanon crisis of 2006, as the USA provided Israel with support in the face of considerable international criticism. Conversely, Syria and Iran were willing to re-arm Hizbullah after the conflict, breaching the arms embargo ordered by the UN under Resolution 1701. Hizbullah boasted that its entire military system was rapidly re-established. In addition, Hizbullah built up an even stronger rocket capacity, ensuring a potent offensive threat to Israel, and one that could be mounted from behind strengthened anti-tank and anti-aircraft defence systems. The threat posed by this rocket capacity may well lead to a resumption of Israeli attack.[21]

Iran, which finances Hizbullah, appears to see Hizbullah's strength as a deterrent to Israeli action against Iran's nuclear programme. In the meanwhile, although Israel did not regard itself as defeated, Hizbullah's proclaimed ability to resist Israel markedly increased its symbolic capital and its prestige within the radical world, ensuring more support from rejectionist powers and groups.[22] This support was an aspect of Hizbullah's ability to shape the information domain, an ability also directed against Israeli public confidence, with television footage being broadcast of Israeli casualties.[23] More generally, the continued strength of Hizbullah and its role as a force for regional instability was displayed in 2008 and thereafter in its successful confrontations with the Lebanese government.

The geopolitics involved are not solely those focused on Israel or Israel and Lebanon as both Iran and Hizbullah are part of the Shia camp in the great divide of the Islamic world between Shia and Sunni. Thus, Hizbullah forces helped the Assad regime of Syria against its opponents in the early 2010s, as the Assad regime is based on a Shia group ruling a country most of which is Sunni and where opposition is supported by Sunni powers, notably Saudi Arabia and Qatar.

The complexity of international alignments was indicated by Iran's pleasure in Hamas' ability to seize the Gaza Strip from the Fatah-dominated Palestinian government in June 2007, and yet Iran's role in supporting the Shia-dominated Iraqi government was also America's basis for stability in the country. Moreover, in 2008, in the aftermath of Israel's successful September 2007 attack on Syrian nuclear facilities, Syria and Israel sought to develop a *modus vivendi*.

Conclusions

As a reminder of the range of circumstances in which Western powers could experience difficulties, France, from 2002, found that its commitment in its former colony of Ivory Coast, an important economic power in West Africa that had hitherto been stable, encountered serious problems due to the interaction of ethnic with religious tensions which led to a bitter civil war in

2002–4. These problems were a marked qualification of the habitual French ability to direct the affairs of most of their former colonies, an ability supported by bases and forces in the Central African Republic, Chad, Djibouti, Gabon, Ivory Coast and Senegal.

The capability of advanced military powers seemed more brittle by late 2006 than had been the case in the immediate aftermath of the invasion of Iraq in 2003, and, in the case of former French Africa, was to become still more brittle by 2012–14. This shift was important not only to military history but also to the politics of the modern world and the future of war. There is also a challenge for analysts. It is easy to see a contrast between what is presented as an apogee of a Western model of warmaking and opposition by the representatives of non-Western systems; but there is a need to be wary of presenting in cultural and geographical terms what is, in part, a more widespread military practice, within as well as between systems, namely the response of the weaker power in an asymmetric relationship.[24] This response classically focuses on developing an anti-strategy, anti-operational method, anti-tactics and anti-weaponry, designed to counter and lessen, if not nullify, the advantages of the stronger.

Yet to focus on fighting may be to ignore the degree to which, and for both sides, the fighting was only part of the equation of conflict. Instead, the emphasis was on affecting the will of the other side, on exploiting its vulnerabilities and on lessening its willingness to fight. Sometimes referred to as 'hearts and minds', this was a strategy pursued by both Western and non-Western combatants, although the emphasis varied greatly. Western powers and their allies sought to win support or, at least, acquiescence in Afghanistan, Iraq, Lebanon, Palestine and elsewhere, while their opponents both resisted this process at the local level and tried to undermine domestic resolve in the Western home populations.

This process entailed two very different issues. On the one hand, there was the struggle with Muslim extremism, both in the Muslim world in South Asia and among Muslim communities in the West; and, on the other, the battle for opinion within Western majority communities. Fighting on the ground was mediated through these different perspectives. In turn, these perspectives were as much, if not more, affected by other aspects of the politics of the conflict. Real or alleged violations of the rights of terrorist suspects, for example, played a role, as, more generally, did the politics of incarceration.

For Western powers, the battle of opinion, in part, involves resisting subversion. Indeed, the latter can be seen as the most effective form of insurrection. Thus, the War on Terror centrally involves opposition to attitudes that countenance radical Islam, and this entails soft power more than the military capability that has also to be available. Such points were not at the forefront of military commentary in the 1990s, but have become far more prominent.

Doctrine has been affected, with much attention to COIN doctrines, as with American Army and Marine Corps' Field Manual 3–24, *Counter Insurgency*, published in December 2006. Secondary literature has also plundered supposedly relevant historical episodes,[25] although the extent to which comparisons can be profitably drawn is unclear. In particular, it is necessary to understand the extent to which insurgencies (like irregular warfare) vary and have the capacity to develop. This emphasis on variety and development is also relevant to the nature of counter-insurgency warfare, which itself has to respond dynamically to changing circumstances; as indeed the Americans did in Iraq, in both situational awareness and response.[26]

This situation posed particular problems for force structure, doctrine and training, as these needs are considerable in counter-insurgency warfare. Published in 2006, John McGrath's historically grounded study of troop density suggested a need for 'about 13.26 troops per 1000 inhabitants', the 13.26 including indigenous police and military as well as contractors, and he argued that, therefore, indigenous units and contractor forces were among the key factors in troop density in Iraq.[27] Indeed, the insurgents, finding American targets very difficult, devoted much effort to assaults on the Iraqi police (as in Mosul in 2004). These, in turn, encouraged the formation of police commando units, which played key roles in both combat and control. McGrath's analysis therefore directed attention to the political factors that affected the viability of relying on indigenous units, as well as the extent to which it was necessary (as well as desirable) for the world's strongest military, in its prime field of commitment, to rely on such units as well as on contractors.

The post-2003 situation in Iraq underlined broader questions about the reliance on COIN, for, aside from the practicality of counter-insurgency operations in particular contexts, it might well be unusual in the future to be able to achieve and afford such a focus in commitments. More generally, military and political practicality and viability are issues, whether or not the intention is in part to rely on allies. The costs to the USA, financial and political, of the Iraq commitment after 2003 also raised the overlapping questions of the strategic value of the commitment, the operational effectiveness of COIN, and whether a long-term 'militarisation' of a political situation was desirable even if victory, however defined, could be won. In short, did recent discussion of the best doctrine for COIN miss the point as the cost was too high, or was this only the case in terms of the particular circumstances and specifications of the Iraq crisis? Taking the example of that crisis, how many campaigns such as Operation Al Fajr (New Dawn), the hard-fought cleaning of the insurgent stronghold of Fallujah in late 2004, could be afforded by the USA or other powers?

Turned round, however, despite their rhetoric, insurgent numbers were/are not unlimited. In addition, focusing counter-insurgency conflict on particular clashes could weaken the insurgents greatly and could break the impression of insurgent success. Moreover, 'if the enemy center of gravity was their leadership',[28] then that could be disrupted or destroyed. Thus, military action could prove a direct part of the political solution. The American use of drone strikes played an important part in this process.

Furthermore, there is the more general point that lack of success is not, as it may seem, the definition of failure, as that may set too high a benchmark for justifying action. Indeed, the very commitment of troops may prevent a more serious situation, as with British Army operations in Northern Ireland from the 1960s to 1990s or, very differently, the dispatch of American National Guard troops to the Mexican border in 2006 to help the Border Patrol limit illegal immigration.[29] Possibly this is the most important conclusion. The use of force may produce a situation that is analogous to that of the police: limiting not ending crime; and/or may lead to a stasis that provides the context for eventual political discussion and negotiation.

Notes

1 Had the buildings been completely destroyed at once without any opportunities for evacuation, far more people, possibly 30,000 in total, would have been killed.

2 M.W.S. Ryan, *Decoding Al-Qaeda's Strategy: The Deep Battle against America* (New York, 2013).

3 M. Mazzetti, *The Way of the Knife: The CIA, a Secret Army, and a War at the Ends of the Earth* (London, 2013).

4 A.H. Cordesman, *The Lessons of Afghanistan* (Washington, 2002); C. Conetta, *Strange Victory: A Critical Appraisal of Operation Enduring Freedom and the Afghanistan War* (Cambridge, Massachusetts, 2002).

5 D.M. Drew, 'U.S. Airpower Theory and the Insurgent Challenge: A Short Journey to Confusion', *Journal of Military History*, 62 (1998), pp. 809–32, esp. pp. 824, 829–30; C. Malkasian, *A History of Modern Wars of Attrition* (Westport, Connecticut, 2002), p. 205.

6 S. Biddle, *Afghanistan and the Future of Warfare: Implications for Army and Defense Policy* (Carlisle, Pennsylvania, 2002), summarised in Biddle, 'Afghanistan and the Future of Warfare', *Foreign Affairs*, 82, 2 (Mar./Apr. 2003), pp. 31–46. For a different approach, S.D. Wrage (ed.), *Immaculate Warfare: Participants Reflect on the Air Campaigns over Kosovo, Afghanistan, and Iraq* (Westport, Connecticut, 2003).

7 R.W. Stewart, *Operation Enduring Freedom* (Washington, 2003), pp. 38–39.

8 C.C. Fair and P. Chalk, *Fortifying Pakistan: The Role of US Internal Security Assistance* (Washington, 2006).

9 J. Zenn, A. Barkindo and N.A. Heras, 'The Ideological Evolution of Boko Haram in Nigeria', *RUSI Journal*, 158, no. 4 (Aug./Sept. 2013), pp. 46–53; S.J. Hansen, *Al-Shabaab in Somalia: The History and Ideology of a Militant Islamist Group, 2005–2012* (London, 2013).

10 J. Keegan, 'How America Can Wreak Vengeance', *Daily Telegraph*, 14 Sept. 2001, p. 22. For a far better-considered response, M. Howard '"9/11" and After: A British View', *Naval War College Review*, 55, 4 (autumn 2002), pp. 12–13.

11 T. Dodge, 'Cake Walk, Coup or Urban Warfare: The Battle for Iraq', in Dodge and S. Simon (eds), *Iraq at the Crossroads: State and Society in the Shadow of Regime Change* (Oxford, 2003), pp. 59, 70–71. For the challenge of cities, D. Kilcullen, *Out of the Mountains: The Coming Age of the Urban Guerrilla* (Oxford, 2013).

12 W. Murray and R.H. Scales, *The Iraq War* (Cambridge, Massachusetts, 2003).

13 M.R. Gordon and B.E. Trainor, *Cobra II: The Inside Story of the Invasion and Occupation of Iraq* (New York, 2007).

14 M. Knights, *Cradle of Conflict: Iraq and the Birth of the Modern US Military* (Annapolis, Maryland, 2005).

15 M. Etherington, *Revolt on the Tigris: The Al-Sadr Uprising and the Governing of Iraq* (London, 2005).

16 J.E. Stiglitz and L. Bilmes, *The Three Trillion Dollar War. The True Cost of the Iraq Conflict* (London, 2008).

17 J.J. Mearsheimer, 'America Unhinged', *The National Interest*, 129 (Jan./Feb. 2014), p. 25.

18 K.W. Eikenberry, 'The Limits of Counterinsurgency Doctrine in Afghanistan: The Other Side of the COIN', *Foreign Affairs*, 92, 5 (Sept./Oct. 2013), pp. 62–63.

19 M.R. Gordon and B.E. Trainor, *The Endgame: The Inside Story of the Struggle for Iraq, from George W. Bush to Barack Obama* (New York, 2012).

20 U.K. Singh, *The State, Democracy and Anti-Terror Laws in India* (New Delhi, 2007).

21 A. Cordesman, 'Preliminary "Lessons" of the Israeli-Hizbullah War', *Centre for Strategic and International Studies* (2006); M. van Creveld, 'Israel's Lebanese War: A Preliminary Assessment', *RUSI Journal*, 151 (Oct. 2006), pp. 40–43.

22 R. Leenders, 'How the Rebel Regained His Cause: Hizbullah and the Sixth Arab-Israeli War', *MIT Electronic Journal of Middle East Studies*, 6 (2006).

23 A.F. Marrero, 'Hezbollah as a Non-State Actor in the Second Lebanon War: An Operational Analysis', in K.D. Gott and M.G. Brooks (eds), *Warfare in the Age of Non-State Actors: Implications for the US Army* (Fort Leavenworth, Kansas, 2007).

24 R. Thornton, *Asymmetric Warfare: Threat and Response in the 21st Century* (London, 2007).

25 J.A. Nagl, *Learning to Eat Soup with a Knife: Counter-insurgency Lessons from Malaya and Vietnam* (Chicago, 2005); D. Galula, *Counter-insurgency Warfare: Theory and Practice* (Westport, Connecticut, 2006); D. Marston and C. Malkasian (eds), *Counterinsurgency in Modern Warfare* (London, 2008).

26 J. Record, *Beating Goliath: Why Insurgencies Win* (Dulles, Virginia, 2007).

27 J.J. McGrath, *Boots on the Ground: Troop Density in Contingency Operations* (Fort Leavenworth, Kansas, 2006), pp. 135, 147.

28 P. Boisson, 'Punishment in Syahcow, Afghanistan, 25 July 2005', in W.G. Robertson (ed.), *In Contact! Case Studies from the Long War* (Fort Leavenworth, Kansas, 2006), p. 120.

29 M.M. Matthews, *The U.S. Army on the Mexican Border: A Historical Perspective* (Fort Leavenworth, Kansas, 2007), p. 83.

6

A MULTITUDE OF CONFLICTS

The problems of the Western militaries considered in chapter 5 reflected the bringing together of the two narratives of warfare separately discussed in chapters 3 and 4. In the 2000s and 2010s, as in the 1990s, these narratives continued to have a separate existence as well as being brought together. This chapter begins with Afghanistan where the bringing together considered in chapter 5 continued chronologically, before focusing on Third World conflict that did not so directly involve the major powers.

The overwhelming majority of states in the world were neither leading military powers nor 'rogue states'. In many countries, especially, but not only, in Africa and Latin America, the prime purpose of the military was internal control, although its position in this respect was rivalled by paramilitary forces. For example, the Iranian Revolutionary Guard Corps, established as a result of the Iranian Revolution of 1979, was, by 2000, better equipped than the Iranian regular army, as well as more important politically and more radical and dangerous in international relations. In territorial terms, the military challenge in many states came, and comes, not so much from foreign powers as from domestic regional opposition to states, some of it separatist in character, or from resistance that has a social dimension, such as peasant risings. The resulting warfare, most of which takes a guerrilla and/or terrorist character on the part of the rebels, is asymmetrical. Yet, there was sometimes an important overlap with the issues centred on Western interventionism.

Afghanistan

To indicate this overlap, the case of Afghanistan is considered here. It could have been separately treated in a chapter on Western interventionism, but to do so would underplay the extent to which the problems facing Western forces are an aspect of a more general limitation for conventional forces in conflicts in many non-Western countries. If, after the fall of the Taliban in 2001, there was not chaos in Afghanistan comparable to that in Liberia, this was only because the weakness of Hamid Karzai's central government was counterpointed by the strength of provincial governors, such as Abdul Rashid

Dostum, Atta Mohammed, Gulbuddin Hikmatyar and Ismail Khan. These, however, were autonomous figures, whose tradition of independence was supported by their own armies which, like those of local militias, were powerful. For example, in 2004, the militia in the northern city of Kunduz had a considerable force of tanks. Rivalry between these warlords – over local dominance and related revenue sources such as land and drug profits – was disruptive and led to conflict, for example between Abdul Rashid Dostum and Atta Mohammed near the northern city of Mazar-e Sharif in late 2003 and in 2004.

Government in Afghanistan indeed involved a process of negotiation with these warlords, a process that accepted their regional power. Peace, in turn, depended on their restraint, but it was threatened by challenges to the regional position of warlords, as well as to that of the central government. A Taliban resurgence led to the collapse of the government position in much of the south and east of the country, with the President, Hamid Karzai, who had not been able to consolidate the new order, wielding scant authority outside the capital.

This resurgence, which gathered pace in 2005, was the cause of renewed Western intervention in the shape of NATO-ISAF (International Security Assistance Force) forces from 2006. The resurgence, however, gravely challenged not only the ineffective and, in part, corrupt Karzai government but also the NATO-ISAF forces deployed to support it. This was particularly the case for the British forces in Helmand province, but also in Kandahar where the Canadians suffered badly from a resistance that was stronger than anticipated. The Taliban benefited greatly from assistance from across the Pakistani frontier. In addition, Taliban forces were more numerous and better led, trained and organised than they had been in 2001–2.

Moreover, the supporting Pakistani military deployment, first in 2001, and then from 2003, in Waziristan in the Federally Administered Tribal Areas (FATA) within Pakistan, did not succeed in destroying the Taliban bases in the region, despite American air and financial support, as well as training. Instead, the Pakistani military, despite deploying 80,000 troops, encountered fierce resistance, both from the Taliban and from much of the local population, and proved unable to hold the initiative or dominate the situation. After what was regarded as unacceptable casualties, and was certainly failure, the Pakistani military withdrew in 2006 and the Taliban were left able to enjoy the shelter of the region. From the FATA, the Taliban could readily intervene in Afghanistan. Furthermore, in October 2006, the army agreed a peace with the tribal leaders that accepted this status quo, although the tribes promised to evict foreigners from their areas. Conflict resumed the following March and remained a backdrop to the war in Afghanistan. In 2009, the army advanced into the Swat region in a challenge to the Taliban's position.

Alongside opposition, support for the Taliban from within the Pakistani system, not least from elements of the Frontier Force, remains important.

There were NATO-ISAF complaints, especially from the Americans, about the Pakistani government and its complicity with the Taliban, and these appear to have been justified, at least in so far as the Inter-Services Intelligence Agency was concerned. Conversely, a standard Pakistani view was of Karzai as lacking legitimacy, not least because he was treated as an American puppet.

At a very different scale to the problems posed by Pakistan, many of the NATO-ISAF forces operating in Afghanistan insisted on 'national caveats' restricting what their forces could do. The resulting rules of engagement proved very varied, which hit at the idea of interoperability. The Germans proved particularly reluctant to make an active contribution in conflict scenarios.

As elsewhere, the 'international' dimension has to be supplemented by a domestic one. Thus, in the FATA, the socio-political structure was also at stake. The Taliban supporters were largely outside the mainstream of traditional tribal structures. Instead, the supporters' leaders were not tribal elders. More-over, clerics were prominent in the leadership of the Taliban supporters, a practice at variance with the traditional ethos in which mullahs were below such elders. Thus, the struggle by Taliban supporters was waged not only in Afghanistan, as well as in the FATA and in the North-West Frontier Province (NWFP) against Pakistani forces, but also against the traditional tribal leadership. The struggle in Pakistan was not restricted to the FATA and NWFP, but spread across Pakistan with suicide bombers attacking the military from the spring of 2007.

This struggle was part of a wider cultural rejection of modernity by militant fundamentalists, one that claimed thousands of lives in the 2000s and 2010s. Thus, in the 2010s, there were attacks on vaccination schemes designed to end endemic polio because these schemes were mistakenly presented as a Western plot to sterilise Muslims. Health workers and escorting police were killed. There was a clear political dimension to the violence. The Taliban and their Punjabi allies, Lashkar-e-Jhangvi, did not tend to launch attacks in the key province of Punjab. Its governor, Shahbaz Sharif, a religious conservative, and his brother Nawaz Sharif, the head of the Pakistan Muslim League, were more sympathetic to the Taliban and critical of the army and the USA than the secular parties. The latter, for example the Pakistan People's Party, suffered at the hands of the militants, with leaders, notably Benazir Bhutto, killed and rallies bombed.

Within Afghanistan itself, the security situation markedly deteriorated from 2006, with Taliban operations becoming far more active and prominent.[1] This pressure tested somewhat complacent British assumptions that their military was more successful than the Americans at counter-insurgency operations, assumptions that were also shown to be mistaken in Iraq. The British deployment in Helmand province was characterised initially by foolish political grandstanding not only about the likely peaceful consequences, but also about the military's ability to understand and direct the situation. Tony

84

Blair told British troops in 2006, 'Here in this extraordinary desert is where the future of world security in the early twenty-first century is going to be played out.' In practice, British forces were in part reduced to the militarised response, without any adequate political strategy, for which they habitually criticised the Americans. The Taliban proved able to put the British under considerable pressures, which, in turn, exposed problems with British weaponry and air–land co-ordination.[2]

More specific problems for the British in Helmand included the terrain: far from being desert, in which the British could employ their superior firepower, their units found themselves deployed in small settlements where walls and orchards provided cover for Taliban assailants. The British were also greatly handicapped by a shortage of helicopters, an issue that caused political difficulties for the government of Gordon Brown in Britain (2007–10). This shortage lessened their firepower and hit both mobility and logistics. Frequently pushed onto the defensive as a result, the British were therefore exposed to Taliban attacks, while the shortage of air mobility led to a use of road links that led to casualties from roadside bombs. The threat from the latter absorbed much military effort.[3]

In both Britain and the USA, there was talk of the difficulty of fighting two wars at once: Iraq and Afghanistan. This argument was reasonable in terms of force numbers and deployments, as well as the more general issue of identifying the main effort.[4] However, irrespective of the Iraq commitment, there was a more fundamental problem in Afghanistan of being able both to win and to stabilise the victory, and each in adverse circumstances, notably with Pakistan a source of renewed opposition and of Taliban resupply. The latter helped explain the military importance of the interdiction of crossing points from Pakistan to Afghanistan, not least in the winter of 2007–8, but the political problem posed by Pakistan was not thereby addressed.

Whereas the USA had had 19,000 troops in Afghanistan in 2004, by the end of 2008 they increased their forces there to about 40,000 men. The election of Barack Obama as President in October 2008 led to a shift in American focus from Iraq. He had fought the election as an opponent of what was presented as a 'bad' war, Iraq, while proclaiming Afghanistan as a 'good', because necessary, conflict. Under a new 'surge' announced in December 2009, 32,000 more troops were sent into Afghanistan. A Pew poll revealed that just under a third of Americans polled supported this commitment.

In very different military and political circumstances, this surge proved less successful than that in Iraq. The unpopularity of the corrupt and unsuccessful Afghan government ensured that there was a weak basis for the 'surge'. Karzai was more concerned about the political legitimacy and control of his government than by the bringing of a peace that he saw as likely to be compromised both by the Taliban and by the NATO-ISAF operations. Karzai would have preferred to see the military effort focused on the Taliban bases in Pakistan. He rejected the very NATO-ISAF strategy of attacking the Taliban in Afghanistan, as well as the operational and tactical methods involved, including raids on alleged Taliban sympathisers, raids that sometimes involved civilian casualties.

In addition, the idea that counter-insurgency could work was challenged by the difficulty of transforming foreign societies.[5] Moreover, the NATO-ISAF mission was challenged by the determination and resilience of the Taliban opposition, and by its ability to draw on bases in Pakistan's borderlands. Taliban resistance in Afghanistan continued, not only in the Taliban heartlands of Helmand and Kandahar but also in other provinces. At the same time, the NATO-ISAF militaries adapted to the specific nature of the military environment and task, in certain cases with considerable success.[6]

Comparisons between wars are valuable, but also risk putting together what is different. The 'surges' in Iraq and Afghanistan worked out differently not only because the situations in the two states were far from identical, but also because Obama sent far fewer troops than the number requested and described as the minimal necessary by his generals. This shortfall may well have contributed to the eventual lack of success, as did his simultaneous announcement that the 'surge' was limited in time, and thus implicitly also in the scope of the mission.

By the 2010s war-weariness among the NATO-ISAF powers led to increased pressure to recall troops. The coalition of those willing to deploy troops unravelled. At the start of 2012, there were 90,000 American combat troops in Afghanistan, as well as 40,000 other foreign troops. Political and governmental support for their presence declined rapidly. As President Obama remarked in March 2012, 'People get weary.' He had certainly become disillusioned.[7] In January 2014, the Pentagon proposed to end the NATO-ISAF military commitment that year, but, under a bilateral security agreement, to retain a 10,000-strong training and support force in Afghanistan, supported by 2,000 other NATO-ISAF troops, after the end of 2014 for two years.

Angola

Afghanistan was an atypical case because of the degree of external intervention. As a reminder of the changing geography of concern in the early twenty-first century, Angola, in contrast, was no longer at the forefront of international attention and confrontation, and the intervention of foreign forces had ceased. Nor was it a failed state. Yet, until the killing of the UNITA leader, Jonas Savimbi, in 2002, Angola faced a debilitating insurrectionary war that rested on ethnic tension, especially Ovimbundu support for UNITA. The conflict was financed by exploitation of the country's diamond wealth. Diamonds were also important in financing conflict in West Africa, especially in Sierra Leone. In turn, the Angolan government benefited greatly from control of the country's oil. As a result, it, like other governments, found its military capability and activity greatly affected by moves in the price of oil.

Having rejected the results of the 1992 election, UNITA had resumed its conflict with the government, which was now weakened by the withdrawal of the Cuban and Soviet assistance that had greatly helped it in the civil war of the 1970s and 1980s. Defeated by the scale of the country, a factor that was also an issue in Afghanistan, Congo and Sudan, neither side was able to win. The operational effectiveness of the government's conventional forces declined in the wet season, which, in turn, favoured UNITA's guerrilla tactics. Each side mounted attacks on the supply systems of the other. These attacks were important to effectiveness, but were without lasting consequences, other than to cause large numbers of civilian casualties and even larger numbers of refugees.

However, international pressure and a failure to win led Savimbi to negotiate anew in 1994, producing a de facto partition of the country that lasted until 1997 when the government attacked UNITA. UNITA now suffered both from the loss of its supply route through Congo, where Mobutu, an ally, had fallen, and from divisions, with Savimbi's leadership under challenge. In 1999, the government mounted intensive attacks, with Russian-made planes, on UNITA bases. It was claimed that they employed napalm and defoliants in addition to conventional explosives. Jamba, where Savimbi had established his capital in 1984, and which the government had failed to take in the 1980s, finally fell. UNITA forces were in a poor position by 2001 and the government used its oil wealth to enhance its military capability. The killing of Savimbi, on 22 February 2002, was rapidly followed, on 4 April, by the signing of a peace agreement.

Sudan

A different type of attempted consolidation of central control over tribal groups and peripheral areas was seen in Sudan. Its government, which was made more intractable by the rise of militant Islam and by its links with Iran, the source of much of its army, confronted the long-standing issue of control over the south. The Comprehensive Peace Agreement, a peace deal with the Sudan People's Liberation Movement, taking them into government and agreeing that, in 2011, the south could decide on secession, was negotiated in 2005, although tension continued. Rising oil revenues made this issue more pressing and became a cause of specific tension, with oil extraction in the south supported by Sudanese troops leading to considerable damage: vital cattle dying from drinking contaminated water. In turn, there were attacks on the oil workers.

In 2011, after a referendum had been held, South Sudan became independent. However, violent clashes with Sudan continued in contested border areas, while each side correctly accused the other of backing rebel groups. In the province of South Kordofan in Sudan, rebels, notably the northern branch of the Sudan People's Liberation Movement, had a considerable impact in 2013, leading the Sudanese government to respond with air attacks.

Moreover, in 2013, ethnic divisions in South Sudan ensured that serious differences within the government led to murderous strife. A dispute within the presidential guard escalated rapidly into street fighting in the capital, Juba, with weapons given to youths. Conflict then spread across the state as local commanders, notably in Jonglei and Unity states, opposed the President, Salva Kiir. Major-General James Koang, the senior commander in Unity, backed the fugitive former Vice-President, Riek Machar; as did General Peter Gadet in Jonglei. Control over oil fields in Unity state was a major issue. The Dinka tribe, the largest ethnic group and that of the President, fought the Nuer, that of Machar. In a pattern seen elsewhere, for example in the Central African Republic in 2013–14, targeted killings led to flight and also to mobilisation for protection, copycat atrocities and revenge. Much of the killing was by hand, involving stones and knives. There was also the chopping of hands from victims, the burning down of huts and the looting of businesses. Outnumbered UN peacekeepers were unable to maintain peace, even though this was the second-largest UN peacekeeping operation after that in the Congo. By the time a fragile ceasefire was negotiated in late January 2014, at least 10,000 people had been killed and about 700,000 had fled. Killings continued.

Aside from the long-lasting conflict in the south, the Sudanese government had faced a serious rebellion in the western Darfur region. Dating to the 1970s, but breaking out with greater intensity in 2003, and mounted by the Sudan Liberation Army and the Justice and Equality Movement, this rebellion was directed against the oppression of non-Arabs by the government. In response, from 2004, the government used its regular forces, including aircraft and infantry moved in trucks, to support an Arab militia, the Janjaweed (much of which rode on horses and camels), in order to slaughter the Fur, Masalit and, in particular, Zaghawa: native tribes in Darfur. Alongside large-scale killing, especially of men and boys, even very young boys, and the systematic rape and mutilation of women, natives were driven away, their cattle and therefore livelihood seized, wells poisoned with corpses, and dams, pumps and buildings destroyed. The government was assisted by serious divisions among the opposition in Darfur, not least over negotiations, and also over whether the goal was partition or a different Sudan.

Militarily, the Sudanese government benefited from its control over the central point, the capital, Khartoum. The government was also greatly helped by the funds gained from resource exploitation, especially of oil. These funds enabled the government to spend large amounts on the army, the basis of the power of the President, Omar al-Bashir, and to buy Chinese, Russian and Iranian arms. The government's use of air power and artillery increased its military effectiveness.

There was a regional dimension, as there had been with Liberia and Sierra Leone and was to be in Libya. The conflict in Sudan spilled over into Chad and the Central African Republic. Chad accused Sudan of backing rebels and, in response, Chad forces crossed the border into Darfur in April 2007 and fought Sudanese troops.

By 2009, fighting had eased in Darfur, and, in 2011, a peace agreement was drawn up in Qatar. However, several of the rebel factions did not accept it, and, in 2011–12, fighting revived, with militia attacks directed anew against the Zaghawa. These attacks were supported in 2011 by the Sudanese use of Russian-supplied aircraft against the Zaghawa base of Shangal Tobay. The violence became more anarchic, with groups on each 'side' fighting each other, notably over resources, particularly water and cattle.

Africa

Ethnic rivalry played a role in internal conflict in many other African states, although often without attracting much international attention, for example in northern Mali in 2004. Violence there only attracted such attention when the government of Mali came close to collapse in 2012–13 and France intervened. The French military found that it was easier to drive back opponents than to ensure stability.

More prominently, the Muslim north of Ivory Coast felt disenfranchised by the government elected in 2000, which was dominated by the Christian south. A rising in 2002 led to the seizure of the north by rebels and to serious fighting until 2004, followed by an agreement in 2007 that left Guillaume Soro, the leader of the rebel New Forces, as Prime Minister. In turn, there were divisions on the rebel side, including fighting in 2004. UN and French peacekeepers played a role in trying to contain the crisis. After an upsurge in violence linked to an election openly contested on sectarian grounds, conflict ended in 2011.

As a stage between Afghanistan and Angola, Congo (formerly Zaire) became both a failed state and one in which regular forces from other African countries intervened in order to influence the direction of conflict there, to dominate neighbouring areas, and to obtain control over raw materials. Mobutu Sese Soko, the dictator of Congo from 1965 and a former general, fell in 1997 as a result of a Rwandan invasion launched in 1996, while another invasion was launched in 1998 in an unsuccessful attempt to overthrow his replacement, Laurent Kabila. Uganda and Rwanda supported competing rebel factions, Rwanda in part in order to defeat the Hutu militias that staged the genocide of 1994 and that took refuge in Congo.

In turn, Zimbabwe, Angola, Chad and Namibia backed Kabila, largely in response to the dynamics of their own internal security situations, but also hoping to benefit from resources they could obtain. Angola wished to stop Congolese support for UNITA, which had been important under Mobutu. As a result of these interventions, Congo was in effect partitioned between the outside powers, which armed their own Congolese allies, particularly, for Rwanda, the Rally for Congolese Democracy and the Union of Congolese

Patriots. These forces overlapped with tribal militia groups, such as those of the Ugandan-backed Lendus, who competed with the Rwandan-allied Hemas in the north-eastern province of Ituri, a major centre of conflict.

Probably between 3.1 and 5.4 million people died in Congo from 1998 to 2003, most of disease and starvation, but many of them in ethnic conflict between tribal militias, as murderous attacks on villages proved a particularly common means of waging war. Far from being at the cutting edge of 'new-generation' warfare, this conflict saw much of the killing with machetes, and bows and arrows and shotguns were employed, alongside the frequent use of mortars and submachine guns. The conflict also led to cannibalism, as well as to the use of child warriors seen in West Africa, Uganda and Nepal and by the Taliban in Afghanistan. Other aspects of African conflict that were distant from Western warfare included the employment of traditional charms and spirit mediums. The degree to which civilians were deliberate targets and victims of war was also seen elsewhere in Africa, and more widely.

Peace talks, which began in 1999, led to an agreement in 2002, but violence continued in Congo after the war officially ended with the leading rebel groups joining a transitional government and their troops joining the national army. The violence continued to be brutal and symbolic. In the Katanga region in 2004 insurgents reputedly cut off the genitals of victims and drank their blood.

Congo's first democratic election, in 2006, was regarded as a possible harbinger of change. The election confirmed Kabila as President. In 2009, after Congo had failed to suppress a rebellion by the Rwandan-backed National Congress for the Defense of the People (CNDP), Congo and Rwanda reached a peace agreement. By this, the CNDP was to be integrated into Congo's army.

However, Rwanda's ambitions in Congo continued unabated. Moreover, the divided government of Congo found force a ready response to discontent, while, in Congo, there were also continuing serious security problems with armed groups, especially in the provinces of North and South Kivu on the eastern border. These problems continued into the 2010s. In 2012, violence was led by the March 23 Movement (M23), named after the date of the 2009 peace agreement which the government was accused of breaching. The fraudulent victory of Kabila in the 2011 presidential and legislative elections was an issue, but more serious was the extent to which the CNDP leader sought to maintain and use control of his organisation: the integration of his men into the army had been limited as the CNDP force was allowed to continue a parallel chain of command within the army, as well as to stay in the Kivu region.[8] Both the badly organised and poorly disciplined army and the insurgents were guilty of serious human rights abuses. The insurgents were backed by Rwanda, which provided military help.

More generally, as also in South Asia, rivalries between African states interacted with insurrections and other civil conflicts elsewhere. Thus, warfare between Eritrea and Ethiopia, which involved large-scale fighting of a conventional type, spilled over into internal conflicts in Somalia. In November 2006, the Prime Minister of Ethiopia called Islamists in Somalia a 'clear and present danger' to Ethiopia, a Christian state, claiming that they were being armed by Eritrea. In turn, the Somali Islamists, the Islamic Courts Union (the Union), met at Mogadishu and declared that they would defend Somalia against a 'reckless and war-thirsty' Ethiopia. Eritrea, Ethiopia and Kenya sent troops into Somalia, and the Islamists were put under considerable pressure by the Ethiopian and Kenyan forces.

Local struggles such as this one were interpreted by outside powers in terms of alleged wider alignments, not only regional but also global, such as the struggle between the USA and Muslim fundamentalists. Thus, in Somalia in 2006, warlord resistance to the fundamentalist attempt to capture Mogadishu was covertly supported by the USA; although, in the event, the capital fell that June to the Union, and the forces of the latter pressed on to attack the Somali transitional government which had taken refuge in the town of Baidoa.

In turn, the American government encouraged the Ethiopian invasion that overthrew the Union and captured Mogadishu in the winter of 2006–7. For the USA, this was a welcome opportunity to benefit from regional animosities, and to leave the military work on the ground to local forces; although the Americans did provide some air support. Subsequently, opposition in Somalia to the Ethiopian-backed transitional government of Abdullahi Yusuf Ahmed continued and became more clearly linked to fundamentalists, notably to the *Shabab* (young men) who sought to overthrow it. The *Shabab* were a continuation of the militias that had supported the Union. Al-Qaeda also played a role in support of the *Shabab*. At the same time, the opposition lacked the benefits enjoyed by the Taliban in Afghanistan, notably a largely safe haven in neighbouring Pakistan and the experience gained by several years of relatively constant conflict. The African Union force in Somalia, mostly from Kenya, Uganda and Burundi, drove the *Shabab* from Mogadishu and the port of Kismayo, but it proved difficult to profit from such successes, because the government remained weak, divided and unable to sustain consent.

Asia

The problem of relating all conflicts to a supposed clash of civilisations was also demonstrated in the far south of Thailand where Muslim separatists are seen as resisting a pro-Western government. There are certainly cultural elements in a conflict that has been ongoing since 2004, but other issues are involved. Not only are the cultural factors more complex than the thesis of a clash of civilisations allows, including the problems of absorbing a largely Malay-speaking Muslim people annexed in 1902 by a Thai-speaking Buddhist state, but in addition, the 'cultural' issues in Thailand, as elsewhere, are often

91

actualised by issues of military brutality, which played a major role in the upsurge of tension in southern Thailand in late 2004 in which troops fired on demonstrators, as well as by exploitation of potential conflicts by politicians and drug barons seeking their own local advantages.

Similarly, in Uzbekistan, the regime of Islam Karimov claimed that opposition was led by Muslim terrorists, a view that neglects the extent to which the dictatorship faces opposition for a number of reasons. In 2005, troops fired on a crowd in the Uzbek city of Andijan demonstrating against the poor economic situation.

Yet, religion could be a key lightning rod for tensions. In 2007, Pakistan forces stormed the Lal Masjd (Red Mosque), a centre of opposition by radical Muslim clergy, in the capital, Islamabad. In response, attacks on the security forces increased. The issues that led to violence might seem trivial, but the tensions were often serious, as in the city of Kaduna in Nigeria in 2002 where Muslim anger about the planned staging of the Miss World competition in the federal capital, Abuja, led to riots in which many were killed.

In Mindanao, the largest island in the southern Philippines, a substantial Muslim minority provided long-standing support for attempts to gain independence. Conflict from the late 1960s led, in 1996, to an agreement on autonomy for some largely Muslim areas. However, this agreement, reached by the Moro National Liberation Front, was rejected by a faction that became the Moro Islamic Liberation Front and that deployed about 12,000 fighters. In turn, this group accepted an agreement in 2014, but other rebel groups did not. Concern about al-Qaeda-linked activity in Mindanao led to an American willingness to support a peace agreement.

Central and West Africa

Sectarian-linked disputes were not the only ones that were portrayed in terms of wider concerns, nor therefore the sole disputes to be internationalised. More widely, foreign assistance was sought and, if necessary, hired to help resist insurrections. Thus, between 1993 and 2003, Ange-Félix Patassé, the President of the Central African Republic, survived seven coup attempts, including one in 2002 by General François Bozizé, one-time head of the army, that involved serious street fighting in the capital, Bangui. Patassé turned for support to Libya, which provided backing until 2002, and then to the Movement for the Liberation of the Congo (MLC) rebel group, but, in 2003, Bozizé, at the head of 1,000 men, overran Bangui. The unpaid army was unwilling to resist, and the MLC did not fight.

Tension between the Christian majority and the Muslim minority was also significant, notably in 2013 when Bozizé was overthrown by the *Séléka*, a rebel group from the mostly Muslim north. Large-scale violence, which, by January 2014, had resulted in about 1 million refugees, led to the intervention of French forces. They found it difficult to prevent sectarian killings, including revenge attacks on Muslims by local Christians. Units from Chad, which had also been deployed as peacekeepers, themselves tended to support their Muslim co-religionists and to attack Christians. Instability in the Central African Republic in part reflected the knock-on effects of war elsewhere, for conflict in Congo hit its trade links down the Congo River.

In West Africa, in 2002 and 2003, the Liberian government under Charles Taylor, whose seizure of power had originally owed much to backing from the Ivory Coast, supported rebels in the three neighbouring states – Sierra Leone, Guinea and the Ivory Coast – before being forced to step down in 2003. Guinea itself was linked to rebels against Taylor, the Liberians United for Reconciliation and Democracy – a misnamed group of thugs – as was the army of the Ivory Coast. France, in turn, intervened to support the government of the Ivory Coast against the *Mouvement patriotique de Côte d'Ivoire* (MPCI): the rebel group that failed to seize power in 2002, but that remained strong in the largely Muslim north. Britain had earlier intervened in Sierra Leone in 2000, supporting UN stabilisation, retraining the army and, in Operation Barras, rescuing hostages from the West Side Boys, one of the gangs that intimidated much of the country. Nigeria also played a role in helping maintain the peace in Sierra Leone.

Coups, military control and the military in politics

In Congo, Laurent Kabila, the President, was assassinated in 2001, while, in 2004, his son and successor, Joseph, overcame an attempt by elements in the Presidential Special Guard to seize power by gaining control of state television and the presidential palace. This attempt was an aspect of the continuing role of force in the seizure and retention of power across parts of the Third World, a role that puts a focus on the attitude of paramilitary units alongside that of the armed forces. Military establishments have a disproportionate autonomy and impact in post-colonial systems where nothing else seems to work very well and where too many countervailing institutions have lost credibility and authority.

Coups, and the possibility of such action, continued to play a major role in military history. In 2000, American and Brazilian pressure on Paraguayan military leaders led them to thwart an attempted coup, and that year the army eventually suppressed an attempted coup on the Pacific island of Fiji. An attempted military coup in Chad failed in 2003. There were also military coups in Fiji and Thailand in 2006, although the Thai army was unable to sustain the political order it sought to create and civilian rule resumed. In 2014, the army seized power again. In Fiji, the coup reflected ethnic conflict between the Indian and Fijian population. In 2012, in the Maldives, Mohammed Nasheed, who had been elected President in 2008, bringing to an end a thirty-year dictatorship, was overthrown in a coup that joined mutinous police to popular protests.

In Indonesia, the military did not return to centre stage after the end of the Suharto regime. Instead, under the 'New Paradigm of the Political Role of the Military', advanced by General Wiranto in 1998, there was a standing back from direct involvement in politics. In his statement on Armed Forces Day in 1998 when he introduced the 'New Paradigm', Wiranto stated that 'the Indonesian National Military would shift its role in politics and the national development process by not always being at the front of leadership, not to occupy but to influence, not in a direct way but indirectly, based on the willingness for political role-sharing with other national groups in Indonesia'.[9] In Myanmar (Burma), in contrast, the government, which was, and still is, army-dominated, began political reforms in 2011. Nevertheless, the constitution guaranteed the armed forces 25 per cent of the seats in Parliament and banned Aung San Suu Kyi, the head of the largest opposition party, from standing as President. The Union Solidarity and Development Party, the dominant party in Parliament, was a proxy for the army.

In Pakistan and, far more conspicuously, Turkey, however, civilian governments weakened the power of the military. Moreover, in 2014, the sacking of senior generals by President Goodluck Jonathan of Nigeria underlined a degree of political weakness in its military not seen in the late twentieth century.

In contrast, in Zimbabwe, in 2008, the military-dominated Joint Operations Command in effect gained a share of power from the weakened Robert Mugabe and orchestrated the use of force in order to maintain him in power against popular pressure and democratic methods. The military, whose members and former members gained assets and government posts, was linked to violent gangs in brutalising opponents. Such violence interacted with economic problems in encouraging large numbers of refugees to flee to neighbouring states, such as Botswana and Zambia, but the economic competition they posed in a situation of high unemployment led to violence against refugees in South Africa. In Egypt, a military coup in 2013 overthrew a government based on the Muslim Brotherhood, and General Abdel Fattah al-Sisi became the country's strongman, before becoming President.

The role of the military in politics is usually considered in terms of the Third World, but that may well underplay its importance elsewhere. If the threshold is that of tanks in the street, then there is only limited sign of this role outside the Third World, although in Ukraine in 2014 the embattled government sought to ensure control of the army. Volodymyr Zamana, Chief of the General Staff and Commander in Chief of the Armed Forces, declared on 1 February, when the government considered imposing a state of emergency, that 'no one had the right to use the armed forces to restrict the rights of citizens'. On 19 February, he was dismissed, but the government soon fell in the face of large-scale popular demonstrations.

The role of the military in politics in more settled circumstances is relevant in three respects. First, and most obviously, the military plays a role in military policy that is often greater than the constitutional situation would allow, and with civilian oversight circumvented. Secondly, an ability to rely on the military is important in giving security to government as well as an ability to implement particular policies. Thirdly, the military may well have greater political influence in specific contexts. As an example, the military has had great influence in Israel in recent decades, not only with former generals, such as Ariel Sharon, playing a major role as politicians, but also with the serving military being important in terms of policy, such as settlements in the occupied territories and relations with other states.

In some states, it is unclear how far the military is under the control of the government, or how far it is in effect autonomous. This question is particularly the case in China, where the military appears far more autonomous than in Japan or India. The regional basis of many Chinese units is an aspect of the situation.

In the Third World, former members of the military were important in democratic politics. This was particularly the case in Latin America. Thus, in 2002, Lucio Gutiérrez, a former colonel, was elected Ecuador's President. However, this was not the happiest precedent as his attempt to pack the Supreme Court was declared unconstitutional and led to his replacement in 2005. Similarly, Hugo Chávez, who was elected President of Venezuela in 1998, had staged an unsuccessful coup in 1992 (for which he served two years in prison), and, in office until he died in 2013, betrayed a willingness to break with democratic norms, although he was re-elected. In Peru, another former military rebel, Ollanta Humala, a lieutenant-colonel sacked for rebellion, stood for President in 2006, but he was defeated. Humala's candidacy was supported by Chávez.

In turn, in some countries, groups outside the military sought to use force to seize, or at least contest, power. Thus, in 2003, an organised criminal group linked to nationalists was responsible for the assassination of the Serbian Prime Minister, Zoran Djindjic; while, in 2004, mercenaries were involved in an unsuccessful plot to overthrow the dictatorial government of the oil-rich Equatorial Guinea, a plot that was allegedly backed by the former colonial power, Spain. Given the nature of dictatorship, the only chance of overthrowing such regimes appeared to be through the use of force. Without suggesting any equivalence, military courts were frequently employed to support governments, as in Egypt where, in 2008, they sentenced members of the Muslim Brotherhood to long prison sentences.

Regional separatism

Alongside the use of force to gain and hold power at the centre, force was widely used against regional separatism. Thus, long-standing southern secessionism in Yemen, from what had been the independent state of South Yemen, was crushed in 1994; the Chinese suppressed Muslim separatism in

Xinjiang in 1990 and 1997; while, in 1998, the Tajik army suppressed a rebellion in the Khojand region of Tajikistan where many Uzbek-speakers live. In 1997, a separatist revolt was suppressed on Anjouan, one of the islands in the Comoros in the Indian Ocean.

However, force frequently did not provide a lasting solution. Muslim separatism continued in Xinjiang, the Russians were unable to bring peace through force to Chechnya, and violence continued in Yemen. In 2012, Ali Abdullah Saleh, President of North Yemen from 1978 and of Yemen since unification in 1990, stepped down in the face of violent opposition, separatist and non-separatist, but violence continued. Separatist opposition was pronounced in a number of Yemen's regions. The resulting disruption was large scale. In February 2014, UN agency figures suggested that conflict between Houthi fighters pressing for autonomy and militia of the al-Ahmar clan had displaced more than 80,000 people.

In Nigeria, the army was used against a number of opponents. The most prominent were tribal separatists in the oil-producing delta of the River Niger, the Movement for the Emancipation of the Niger Delta, which exploited the importance to Nigeria of oil production and responded to anger about the poor treatment of the delta region, and, increasingly, the Islamist Boko Haram group. Based in the Muslim north, and therefore a regional revolt with national aspirations, the latter seeks an Islamic state in Nigeria. Iran, al-Qaeda and the Taliban all provided inspiration for Boko Haram, which has violently opposed the state since 2009.

The breakdown in May 2003 of a five-month ceasefire in the Aceh region of Sumatra led the Indonesian army to announce that it would destroy the Gam separatist movement, in part by moving the local population into tented camps so as to deny them cover. This conflict, which had begun in 1976, opposed a military using the means of conventional warfare, including ground attack, aircraft, amphibious landings, parachutists and tanks, against a smaller guerrilla force lacking international support but strong in determination. After the tsunami (tidal wave) disaster of December 2004, it proved possible to solve the crisis, in part because President Yudhoyono of Indonesia was able to sideline hardline elements within the military. Moreover, concessions were made to demands in Aceh for Islamic courts.

Supporting separatists from India in Kashmir, Pakistan, in turn, used harsh measures to oppose the Baluch Liberation Army, the separatist insurgents in Baluchistan who, according to the Pakistani army, are financed by India. There were large-scale arrests and 'disappearances', torture and the use of air attack on areas of Baluchistan deemed particularly dissident.

Conflict was more sustained in Sri Lanka, with civil war between the Liberation Tigers of Tamil Eelam (LTTE) and the government from 1983 until a ceasefire in 2002, and then the resumption of open military confrontation from 2006 until 2009. This conflict cost over 60,000 lives, including about 18,000 combatants on each side, left over 2 million refugees, and imposed a formidable economic burden. The war drew heavily on Tamil separatism, which was opposed by most of the Sinhalese majority; although not all Tamils supported the LTTE. The LTTE relied on guerrilla operations in the Tamil heartland and terrorist strikes elsewhere. The government used its more extensive military resources, not least naval and air power, to contest the heartland, especially the Jaffna peninsula, but found it difficult to hold the initiative. The disruptive capacity of the LTTE was demonstrated in 2007 when they launched air attacks on the capital Colombo, using propeller-powered trainer planes. Nevertheless, most of the east had been cleared of separatist fighters by 2008. The LTTE suffered from strategic failures, notably a shift to conventional warfare, while it also lost support among the Tamil population as a result of the continuation of the war and its own brutal techniques. The Sri Lankan military, which benefited from a qualitative improvement, scarcely provided a 'hearts-and-minds' policy, and, in 2009, the insurgency was crushed with heavy civilian casualties.[10]

A key element, as for so many insurrections, was that of the broader international context. In particular, whereas, in 1971, India had intervened in support of rebellion in East Pakistan, the LTTE seriously alienated the Indian government. Its peacekeeping force ended up fighting against the LTTE and a suicide bomber from the latter killed Rajiv Gandhi, the Prime Minister, in 1991.[11]

Civil wars

In the case of some insurrections, separatism was not the issue. Thus, from 1996, Nepal faced a serious Maoist insurgency which posed major problems for its military, providing ample evidence of the difficulty of suppressing a determined insurrection. Helped by the mountainous and forested terrain, Chinese assistance from across the Tibetan border, and their own brutality, the guerrillas were able to avoid defeat and to continue attacking, which ensured that they remained a factor in politics. In 2006, having seized absolute power the previous year, the autocratic ruler, King Gyanendra, lost control in the face of street protests, and, in 2008, the Maoists won the position of leading party in an election (the monarchy had been provisionally abolished in 2007). This outcome led to a coalition government in which the Maoists played a leading role, creating the problem of merging army and guerrillas in a reconstituted defence force. The future stability of Nepal is unclear, and this may become a serious issue in Indian–Chinese relations.

The struggle between Fatah and Hamas in Palestine, a struggle that came to a head in June 2007, was not separatist in origin, as each wished to rule the entire authority; but it became separatist in character because Hamas ended up successful in Gaza and Fatah on the West Bank. Conflict between the two movements continued, notably in Gaza in 2008.

Arms expenditure

Sales of arms continue to provide fresh munitions for Third World forces, and their governments, encouraged by international competition as well as by concern over domestic stability, have been only too willing to spend money on the military. In 2002, African states alone spent about $14 billion on defence. Expenditure on arms by terrorist movements was restricted by measures, including attempts to restrict money laundering; but, despite the repeated efforts of aid donors, no such restraint limited states as a whole. Instead, developments in their military capability were affected by attempts to control the trade in weaponry to specific states, such as North Korea, and also by efforts to restrict the sale of components for weapons of mass destruction.

Despite the terrible poverty of much of their population, India pushed up defence spending by 14 per cent in 1999 alone and Pakistan by 8.5 per cent, to total allocations of $9.9 billion and $3.3 billion, respectively. Moreover, Pakistan's nuclear weaponry programme may have been funded by Saudi Arabia, as well as by the sale of weapons technology to North Korea, Iraq, Iran, Libya and, probably, Egypt and Syria. The key figure, the scientist Abdul Qadeer Khan, who ran an international nuclear smuggling ring, was disavowed by the Pakistani government, but in a scarcely convincing fashion. As India also developed an atomic capability, Pakistan was unable to achieve a competitive edge that would permit it to cut conventional defence expenditure, although that was scarcely the priority of the powerful army.[12]

Rivalry over Kashmir between India and Pakistan led to the Kargil conflict in 1999 and took them close to war in 2002, with the Indians moving over 600,000 troops to the frontier. Religious hatred between Muslim Pakistan and Hindu-dominated India exacerbated national rivalry. India accused Pakistan of providing a base for a terrorist attack on the Indian Parliament in 2001. The rivalry of the two powers was made more serious by their increased nuclear capability, which led, first, India and, then, Pakistan to test nuclear weapons in 1998. That year, moreover, Pakistan test-fired its new Ghauri intermediate-range missile, while India fired its new long-range Agni 2 missile the following year. Its range is 2,000–3,000 kilometres, extending to Tehran, the capital of Iran, and covering most of China and South-East Asia. In 2003, both states test-fired short-range, surface-to-surface missiles that could have been used to carry nuclear warheads. The Indian Agni 5 missile, tested in April 2012, offered an intercontinental capacity with a range of 5,000 kilometres, and was seen as a way to lessen the military gap with China. The Pakistanis have also fitted their F-16 fighters to be able to deliver atomic bombs.

These and other weapons programmes were designed to provide regimes with the ability to counter the military superiority or plans of other states. Thus, North Korea, which appears to have provided Pakistan with the technology for its Ghauri missiles, saw atomic weaponry as a counter to American power. Pakistan provided relevant information. In 2005, North Korea claimed to possess nuclear weaponry in a tunnel at Punggye. This was a clear defiance of any idea of non-proliferation, and one that was made more serious by the difficulty in obtaining information on North Korean capability and intentions.[13]

In 2006, North Korea staged long-range missile tests and tested a nuclear weapon. Meanwhile, Syria sought to develop chemical and biological weapons in response to Israeli conventional military superiority. On 6 September 2007, the Israeli air force attacked a military construction site in Syria. Rumoured to be a location for a nuclear programme drawing on North Korean technology, this site may, instead, have been linked to other dangerous weapons capabilities. The Israelis, in turn, built up a substantial stockpile of nuclear bombs, in part in response to the chemical weapons and nuclear plans of its Arab neighbours. The Iraqi nuclear programme was delayed by the Israeli destruction of the reactor at Osirak in 1981, a bold and brilliantly executed air attack, and was definitively ended by the overthrow of Saddam Hussein in 2003, while, later that year, Libya abandoned its own programme.

Iran, however, proved unwilling to follow suit even after its violations of nuclear safeguards on nuclear proliferation were exposed in 2002 with the revelation of secret nuclear facilities at Arak and Natanz. Having suspended uranium enrichment, a more radical Iranian government resumed it in 2005, and subsequently ignored UN Security Council resolutions that it suspend anew. Iran pushed on with work on a cone for its Shahab-3 missiles designed to ensure that the cone can carry a nuclear warhead. Concern about Iranian moves led to Israeli plans for action. These, however, faced practical problems (distance, refuelling, extent of reliable information about targets), as well as the likelihood that an attack would unite domestic support behind the Iranian government (such support is a goal of the nuclear programme) and lead to a measure of international backing for Iran, and that, after an attack, Iran would be able to restart operations. The probability of Iranian reprisals in Afghanistan, Iraq and the Gulf were less a matter of concern for Israel and, instead, offered the encouragement that they might lessen support for Iran as well as binding Israel and the USA closer together. An international agreement to limit the development of a Iranian nuclear military capacity was reached in late 2013, but it is unclear how lasting it will prove. Israel rejects the agreement as a form of appeasement but, more significantly, the strength of the reform candidate, Hassan Rouhani, elected President in June 2013, is uncertain.

Weapons were (and are) not only purchased by states. They were (and are) also freely available across much of the Third World, which contributes greatly to crime, and can be linked to threats to political and social stability. The case of the USA, where guns are readily available, shows that high rates of crime do not have to lead to social or political instability at the national level, but the situation elsewhere is less promising.

Conflict and criminality

Indeed, asymmetrical warfare can overlap considerably with struggles against crime, specifically wars on drugs. Thus in Mexico in the 2000s and 2010s, the army was used against the powerful drugs gangs, such as the Zetas, while a paramilitary Federal Investigations Agency was established to the same end. The firepower used by both sides was considerable. Allegedly over 70,000 people were killed in drug-linked violence in 2006–12. In 2013, the army, navy and federal police took over the port of Lázaro Cárdenas, the second biggest in Mexico, in order to challenge the power of one of the gangs, the Knights Templar. As the drug wars spilled over the border into the USA, there was growing pressure there to use the National Guard to protect the border.

In Central America as a whole, arms left over from the Cold War exacerbated conflict over drug assets, routes and markets. The same was true of conflicts in Central Asia, notably Afghanistan, while drugs also played a major role in conflict within Myanmar (Burma), notably as the state sought to impose its control over frontier regions.

In Colombia, the left-wing Revolutionary Armed Forces of Colombia (FARC) guerrillas and the right-wing United Self-Defence Forces of Colombia (AUC) paramilitaries were both involved heavily in drugs, and this ensured that their operations were often designed to ensure control over drug-producing areas. In 2004, the two groups clashed over control of the department of Norte de Santander, an area on the Venezuelan border important for the export of drugs and the import of arms. The relationship between these groups and organised crime was close, but FARC also had a clear politico-military agenda, in which force was applied to pursue political goals. In 2002, FARC was able to put pressure on the capital, Bogotá, firing rockets at the presidential palace during the swearing in of the President (they missed and killed nineteen in a working-class district); but the American- and British-backed military was then able to drive it back into distant mountain and jungle regions.

Concern about drugs, radicalism and the possibility that Colombia would become a failed state, led the USA, under the 'Plan Colombia' initiative, to provide aid: over \$8 billion in 2000–2012, much to the army, with an annual level in 2006 of \$600 million. Equipment as well as money was provided. Helicopter-borne mobility proved a key advantage for the military in operating in the difficult terrain. This mobility assisted in the recovery of the initiative from FARC, which was driven from the major cities into the peripheries, with its number of combatants falling from about 20,000 in 2002 to about 8,000 in 2013. Colombian forces received GPS equipment that helped produce the precision-guided munitions capable of targeting FARC leaders. Eavesdropping information assisted greatly by providing the necessary real-time intelligence on the leaders' location.

As an instance, however, of the problems posed by drug wealth, some of the army units, in Colombia and elsewhere, intended to fight drug trafficking were, in turn, linked to that drug traffic and its massive profits. In 2014, General Leonardo Barrero, the head of the armed forces, was dismissed for criticising the prosecution of the military for the extra-judicial killing of civilians who were falsely presented as guerrillas killed in combat.

As always, the political context was important. The Colombian government signed a peace agreement with the AUC in 2003 which led to its demobilisation. Similar progress appears to be the case with the National Liberation Army, FARC's rival on the Left, and with FARC itself in negotiations that began in 2012. The disruption caused by warfare between the mid-1960s and 2013 left almost 220,000 dead, 45,000 missing and over 5.7 million refugees within Colombia.[14]

In Afghanistan, the War on Terror intersects with heroin production and trafficking, as well as religion and warlordism. The problem of drug-financed armed force is a matter, however, not simply of supply in poor countries, but also of demand in rich ones. Indeed, the American 'War on Drugs' contributes to the profits of the trade, which is handled by criminal gangs that in part are able to force or buy protection from government regulation, more particularly where governments are weak. The term 'War on Drugs' highlights the cultural tendency to view problems through the lenses of conflict.

Conflict and society

The porous and contested definition of war suggested by its current usage, as in war on drugs, or war on terror, let alone war on crime or poverty or cancer, further complicates understandings of force and legitimacy, and makes it difficult to define the military. If the War on Terror is crucial, then the Saudi security forces carrying out armed raids against al-Qaeda suspects in which people are killed, or the Indian Border Security Force resisting the United Liberation Front of Asom in Assam, are as much part of the military as conventional armed forces. Similarly, troops are employed for policing duties, as in Quetta in Pakistan in 2004 to restore order after a riot following a terrorist attack on a Shia procession.

Crime also overlaps with social tension, if not 'class warfare', as in kidnapping, practised, for example in Mexico, in order to raise money but also associated with hatred of the better off. In the 2000s, almost half the world's kidnappings occurred in Latin America, and they represented a formidable strain on society in total terms.

More generally, the rate of crime in Latin America was a form of war on society. The 2013 UN's Development Programme report *Citizen Security with a Human Face* noted that, in the 2000s, over a million Latin Americans had died as a result of criminal violence, with about four-fifths of murders committed with firearms. Over the quarter-century 1985–2010, robberies had

A MULTITUDE OF CONFLICTS

tripled, 60 per cent of them involving violence, and nearly two-thirds of Latin Americans avoided going out at night for fear of crime. In January and February 2004 combined, there were 3,290 officially recorded murders in Colombia. The small state of El Salvador had 3,761 murders in 2005 according to Amnesty International out of a population of 6 million. The following year, the Brazilian murder rate was 23.8 per 100,000, although this had fallen in cities such as Sao Paulo. In 2013, Venezuela had almost 25,000 murders out of a population of 30 million.

Widespread ownership of weaponry complicates these, and other, problems. By 2003, there were estimated to be more than three guns for every Yemeni, and the ability of the government to control the country was limited. This problem made the presence in Yemen of al-Qaeda in the Arabian Peninsula more serious and, more generally, contributed to Yemeni resistance to the government. In 2004, for example, the army launched an operation in the north of Yemen against Sheikh Hussein Badr Eddin al-Huthi, a Muslim preacher leading a rebellion. In response to the role of al-Qaeda, the USA provided assistance to the Yemeni government and also launched drone strikes, killing up to 891 people in 2002–13.

In Haiti, as in Yemen, large-scale ownership of guns exacerbated problems stemming from mass unemployment and poverty. A powerful drugs and drug-smuggling culture was also an issue in Haiti, where gun ownership challenged the country's political stability, leading to a major role for street gangs or *chimeras*. In Brazil, criminal groups were able to challenge public order, though not governmental stability at the federal level. Thus, in May 2006, the *Primeiro Comando da Capital* attacked Sao Paulo, killing policemen, firebombing buses and banks and producing chaos. This chaos led to a police response that was equally forceful. One hundred and fifty people were killed in the crisis. In El Salvador, Barrio 18, a vicious gang, and its rival, Mara Salvatrucha, were responsible for a high rate of violence until, in 2012, the government arranged a truce between the gangs. The estimated size of the gangs in El Salvador, 60,000 members in total, is greater than that of many armies.

The high rate of gun ownership in Iraq posed a serious problem with the overthrow of the regime in 2003. Alongside political opposition from insurgents in Iraq came large-scale property crime, as well as activity by well-armed criminal gangs, especially smugglers trying to profit from new circumstances. In Lebanon, where there is also large-scale gun ownership, the autonomous nature of the Palestinian camps is one of the many problems confronting the government. In 2007, the Fatah Al-Islam militants in the Nahr Al-Bared camp outside Tripoli in Lebanon were able to mount deadly resistance to the army for nearly four months.

As an instance of military action in a different context, in 2007 the Kenyan army launched an operation in the Mathare slum area of Nairobi, a step directed against the Mungiki, a gang that ran the area and violently resisted police activity. Similarly, the army has been used in Jamaica against gangs. The

Kenyan army is also deployed against cattle-rustling on the Somali frontier, a deployment that is of value to the USA, which is concerned about al-Qaeda operations based in neighbouring Somalia, the classic failed state. In 2007, concern about Islamist forces escaping from Somalia led the Kenyan army to move up to the frontier. Such action contributed to a terrorist response in Kenya, notably in Nairobi in 2013 and against tourist resorts in 2014.

Civil violence and interventionism

The challenge to states from domestic opposition is internationalised in so far as there may be foreign support for such opposition, or international humanitarian concern about the issue, as in Zimbabwe where the army has acted as a brutal adjunct of the corrupt Mugabe regime. On the whole, however, the nature of conflict reflects an important aspect of international relations; namely, the extent to which the use of force within sovereign areas (i.e. states) is generally accepted by many other states. Moreover, international pressure for action could be countered by foreign powers willing to sponsor the regime in question. This proved a particular issue affecting the Western response to Syria in the 2010s as the Assad regime was supported by Russia, China and Iran, the first two thwarting the prospect of UN action. As a result, the regime was able to wage war on much of its public. Aside from large-scale military action, there was also appalling systemic brutality, notably by security officials in Syria's prisons. This brutality was a major aspect of the counter-insurgency policy of the regime, and thus of its warfare.

This practice of force is seen as a challenge to humanitarian interventionist precepts, but the latter usually lack military capability unless they conform to the goals of great power diplomacy. A more typical instance of intervention is that in Uganda. The brutal rebellion by the Lord's Resistance Army (LRA), a maverick Christian group in the north of the country, a rebellion which broke out in 1986, was backed by the Muslim government in Sudan in response to Ugandan government support for the rebels in southern Sudan. Similar patterns of activity have occurred in the last two decades in West Africa, linking Guinea, Sierra Leone and Ivory Coast, as well as also centring on Congo. In Uganda, the rebels targeted children for abduction as fighters or sex slaves, and the rebellion had, by 2004, led about 95 per cent of the region's population, over one and a half million people, to flee. By 2012, the LRA was down to 200 soldiers, a big fall from its peak of 2,000, but, operating on the borderlands of Congo, Uganda, South Sudan and the Central African Republic, it was able to exploit the weakness of Congo in particular. In 2011, the LRA mounted 278 attacks. Child abductions and the mutilation of victims continued.

In this and other conflicts, aside from deaths due to slaughter, there was also the destruction of the economy, as military units focused on plundering villages. Moreover, the infrastructure collapsed, with resulting deaths from privation, as well as from disease. In part, a rise in disease reflected disruption, for example to water supplies, but the spread of disease by both troops and refugees was also important. In Africa, refugees spread malaria. The Angolan civil war led to over 3 million people being displaced.

Such instability is particularly savage in Africa and the Middle East, but is not restricted to them. For example, the situation in Oceania, the islands of the Pacific, became more unstable as imperial presences receded. Internal disputes over jobs and other opportunities were exacerbated by economic problems, and the resulting disagreements led to a high level of tension in which violence became common and sapped any sense of security. The results were endemic strife, and armed gangs of unemployed youths challenge the social order in Papua New Guinea. In the Solomon Islands, serious ethnic conflicts led to a coup in 2000, the year in which there was also an attempted coup in Fiji that included a bloody, but unsuccessful, army mutiny. In 2006, rioting and conflict between police and army led to a collapse of security in East Timor, while a coup occurred in Fiji. Paradoxically, this disorder led former imperial powers to send troops and police back into the region. In 2006, Australian and New Zealand troops and police were sent into East Timor, the Solomon Islands and Tonga to try to preserve civil order.

The overlap between political disorder and civil conflict was also seen in South Asia. Thus, in Bangladesh, the two main political parties, the Bangladesh Nationalist Party and the Awami League, compete violently as well as electorally, with mob violence, strikes, targeted assassinations and politicised judicial decisions all part of the political and electoral processes. Weapons, especially staves, are used in street battles, while politicians wear bullet-proof vests. Such a level of violence threatens to effect a transition, from what can be seen as politics by other means, to a subversion of politics, as in 2004 when the leader of the Bangladesh opposition was nearly killed by a grenade attack at an election rally. The military feels itself obliged to try to contain the political violence. In India, there was religious violence in 2002, especially attacks on Muslims in Gujarat. Possibly 2,000 were killed in the latter.

The overlap of such disorder with international tensions is widespread. In the case of India, bomb blasts in Mumbai in 2008 were seen as a response to the Gujarat violence and were blamed on Muslim extremists based in Pakistan. In Turkey, external intervention played a key role, with Kurdish insurgents operating from bases in northern Iraq. In turn, this action led to incursions by Turkish forces into Iraq, as in 2008. These incursions reflected the degree to which Turkish nationalism is directed against the Kurds: the Turkish army sees its role in part as the resister of Kurdish aspirations. As a result, Turkey viewed the collapse of Syria with concern as it resulted in the Kurdish parts of Syria becoming in effect independent and thus joining those of Iraq in acting as a model for the Turkish Kurds.

In part, such conflicts also arise from the contested nature of international frontiers and their interaction with rival states, ideologies and nationalisms.

While it is a commonplace to blame the legacy of Western imperial power for this situation, this blame frequently presumes the alternative of a clear border that, in practice, is generally far from the case. At any rate, frontier disputes remain part of the agenda of international relations and frequently, such as that between Thailand and Cambodia in 2008, lead to military confrontations or, as between Ethiopia and Eritrea in 1998–2000, large-scale conflict.

The interaction between civil violence and external intervention provides a way to consider not only conflict across the Third World but also those specific conflicts in which Western powers have committed troops; in short, it diminishes the difference and contextualises the latter. At the same time, this comparison poses a difficulty for Western intervention, as it indicates the extent to which civil conflict is frequent, if not, in some countries, constant. Thus, such intervention is unlikely to end it. Moreover, this approach questions the analysis that sees violence largely in terms of resistance to the Western powers. Instead, as in Afghanistan and Iraq (in the second of which the insurgents had particularly disparate goals), it is appropriate to note the high levels of civil violence. Furthermore, this violence cannot be readily contained in the terms of Western intervention or by means of the attrition of killing insurgents. The aftermath of Western intervention in Libya in 2011 and of French intervention in Mali in 2013 demonstrated these points, and they would also have been pertinent had there been intervention in the Syrian civil war in 2013.

In Libya, the Gaddafi regime was rapidly overthrown following Western intervention in the civil war that began in February 2011 when Islamist militia rebelled in Benghazi. The rebellion gathered momentum because Abdel Fatah Younis, the Interior Minister, who was sent to suppress it, instead, decided to try to lead it, a key aspect of the divisions within the regime that helped weaken it. The anti-Gaddafi insurgents made plentiful use of unarmoured vehicles, both to transport themselves and to mount weapons, especially anti-aircraft guns. By aiding speedy advances and retreats, these vehicles provided a mobility that helped explain rapid changes of fortune in the campaigning. The heavier conventional units of the Libyan army, both tanks and artillery, were more deadly, but they were countered, and then seriously damaged, by NATO air attacks, despite the major problems the latter faced due to a lack of reliable reconnaissance information. The key role in the air was played by Britain and France, operating from Italian bases, although American stealth bombers were central to the original assault on the Libyan air force and the Americans also played a vital role in air-to-air refuelling and in intelligence provision.

An air umbrella provided crucial support for the Libyan insurgents. The provision of NATO advisers and arms, notably firearms, night-warfare optics and communication equipment, as well as money from Qatar, also helped the generally poorly organised insurgents. They captured the capital, Tripoli, that August, overthrowing the Gaddafi regime. Continuing to resist, Gaddafi was captured and killed in October. The Libyan intervention suggested that air power would be most effective as part of a joint strategy, although in Libya the situation on the ground was more propitious than in Kosovo in 1999.

Foreign intervention in Libya did not bring stability, not least because long-standing regional tensions continued, notably demands in eastern Libya for more autonomy. Struggles between rival *thuwwar* (militias) exacerbated these tensions and had a dynamic of their own. Thus, in June 2013, tribesmen protesting against the killing of a kin member by a patrol of Libya Shield No. 1, a leading Islamist militia, attacked its base in Benghazi, being joined by al-Saiqa, a special force initially established by Gaddafi, but which had abandoned him in 2011. The militia was forced to flee. Sniping and the use of rocket-propelled grenades were key elements in the conflict. The role of the al-Saiqa reflected the extent to which, in many revolutionary and post-revolutionary contexts, there was division over the monopolisation of military authority. In Libya, the Islamist militias were co-opted by the new government into ten Libya Shields, and thereby authorised (and paid) as a form of parallel National Guard, only to be dissolved by order of the new Army Chief of Staff in June 2013. As an instance of more general chaos, many Libyan ports and other positions have been seized by local militiamen who have thereby gained control of trade, notably oil exports. The threat by the central government to use force to regain control has proved fruitless. In 2014, a senior army officer found no military support when he announced a coup, but the Tripoli-based Qaqa militia and the Zintan-based Sawaiq militia demanded that Parliament disband, a push opposed by other militias. Unlike in Afghanistan, however, no Western forces were involved in propping up the new government against opposition.

In 2013, there was French intervention in Mali, with the stress again being on air attack. The Tuareg insurgents who had threatened the overthrow of the government were rapidly pushed back by Malian forces assisted by the French. As an instance of the more general extent to which struggles in one state could lead to conflict elsewhere, the insurrection in Mali owed something to the return home of men who had served Gaddafi, as well as to long-established separatist tendencies in northern Mali.

Instead of focusing on Western intervention in these and other cases, it is appropriate to note the centrality of the divisions within the individual states that were affected, and the extent to which the international interaction of these crises did not necessarily involve Western forces. This was very much the case with the 'Arab Spring' of 2011 and its aftermath. Resistance to the authority of particular rulers was encouraged by outside regional powers, while others sent assistance to them. Saudi Arabia and Qatar provided assistance to the opposition to Colonel Gaddafi in Libya in 2011, and that to the Assad regime in Syria from 2012. Saudi Arabia also encouraged the Egyptian army when it overthrew the Muslim Brotherhood government in 2013. In turn, in 2011, Saudi forces were sent to Bahrain to help the military there suppress Iranian-influenced Shia discontent. Moreover, Iran and Hizbullah provided highly effective assistance to the Assad regime.

Syria

In Syria, fighting began in May 2011 when protesters in the city of Homs, a long-standing centre of opposition, were confronted by the army. Treating the opposition as terrorists, the Assad regime automatically resorted to force, which led its opponents to do likewise. The intractable nature of the Syrian civil war, its sectarian character and the willingness to attack civilians led to widespread civilian casualties. According to the International Committee for the Red Cross on 22 December 2013, the conflict had led to 126,000 killed, over half a million wounded, 5 million people displaced within Syria and 2.2 million refugees abroad. The bombing by the government of rebel-held areas, such as the cities of Aleppo and Homs, was particularly destructive. The killing of over 1,400 people as a result of the regime's use of sarin gas in the Damascus suburb of Ghouta on 21 August 2013 excited widespread outrage.

The killing of civilians extended across society. Children proved particular targets. They were used as human shields from 2011, shot by government snipers, raped, tortured and maimed. Rebel groups sought to recruit children after the death of their parents, when they were particularly vulnerable. A UN estimate in February 2014 suggested that thousands of children had been killed.

The 2013 gas attack raised the possibility of international intervention, but the prospect of action against the Assad regime by the USA, France and Britain fell victim to domestic political hesitation. Russia, Assad's ally, negotiated a solution to that crisis in the shape of the removal of the arsenal of chemical weapons. At the same time, Russia and Iran provided extensive military support, whereas the USA offered scant support to the opposition. The degree to which the latter had become increasingly characterised by jihadist views, rather than, as originally, by opposition to the regime's human rights abuses, led to considerable Western disquiet. In turn, the funding of opposition by Qatar and Saudi Arabia accentuated the sectarian character of the civil war. The belief by Russia and Iran that a military solution was possible was exemplified by the support of weaponry and advisers. Thus, by the winter of 2013–14, the Russians were operating reconnaissance drones able to provide the Syrian army with accurate information on their opponents to help targeting.

The regime made plentiful use of artillery, shelling rebel-held regions in order to make life in them unbearable. This process was taken further by blockades that prevented food supplies and by cutting off gas and water. At the same time, concern about its own military casualties ensured that the regime was reluctant to order attacks by ground forces unless near strategic routes. The blockades and bombardments were supported by local negotiations designed to end opposition. They had a degree of success in early 2014.

The convergence of the local conflict in Syria with regional rivalries and international tensions created a dangerously unstable situation. Looked at differently, this was similar, in realist terms, in many respects to the position during the Cold War.

Notes

1 A. Giustozzi, *Koran, Kalashnikov and Laptop: The Neo-Taliban Insurgency in Afghanistan* (London, 2007).

2 J. Fergusson, *A Million Bullets: The Real Story of the British Army in Afghanistan* (London, 2008).

3 F. Ledwige, *Investment in Blood: The True Cost of Britain's Afghan War* (New Haven, Connecticut, 2013).

4 J. Burk (ed.), *How 9/11 Changed Our Ways of War* (Stanford, California, 2013).

5 G. Gentile, *Wrong Turn: America's Deadly Embrace of Counterinsurgency* (New York, 2013), esp. pp. 135–40.

6 T. Farrell, F. Osinga and J.A. Russell, *Military Adaptation in Afghanistan* (Stanford, California, 2013).

7 R. Gates, *Duty* (Washington, 2014).

8 J.K. Stearns, *Dancing in the Glory of Monsters: The Collapse of the Congo and the Great War of Africa* (New York, 2011).

9 S. Said, *Legitimizing Military Rule: Indonesian Armed Forces Ideology, 1958–2000* (Jakarta, 2006).

10 A.S. Hashim, *When Counterinsurgency Wins: Sri Lanka's Defeat of the Tamil Tigers* (Philadelphia, 2013).

11 S. Gates and K. Roy, *Unconventional Warfare in South Asia: Shadow Warriors and Counterinsurgency* (Farnham, 2014), p. 188.

12 A. Levy and C. Scott-Clark, *Deception: Pakistan, the United States and the Global Nuclear Weapons Conspiracy* (New York, 2007); G. Perkovich, *India's Nuclear Bomb: The Impact on Global Proliferation* (Berkeley, California, 1999).

13 B.E. Bechtol, *Red Rogue: The Persistent Challenge of North Korea* (Dulles, Virginia, 2007); J. Becker, *Rogue Regime: Kim Jong II and the Looming Threat of North Korea* (Oxford, 2007); G.D. Chang, *Nuclear Showdown: North Korea Takes on the World* (London, 2007); M.V. Creekmore, *A Moment of Crisis: Jimmy Carter, the Power of a Peacemaker, and North Korea's Nuclear Ambitions* (London, 2007).

14 M. Ince, 'Filling the FARC-Shaped Void', *RUSI Journal*, 158, no. 5 (Oct./Nov. 2013), p. 26.

7

INTO THE FUTURE

The rivalry of major powers?

An understanding of the diversity of future wars helps explain the range of future conflict. There will be no one type of war, and, thus, no one way of waging or winning war. Military goals will vary greatly, as will political contexts; and the two are closely linked. Yet the linkage is also uncertain because there is a degree of autonomy from political contexts and taskings: while war may be the pursuit of politics, the institutions for, and demands of, conflict have needs of their own that do not readily respond to political requirements.

Much of the assessment of future high-tech confrontation or war depends, at least in the short term, on two concepts: synergy (profitable combination) and information warfare. Both are seen as of importance to the rivalry of major powers, which indeed is the suppressed theme of the 2000s and early 2010s: at the same time that the War on Terror engaged the bulk of American attention, a deterioration of relations affecting China, India, Russia and the USA was of considerable importance.

This deterioration led to public shows of friction, notably between the USA and both Russia and China. These shows of friction included, in 2007–8, Russian opposition to American plans to extend the Ballistic Missile Defence shield to cover Eastern Europe, and to encourage Georgia and Ukraine to join NATO, as well as Russian withdrawal, in 2007, from the Conventional Armed Forces in Europe Treaty. Hostilities between Georgia and Russia in 2008 can very much be seen in this context, as can large-scale Russian exercises in 2009 that focused on a simulated invasion of the Baltic states (Estonia, Latvia, Lithuania) and on a nuclear attack on Poland. In 2013, Russia and Belarus conducted a large-scale military exercise, NATO a small one that simulated the protection of Estonia from invasion, and Russia staged dummy air attacks on Sweden, Poland and Lithuania. In early 2014, Russia occupied Crimea in a crisis over Ukraine that also involved the deployment of possible invasion forces.

However, whereas Russian intentions troubled NATO, the USA was more worried, in the case of major powers, by China. At the close of the Cold War in 1989, 213,000 American forces were based in Europe, but, by 2013, the number was down to 30,000.

The concept of synergy suggests that, in any future conflict, success will hinge on the ability to achieve a successful combination of land, air and sea forces, which requires the development of new organisational structures, as well as the careful training of commanders and units, and appropriate systems of command, control, communications, and information appraisal and analysis. Advanced technology, and a sense that technology could, would, indeed must continue to advance, and that this has to be planned for, greatly contributes to ideas of synergetical warfare. These ideas reflect an awareness of the requirement for a more sophisticated command and planning environment, and also a need to do more than simply respond to the possibilities created by new weapons. Instead of treating these factors in isolation, their impact is to be multiplied by careful co-operation within, and outside of, new organisational structures. Thus, for example, as has been discussed, if high-speed aircraft capable of 'skipping' on the upper atmosphere and, thereby, of transporting troops anywhere in the world within two hours are developed, then their successful operational usage will depend, to a considerable extent, on such co-operation.

China and Russia

Given that most discussion of future war between major powers focuses on American, or, at least, Western forces, weaponry and doctrine, competing with those of autocratic governments, especially China and Russia,[1] it is worth noting that future war, or, at least, confrontation, could also be between China and India, or even China and Russia, however improbable the latter currently is. Discussion of these possibilities serves to clarify the range of factors that may be involved in future conflict, or its prevention. Such discussion can seem more or less plausible depending on which timescale is employed.

Whereas, in the 1960s, India and Russia would have found the Chinese stronger on numbers than weapons, the situation is different now. Furthermore, in contrast to the emphasis in modern discussion on a lack of Western interest in territorial expansion, it is appropriate to note the role of frontier disputes and issues between China and both India and Russia. In the former case, dispute over the contested Himalayan frontier, a contest China blamed on the imperial ambitions of Britain when it ruled India, led to a short war in 1962 that was won by China. This victory makes China keen on the regional status quo, linking in to Chinese sensitivities over Tibet, and also relates to Chinese interest in frontier disputes between India and Pakistan and in keeping Nepal out of an Indian bloc.

In the case of Russia, there is still a Chinese grievance. Russia gained the Amur region in 1858 and the Ussuri region in 1860, a frontier delimited by the Treaty of Beijing of 1860, which was wrung from the Chinese in a year of defeat and humiliation: Beijing was occupied by Anglo-French forces that year. Although far from being at the forefront of strategic concerns at present, this is unfinished business, and the past Chinese concern to regain Hong Kong and Macao from Britain and Portugal, respectively, both achieved without conflict in the 1990s, is a reminder of sensitivity to these nineteenth-century losses. Regaining these territories, however, would undermine the Russian position in Siberia and would provide opportunities for enhanced Chinese influence and resource sequestration, whether in co-operation with, or in opposition to, the Russians.

While such a conflict appears implausible in a world defined in terms of Western action, and the reaction to it, this prospectus of Sino-Russian conflict seems less implausible if the emphasis is on future resource competition, not least in order to meet the demanding needs of Chinese demographic and economic expansion. By the 2010s, China had a population of 1.2 billion. Land and water are prime resources, and Siberia has both, whereas northern China has particular shortages of water and cultivable land. Indeed, the tensions of scarcity discussed in the next chapter may prove as potent in the case of major powers.

Were a conflict to occur between China and Russia, it is likely to be waged without the concern to minimise civilian and military losses that characterises Western operations. However, it would be unclear whether it would be possible to contain the conflict or whether nuclear weaponry would be employed. At the operational level, there is likely to be a similar emphasis on mobility to that in Western warfare, but also a greater reliance on the attritional characteristics of firepower, and a greater willingness to engage in frontal attacks (provided that there is a firepower advantage), rather than searching for a vulnerable flank as the Americans did against Iraq in the Gulf Wars.

The vulnerability of the Russian Far East to Chinese attack from Manchuria makes the situation very different to operating into Siberia. For the Chinese, an advance overland to the Sea of Okhotsk in order to cut off the region, followed by the capture of Vladivostok might appear a tempting 'small war', especially if Russian control of the Far East had already ceased to be effective and/or if the Russians were already heavily engaged in Central Asia and the Caucasus. The extent to which 'small wars' between nuclear powers have been made redundant by their weaponry has been challenged by the experience of sabre-rattling between India and Pakistan, and, rather than making such conflict redundant, it may keep it limited.

At present, a common concern about the USA helps ensure that Russia has relatively close relations with China, not least through the Shanghai Co-Operation Organization, which, in 2005 and 2007, held joint military manoeuvres: Peace Mission 2005 and Peace Mission 2007. The first appeared to be a practice for an amphibious attack on Taiwan. In 2013, China and, even more, Russia made clear their opposition to any American-led military action against the Assad regime in Syria.

Yet, a Russia determined to retain its position in the Far East, needing to secure its Siberian resources, and wary of Chinese–Islamic links, for example co-operation with Iran and Chinese interest in Central Asian resources, may come to see China as hostile, especially if America's role becomes less prominent. East of the Ural Mountains, the ratio of Chinese to Russian is 100:1, which will pose further challenges to stability in the region as competition for resources only worsens in the years to come.

However, Russian anger with defeat in the Cold War and concern over American globalist pretensions and particular policies, anger and concern amply demonstrated in 2007–14, for example in response to the overthrow of the Gaddafi regime in Libya in 2011, have led to an identification of the USA as a threat that has encouraged a positive Russian response to Chinese approaches. This response has been clearly revealed by the large-scale arms sales to China that have helped keep the Russian arms industry buoyant.

More generally, this industry has benefited from a revival in Russian military expenditure, up 26 per cent in 2013 alone. The Russians have also profited from the end of the Cold War in that they are able to sell to former opponents elsewhere in the world. Moreover, the Russians, like the Chinese, lack the restraints stemming from humanitarian and ideological concerns that have restrained Western governments from approving sales.

The USA and possible partners

The USA has a number of strategic partners in the event of deteriorating relations with China. For long, Japan was the key one, but the Bush and Obama years saw the pronounced strengthening of the strategic partnership with Australia, and the creation of a new one with India. The latter was based on American support for Indian nuclear ambitions, a policy that breached agreements on nuclear non-proliferation, and, on the American side, was driven by concern about the need for allies. This need linked two American strategic concerns: China and the Islamic world.

Both India and Japan are major military powers, and each feels challenged by another state that is unpredictable and that may be supported by China: Pakistan and North Korea, respectively. In 2007, the USA reaffirmed its commitment to protect Japan against both conventional and nuclear threats, a key shield against North Korea, as well as agreeing to give this commitment teeth by deploying anti-ballistic missile systems. The Japanese economy and fiscal system will probably remain well integrated with that of the USA, and that of India will become more so as the state socialism of the past is abandoned. Fresh assurances to Japan were offered in 2014.

In 2005, India and the USA agreed a defence pact designed to improve co-operation, notably in weapons procurement. The same year, agreement was reached on co-operation in civil nuclear technology, an agreement preserved in 2008 when Indian internal politics threatened to derail it. The development of a new strategic partnership between India and the USA was a break with former tensions arising from India's interpretation of its non-aligned stance and from American sanctions due to India's stance on nuclear weaponry. India's economic growth and rising self-confidence make it more attractive as a partner; although, in 2013, India's growth rate fell significantly. In addition, in March 2012, General V.K. Singh, the army chief, in a leaked letter to the Prime Minister, described the armed forces as 'obsolete' and 'woefully short' of weapons.

Moreover, India is not comfortable in the role of ally for America against China. It feels vulnerable to Chinese attack, and rightly so, and neither wishes to lose the degree of flexibility about policy that it currently possesses. China is India's largest trading power, and India is looking for a growth in co-operation with China, not competition. Similarly, China has tried to get on with India, to that end separating its India policy from its Pakistan policy. China's priority is Taiwan, and the East and South China Seas, not the Indian Ocean. In addition, despite considerable investment in military modernisation, Indian and Japanese force structures and doctrines are not designed for an offensive war against China.

If, in the event of confrontation between China and the USA, India and Japan simply protect their space against Chinese attack that will be of only limited value to the Americans. The failure of the much-subsidised Pakistani and Turkish militaries to come to the support of the USA in the Gulf War of 1990–91, let alone in 2003, and the refusal of Turkey to permit use of its territory for operations against Iraq in 2003, are warnings about any reliance on India and Japan. For political reasons, these states are unlikely to take part in operations against China, and, indeed, in the event of such a war, the Indian military is likely to be most concerned about Pakistan. The election of a more nationalist Indian government in 2014 may lead to a more assertive policy, but the consequences are unclear.

Other allies will probably be found wanting in any American clash with China, for states as varied as Australia, Israel, Canada, Germany and Britain are unlikely to meet the requirements of American policy. Indeed, past examples, such as the Vietnam War, the two Gulf Wars, and the 2013 Syria crisis, reveal a conditionality in support that is unwelcome to America. On the other hand, allies feel a lack of consultation and a concern about American policy-making processes and perceive a conditionality on the part of America.

The problem of alliances involves not simply the tussle of interests, but also serious issues of comprehension because, whatever the rhetoric of shared values, there are differences. These, however, become greatly magnified by the habit of extrapolating differences onto the background of two different states rather than understanding them, more appropriately, in terms of the continuum of values present in most states and the accompanying differences and tension. The latter is certainly the case with the USA, but there is a habit (understandable and seen also elsewhere) of ignoring this tension and, instead, expecting allies to meet American governmental expectations.

Concern about consultation is fully understandable in political terms, but poses difficulties for military planning in both the pre-conflict and conflict stages of any confrontation or war: both stages are now very high tempo, while alliance co-operation raises issues of security as well as speed, as was seen in the Kosovo War of 1999. Yet, the consequence of democratisation and popular politics is a demand for accountability in government that makes it difficult for states to accept the leadership of another or, indeed, the consequences of membership in an alliance. The notion that alliances may lead to unwelcome steps is antipathetical to the democratising principles and practices already referred to, which reflects the extent to which nationhood does not act as a building block for global co-operation, but rather as both a delimitation of concern and a demand for independence. This situation is abundantly the case as far as trade is concerned, but is also the case for military action and for espionage activities. Thus, in 2013, opposition in Parliament led to Britain abandoning the promise of support for participation in American-led military action against Syria in order to destroy its chemical arms.

From a different angle, globalism and worldwide commitments will continue to pose major problems of prioritisation for the West, which may encourage restraint or, alternatively, a resort to war in order to try to settle an issue. The multiplicity of problems and commitments facing Western powers will limit the ability to respond to fresh problems: an issue dramatised for the USA by the need to plan for 'two-front' commitments. This need may lead to the reliance on a rapid response in a particular crisis – the use of force in order to end the need to use force – which risks proving as unsuccessful in the future as it has often done in the past.

China

Chinese strategic culture has attracted considerable interest, not least the question of the degree of aggressiveness and expansionism involved.[2] The Chinese showed, with their intervention in Korea in 1950–53, their successful conflict with India in 1962, and their less successful invasion of Vietnam in 1979, that they were determined to assert their power when it seemed both necessary and possible. Chinese prosperity – in 2010 China passed Japan to become the world's second-largest economy – has helped to make it more assertive. So also has the strong sense of a need to return to an intrinsic great power status that was compromised by the West in the nineteenth century. This argument has very much been seen with Xi Jinping, who became President in 2013, and, more generally, is a staple of Chinese discussion.

Russian weakness (whatever the aggression towards Georgia displayed in 2008) and the absence of a universalist Russian ideology comparable to the liberal global interventionism of the USA have made it more likely that China's opponent in any great power struggle will be the USA. This situation will also reflect America's specific interests in East Asia and the West Pacific and, to a lesser extent, South-East Asia, as well as a more general American concern to preserve the international order that it has created. Revisionism as a goal, expansionism as a policy, and aggression as a method will all clash with American norms.

In the case of China, there is also a tradition of American wariness, alongside the search for better relations. This tradition, and its location in terms of the political culture of the two states, provides both sides with a ready vocabulary for dispute. The 'comprehensive engagement' that America under President Clinton (1993–2001) sought with China was designed to limit Chinese revisionism of the international order, and included unsuccessful attempts to dissuade the Chinese from transferring advanced weaponry to hostile states. China had demonstrated its aggressiveness with the Taiwan Strait crisis of 1995–96, and indeed Taiwan has been described as the Alsace-Lorraine of the twenty-first century, in short as the cause of revisionism.[3] The effective display of American naval power in that crisis led China to develop anti-ship ballistic missiles.

Under President George W. Bush (2001–9), constructive engagement was constrained by greater American criticism of what were seen as hostile Chinese policies. However, the wish to secure Chinese acceptance of American policy towards, first, Afghanistan and, subsequently, Iraq helped temper earlier tension, tension which had been dramatised with the Chinese detention of an American surveillance plane in 2001.

In 2000, the American government was warned that plans for a comprehensive missile defence system might lead the Chinese to increase dramatically their number of warheads in order to be able to overcome whatever system the Americans could deploy. To this end, China sought to upgrade its intercontinental ballistic missiles, making the missiles more mobile and the warheads more accurate. The entry of India and Pakistan into the ranks of the nuclear powers made China's position look less secure and has increased the sensitivity of the issue of missile defence and deployment. Chinese interest in developing intermediate-range missile systems is, in part, a reply. Any increase in Chinese nuclear weaponry will lead to a response by India.

China's long-term Versailles complex – the sense, with reference to Germans after 1919, that it has been wronged by history – remains powerful, has become stronger over the last decade, and needs to be considered when reassurance is offered about the intentions of the current generation of Communist leaders. The return of Hong Kong and Macao by Britain and Portugal, respectively, in the 1990s removed prime irritants in relations with the West, but foreign concern about human rights within China, especially those of religious groups and Tibetans, is seen as unacceptable interference and a challenge to the Chinese system. This concern has greatly affected relations with the USA, a reminder that conventional 'realist' approaches to international relations[4] have to be expanded to take note of ideological alignments and dynamics.

Furthermore, the very fact of American power in East Asia, let alone the ability of America to act to defend Taiwanese sovereignty and Japan's territorial position in the East China Sea, while it gives America great political and economic leverage,[5] is unacceptable to Chinese policy-makers and may become more so in the future. This parallel with French attitudes after the Congress of Vienna in 1814–15, and German revisionism after the Peace of Versailles of 1919, serves as a clear warning that the idea that the status quo should be the basis for future relations is inherently unacceptable to certain powers, as the status quo is perceived by them as both cause and symbol of mistreatment and international instability.

Revisionist powers are generally regarded as rogue states when they seek to alter the situation by means outside those of peaceful negotiation; although, being realistic, such negotiation rarely serves the causes of revision, and to pretend otherwise would be complacent. As a consequence, revisionism is inherently a cause of instability, as, usually, is the response to it in terms of protecting the status quo. Aside from revisionism, the role of traditional disputes, tensions and threats remains pertinent in East Asia, most obviously between China and Taiwan, and China and Japan. In Europe, in contrast, outside the Balkans, such tensions are contained within federal and collective entities. This is clear in the case of tension over Gibraltar between Britain and Spain. In 2013, the EU expressed a view when there was an upsurge in such tension.

Aside from differences in South-East and East Asia, and resource competition in Africa and the Middle East, it is possible that China and the USA will clash in the future as a consequence of growing instability in the Pacific, where economic tensions in many of the island groups have exacerbated, and been accentuated by, ethnic tensions. In 2000 alone, this situation led to violent attempted coups in Fiji and the Solomon Islands. Since 1945, the Pacific has not been an international battlefield, as the defeat of Japan in World War Two was followed by an American hegemony that was enhanced by the support of Australia and a rearmed Japan. A China with a stronger navy, however, may seek to challenge American interests.

This navy is certainly designed to be able to protect China's capacity to act against Taiwan, for example by ensuring a blockade or mounting an invasion, and to provide defence against a 1999 Kosovo crisis-type strike on China mounted from oceanic directions. This capacity is linked to the long-term maritime strategy outlined by Admiral Liu Huaqing in 1987. This strategy has been adjusted from one of peace-time building to one of war preparation, with more planning for joint operations. Chinese plans in this respect include not only amphibious campaigns and missile strikes, but also submarine ambushes to restrict American access to crucial areas. This stance was taken forward in part due to an episode linked to the Kosovo 1999 crisis; namely, the accidental American cruise missile attack on the Chinese embassy in Belgrade. This episode encouraged interest in an advanced military capability.[6]

The launching of major surface warships by China in the 2000s was at more than twice the rate of the 1990s. Access-denial operations are seen by

Chinese planners as crucial for conflict over Taiwan, for any war with the USA and for a role for the Chinese navy. The doctrine of sea denial provides the weaker navy with an opportunity to thwart the stronger (American) navy, and this entails asymmetric capabilities such as saturation missile strikes against carrier battle groups. The sea trials in 2011 of China's first aircraft carrier intensified speculation about strategic rivalry with the USA, as did tensions when it was deployed in 2013.

It is possible that Chinese membership, alongside Japan, South Korea and the Association of South-East Asian Nations (ASEAN), in the ASEAN+3 network may temper Sino-US tensions, as many fellow members have close ties with the West. Yet, in the long term, if global economic tensions become more serious, this membership may also provide China with a degree of regional support. China indeed has been trying to persuade Asian powers such as Malaysia and Indonesia that their economic interests are best served by looking to it, rather than to the USA or Japan; although critical references to Japanese conduct in World War Two and to Japanese revisionism have only really struck an echo in South Korea. Talk of Asian values, however, has become more pronounced in Singapore.

America's proclaimed 'pivot' towards Asia in 2013 did not command much credibility in East Asia. In part, this was a reflection of a sense of general American weakness as the Afghan commitment was wound up, as the USA struggled with very weak public finances, and as American resolve was doubled.

More generally, there is the question with East Asia of the relationship between economic progress and peace, a question similar to that about whether democracies engage in war with each other. Although capitalism (like democracy) has been seen as a force for peace, capitalist powers have fought each other, as in World War One, and, whatever their strongly shared interests through trade (with the US the second-largest destination for Chinese exports after the EU), it is far from clear that a capitalist China will automatically be a more welcome partner for a capitalist USA than Communist China was. Indeed, a free-market China may find it easier to capitalise on East Asian disquiet with Western economic policies and financial hegemony. This disquiet grew after the 1997–98 financial crisis, because the feeling that the West, through institutions such as the International Monetary Fund (IMF), was responsible for the crisis (rather than incompetent, if not corrupt, East Asian fiscal policies) is deeply ingrained. This attitude encouraged an East Asian search for economic autonomy. Similar questions about the restraining role of economic links arise in the case of China and Japan.

American and European protectionism and/or limited economic growth will accentuate these tensions with East Asian powers. The notion of an effective Asian regional pact may appear incredible, but the EU has shown that long-standing enemies, such as France and Germany, can readily co-operate. However, China's ability to act as a regional leader will be undermined by continued suspicion of its intentions, especially from Japan, South Korea and

Taiwan. The Russian attack on Georgia in 2008 served as a warning that major states would not necessarily be willing to see their interests thwarted. This warning was of particular note in East and South-East Asia.

Alongside the ASEAN dimension, China's membership in the Shanghai Co-Operation Organization, combined with its key role in seeking resources in Central Asia, has dramatically increased its influence in East Asia, understood in the widest terms. Moreover, there are important military, strategic, political and economic links between China and both Myanmar and Sri Lanka. Such alliance-links ensure that future confrontations and clashes between major powers would have a ripple effect. This effect can be seen in the Caucasus, with American links to Georgia and Azerbaijan countered by Russian links with Armenia (where troops, planes and air-defence units are based) and Russian support for secessionist regions of Georgia, support which led to conflict in 2008.

Russo-American tensions have an impact in the Caucasus, as do American–Iranian counterparts. Iran has threatened to attack Georgia and Azerbaijan if they accept an American military presence. Tensions also move upwards, with the danger that regional disputes, such as that between Armenia and Azerbaijan over Nagorno-Karabakh (itself a disputed term for Karabakh), or between Armenia and Turkey, might draw in major powers. There are Turkish military advisers with the armed forces of Azerbaijan, while the latter has turned to Ukraine for co-operation in procurement. The resulting rivalry helps destabilise the region, as well as encourages further militarisation.

A conflict between the USA and China would test not only their military effectiveness, but also that of their allies. It is far from clear that such a conflict would be settled by a technological lead. However, it is also worth noting that, while such a remark would generally be seen as a warning against the inevitability of American victory, the Chinese themselves have made major advances in their military capability, in part from borrowing American capability by trade, purchase and espionage. Having put the emphasis initially on asymmetric responses, notably 'assassins mace' weapons,[7] the Chinese now can also hope to mount a viable symmetrical challenge to the USA.

The relative ease of borrowing and development serves as a reminder of the difficulty of maintaining a lead in technology, provided the industrial infrastructure to permit production is present in both countries. Indeed, the continued spread of advanced engineering and electronics will ensure that, in the future, the Western dominance of advanced weaponry and the relevant control systems will be increasingly challenged. Yet, in turn, American investment in research on such weaponry and systems is unmatched, and the nature of China's military-industrial base is such that recent expenditure on the military and on this base has not remedied their major weaknesses vis-à-vis the USA. In 2010, for example, the USA had 6,302 main battle tanks, whereas China had 2,800. The tank was not to the forefront in Sino-American tension, but there were American leads with other weapons systems, notably aircraft carriers and submarines.

The Chinese need to purchase advanced weaponry from Russia, which, so far, includes guided missile destroyers, submarines and modern fighters, is significant, while the display of American conventional capability in conflicts from 1991 has indicated China's relative weakness. This impression encouraged a marked increase in expenditure on the military from the 1990s, a policy pushed under Jiang Zemin (President 1993–2002) and his successor Hu Jintao (2002–13). The sensitivity of military command was indicated by Jiang, a keen advocate of military modernisation, remaining Chairman of the Central Military Commission until 2004, when Hu succeeded him. This expenditure, designed to encourage a modernisation enabling China to fight a high-tech limited war, contrasted with lower expenditure from the 1960s to the 1980s.[8]

China's expenditure rose by about 12 per cent a year from 2002–12, although it has been suggested that, owing to deliberately misleading figures, its real military budget could be much higher than announced: about $160 billion in 2012 not, as announced, $106 billion. There has been speculation that Chinese defence spending will pass that of the USA, with various dates offered, including as early as 2025, an implausible date.

Chinese military plans include a major naval enhancement. The Chinese carrier will be unable to counter superior American carrier strength, which, instead, is threatened by Chinese submarine development. In October 2007, a Chinese submarine was able to surface five miles from the American carrier USS *Kitty Hawk* and its battle group without apparently being detected prior to that. A different type of threat is indicated by the Chinese nuclear missile submarines equipped with 8,000-kilometre-range ballistic missiles with nuclear warheads. Submarines, specifically the Class 094, of which six should be operable by the end of 2018, will give the Chinese a potent second-strike capability in any nuclear conflict. These developments mean that the USA has revitalised its anti-submarine warfare capacity, which had been downgraded with the end of the Cold War and the decline of the Soviet navy. At a different level, Chinese naval forces were deployed to advance and protect China's territorial claims and oil interests in nearby waters. The key change is from a coastal navy to one capable of true blue water policies, including protecting against piracy in the Indian Ocean.[9] The Chinese have also challenged the US dominance of space by demonstrating an anti-satellite capability.

The Chinese challenge is also apparent as an aspect of an increasingly far-flung Chinese defence system. For example, China's alliance with Iran threatens Western interests in the Middle East and South Asia, especially trade routes in, and from, the Persian Gulf. The provision of Chinese weaponry is part of the problem. Advanced C-series Chinese-supplied missiles make the Strait of Hormuz a choke point vulnerable to Iranian power, and this risk is exacerbated by the availability of Russian Kilo-class submarines as well as by Iran's mine-laying capability, mobile land-based missile batteries, cruise missiles, speedboats and midget submarines.

Fracking is altering the geostrategy of energy, ensuring that the USA moves towards oil-independence. However, in 2008, over half of the world's proven oil reserves were in countries that adjoin the Gulf (in order: Saudi Arabia, Iran, Iraq, Kuwait, United Arab Emirates). Moreover, these states were more able to sustain production at current rates than others elsewhere (in order: Iraq, Kuwait, United Arab Emirates, Iran, Saudi Arabia).[10] As a result, the security of the maritime route within the Gulf, and from it, is clearly foremost, and this will remain so even if the relevant percentages decrease. In 2012, the aircraft carrier USS *Abraham Lincoln*, supported by five other warships, sailed through the Strait of Hormuz in order to underline the right of passage under international law. Nevertheless, it remains a key issue in the event of hostilities between the USA and China. Indian support for the USA is relevant in the Indian Ocean, not least as India may be able to block, or at least challenge, Chinese naval moves beyond the Strait of Malacca.

If advanced weaponry was used by the Americans in an all-out conflict with China, it is not clear whether it could fulfil objectives or survive a rapid depletion rate. As in the Vietnam War, the timetable of conflict by the two sides might be very different, and such that the short-term, high-intensity use of advanced technology by the Americans achieves devastating results, but without destroying the Chinese military system or overcoming the political determination to refuse American terms. In addition, recent experience, for example in the 1999 Kosovo campaign, suggests that 'just-in-time' procurement systems are inadequate, as they provide neither sufficient weaponry nor the sense of confidence in reserves that is necessary for operational choice and for planning. This inadequacy is a product of financial stringency and of a rate of technological change that discourages stockpiling. The difficulty of sustaining a conventional war might lead a clash between America and China to face parameters different in type, but similar in some respects, to those had there been a nuclear war.

Weapons procurement

The prospect of a nuclear war was, is and will be increased by nuclear proliferation. Were Iran to gain an atomic capability, then other regional powers would probably want one. If indeed Egypt, Saudi Arabia, Syria and Turkey joined Israel, Iran, Pakistan and India in having such a capability, or Japan, South Korea and Taiwan joined China, then the possibility of avoiding nuclear confrontations might be remote. Similar points could be made about East and South-East Asia, areas of marked military build-up. The wealth gained by the Tiger Economies of East Asia and the oil states helped to fuel the modernisation of their militaries, especially, but not only, in terms of procurement. The obsolescence of weapons systems purchased in the 1960s and 1970s has led to pressure for their replacement.

This investment is largely in terms of conventional military power, with less interest in counter-insurgency doctrine and needs than at present in the West.

Thus, Singapore constructed 6 new frigates; India, in 2007, invited bids for 126 medium-range, multi-role combat aircraft and, in 2012, decided to give preferred bidder status to French jets; and, in 2013, the United Arab Emirates decided to upgrade its air force with 60 French jets. Sudan, a very different type of state, spent much of its oil wealth on internal conflicts.

Economic growth and resource yields, in short, are recycled militarily. The resulting strength of regional powers then gives added edge to tensions, such as that between Iran and Saudi Arabia, as the latter seeks to resist what it sees as an ascendant Shia movement. To a considerable extent, the Western powers are manipulated by, as much as they manipulate, such tensions, and this dimension of the Iraq crisis and the Arab Spring, and its aftermath, repays consideration.

Weaponry is also purchased by deficit financing, borrowing in short. This was the prime means used by the USA and ensured investment in a series of new weapons systems, including the biggest military programme in history: the F-35 Joint Strike Fighter. This is the latest in a series of projects for a single plane for that function, for example the TFX of the 1960s, which became the F-111 built by General Dynamics, while the carrier variant, the F-111B, was cancelled. The contract for what became known as the F-35 was awarded to Lockheed Martin in 2001, and, at that time, it appeared to have a lot to offer and to be value for money. The F-35 was designed as a comparatively inexpensive tactical aircraft intended to achieve air superiority and as a ground attack tool. The F-35 was also seen as at the cutting edge in technology as it was planned with the stealth capability that defeats radar recognition as well as with advanced software and sensors. Designed to replace at least four other types in service, the F-35 was intended as the central American fighter for the next half-century as well as the basis for allied air forces.

It was planned that the USA would purchase 2,443 F-35s, ensuring that, alongside orders from allies, at least 3,000 could be ordered from the outset. This bulk order was intended to produce major efficiencies of scale, both in procurement and in subsequent maintenance and support. In doing so, it was planned to counter the great expense of producing and delivering a new aircraft. These costs were such that the economic viability of air power had diminished notably, as measured in the number of firms and countries able to manufacture aircraft and the number of countries capable of supporting a significant state-of-the-art air force. As a result, coalitions of interest were required, as with the F-35 or the Eurofighter Typhoon fighter.

These coalitions of interest underline the extent to which political decisions played, and play, a key role in purchasing weapons. For example, in 1963, India bought MiG-21 fighters from the Soviet Union, rather than British Lightnings, in order to demonstrate India's distance from the West. Subsequently, American support for Pakistan encouraged the Indians to stick with the Soviet Union and, then, Russia. In turn, improved relations with the USA from the mid-2000s led India to show greater interest in purchasing American fighters and helped lead Japan to settle on the F-35 in 2011. In 2012, India preferred French to British fighters. Read back, this factor of political preference, which appears so obvious in the modern world, suggests the need for caution when criticising what appears to be the acquisition, and therefore use, of sub-optimal technology in the past.

Deliveries of the F-35 were supposed to start in 2010, but, by the summer of 2011, the date for entering service had been postponed to 2016. Moreover, the average price of each plane had nearly doubled, from $81 million to $156 million, and programme costs had risen to $382 billion. The cost of operating and maintaining the aircraft has also risen significantly, ensuring that the F-35 would be more expensive than the planes it was intended to replace. The scale of America's fiscal crisis, which, in part, is due to expensive wars in the 2000s, made this unacceptable.

Moreover, changes in the strategic environment and the nature of weaponry make the value of the F-35 increasingly questionable. There is doubt about its stealth capacity and its related ability to cope with the most modern air-defence system that it may have to face. Range is also an issue. Whereas the USA had nearby bases from which to confront the Soviet Union, Iraq and Iran, for example in Abu Dhabi, the range of about 600 miles is less helpful in opposing China, whose deployment of new planes, including Su-30 MK2 fighters and JH-7A fighter-bombers, increases its challenge.[11] Moreover, the development of anti-ship missiles by China able to challenge American aircraft carriers, notably the DF-21F intermediate-range ballistic missile fitted with a manoeuvring re-entry head containing an anti-ship seeker, poses a major problem. As a result, the carriers may have to operate well to the east of Taiwan, in other words beyond the range of the American navy's F-35s. The new anti-carrier technology has led to a call for doctrinal flexibility in defining the role of carriers as they cease to be the clear supreme arbiter of (American) naval power.[12] Obsolescence for the F-35 was further underlined by planned developments for rival weapons systems, both drones and hypersonic cruise missiles.

In addition, the F-35 indicated classic problems that need to be borne in mind when discussing effectiveness. The F-35's costs and performance were compromised by being expected to fulfil many roles, which, in turn, led to an overly complicated design. In particular, the F-35 was intended for the American air force, replacing its F-16s and A-10s; as well as for the navy, providing a conventional take-off and landing version (the F-35B) to replace its F-18s; and, also, for the marines, to replace their AV-8B jump jets with a short take-off and vertical landing version (the F-35C). Aside from its much more limited range and payload, the last caused particular problems, both with structure and propulsion and was placed on 'probation' in 2011 (although it subsequently came out of it). F-35C caused problems with the location of its arrester hook, based on the plane's radar-avoiding stealth 'design', proving inadequate for catching the wire on landing. That was not the sole issue for there are also difficulties in integrating and testing the complex software that runs the F-35's electronics and sensors. In August 2011, test flights were stopped when a defective valve in the power system was discovered. This was part of a crisis of system failures that saw the F-22 Raptor grounded after a defect was found with its oxygen system. Indeed, the F-22 has been beset by problems since it began to enter service in 2006.

The F-35 may prove to be an expense too far and an entirely unnecessary system. Indeed, the loss of all or part of the programme was mentioned in late 2011 as a possible outcome of defence cuts.[13] At any rate, the fate of the F-35 reflects the rapid rise of obsolescence, but also the abiding issues of confusion in goals, limitations in function, and changing tactical, operational and strategic parameters. These factors will remain important. At the same time, it would be mistaken to treat air power simply as a lesson in failure. The hopes of its advocates were frequently misplaced, notably in terms of outcomes or political consequences, but air power has dramatically changed equations of firepower and mobility. Both in its own right, and as part of combined arms operations, air power has made manoeuvre warfare a more central part of conflict, and thus increased the tempo of war.

The cost dimension of advanced weaponry varies. In the USA, alongside the high cost of planes has come the far more modest cost of drones. In addition, in 2014, America deployed its first laser gun, or, rather, weapon. This involves six lasers, with a combined output of 1,000 kilowatts, a beam director, a target-tracking sensor and a radio frequency sensor, mounted on a tracking mount. This laser weapon, which can be fired continuously, is designed to target asymmetrical threats, including drones, speedboats and swarm boats, in short, weaponry the Iranians threaten to deploy in the Gulf. The laser weapon directs a beam of energy capable of burning through a target or destroying its electronics. A single sailor can operate the weapon and it is inexpensive compared with missiles. Lasers, however, are affected by rain, dust and atmospheric turbulence. In 2016, the American navy is due to deploy an electromagnetic rail gun prototype capable of firing projectiles at six or seven times the speed of sound, a velocity capable of causing severe damage. However, vast amounts of electricity are required to launch the projectile. At the operational, and possibly strategic, level, cyberwar offers other possibilities, although its capability may well be exaggerated.[14]

The specialist military

Looking to the future, it is difficult, despite the rise of private military companies, especially, but not only, in security and paramilitary roles,[15] most famously Blackwater, to see any abandonment of the notion of a specialist military. Indeed, the RMA, in this respect, is simply another stage in the move away from the notion and practice of the citizenry under arms. As a result of force cuts and of the abandonment of conscription in many states, there are several million fewer troops today than in 1989. Thus, the RMA is part of the search for continued military potency by societies that can no longer countenance the mass mobilisation and ideological and social militarism that characterised the conflict with totalitarian regimes in World War Two and the first two decades of the Cold War.

To defeat Germany and Japan, and to forestall Communism, it had proved necessary to match the impressment and ideological coherence (at least over foreign policy) shown by these armed nations. Yet, both were inappropriate for Western social politics from the 1960s, let alone for the pattern of their economic development. As a consequence, the notion of the armed nation had to be reconceptualised, back towards professionalism, with the citizenry paying the bill through taxation. This shift not only matched political needs and military doctrine, but also ensured that a diminished percentage of the population – the electorate, the taxpayers and the politicians – had seen military service and thus (on the whole) been habituated to military assumptions.

A true military revolution, in the sense of an abrupt change, would be a return to the citizenry under arms, but such a return, although periodically suggested by non-specialist commentators, is definitely not necessary nor appropriate in terms of modern military technology. The equation varies by country: Iran, a state that has the ethos necessary for mass mobilisation, as it showed in its 1980–88 war with Iraq, is currently developing or purchasing and integrating specialised high-tech capability, such as missiles, submarines and atomic power. Nevertheless, the likely speed of a future major war is such that there would not be the time for combatants to move from specialised to mass forces, nor would there be sufficient advanced weaponry.

Thus, looking to the future, the language of total commitment will be employed to explain, justify and encourage economic direction, the retrenchment of consumption and the curtailing of civil liberties, rather than the mass mobilisation of potential combatants. As the Iraq crisis of 2003–11 suggested, however, this assessment may require supplementing because confrontations and interventions (as opposed to a campaign of conquest or deployment) could be very lengthy, while the use of the military for policing units requires a higher density on the ground and thus more troops. The new version of the American Army's *Field Manual 3–0*, released in February 2008, emphasised the need to understand post-conflict stability operations as an important role by making them equal with traditional priorities. The first task in practice overlaps greatly with the functions of other agencies of government in such a crisis, as well as of non-governmental organisations, but in a situation like Iraq, there is an important military dimension to the task.

The Iraq War placed severe strains on the American army, much of which passed through Iraq, but not ones that are comparable with those experienced as a result of the Vietnam War. Instead, it is the strains placed on American public finances, and the very serious consequences these may have for future military procurement and activity, that may be more significant. However, these strains and consequences have to be considered within the context, first, of the general fiscal policy of the Bush presidency, not least the reduction of taxation, and, subsequently, in the automatic budget cuts of the sequester during the Obama presidency. An additional context is that of American economic developments, including an unprecedented trade gap and a crisis in the traditional industrial base.

Thus, yet again, military capability has to be set in wider contexts, notably political, but also economic, social and cultural. In 2011, the American budget deficit reached $1.3 trillion, although the USA remained well able to issue debt to foreigners and at low interest rates. Moreover, foreign investment in the USA and investor confidence in the dollar as a medium of exchange both remained high, with the USA again being clearly in the leading position. The crisis of the Euro from the late 2000s encouraged this situation, as did issues over repatriating profit from China. The development of energy production through fracking fostered confidence.

The specific character of American military culture and power is also pertinent. As far as violent challenges to authority within the USA itself are concerned, challenges that at present and in prospect are very limited, the government has a key ability to deploy, and preference for the deployment of, paramilitary units, the citizen National Guard, rather than the regular armed forces. Moreover, given the depoliced nature of the latter, it is probable that the USA will be able to continue to regard internal violence as separate from war and, crucially, as not part of the function of its military.

This approach again captures American military exceptionalism, and also helps to explain why the Americans underrate the infantryman. In practice, the latter is, at once, the most flexible tool of war and the prime point of contact between responses to external confrontation and to internal challenges. The general American attitude to the use of the military internally also conditions American ambivalence or hostility to the use of the military to maintain control and 'order' in other states, whether by America's allies, by its opponents or by other powers. The American occupation of Iraq proved a challenge to this approach, not least forcing to the fore an emphasis on winning the peace.[16]

Europe

It is reasonable for a British author to ask where this all leaves Britain. In part, there is the question of whether Britain should indeed be included as a major power. Aside from what, at times, has seemed like a running down of the military, particularly the army and navy, entailing major questions about capability, there are also serious questions about the strength and stability of the British state. These arise from a host of issues and problems, including relations between the parts of the United Kingdom, notably Scottish separatism, and between Britain and the EU, as well as the legacy of acute fiscal difficulties. Scottish separatism raises questions about the future viability of the British nuclear deterrent as the relevant submarine base is in Scotland.

There are also the more general problems of the sapping of effort and will, a sapping linked closely to the dependency culture and the sense of entitlement that government has fostered. In many respects, the social policies of dependency and entitlement have been out of step with the active policy of international military engagement that the Labour governments of Tony Blair (1997–2007) and Gordon Brown (2007–10) followed, and this point represents a fundamental issue of strategic conception. A measure of this is money, although that is what money is: a measure of a more fundamental clash of values. The expenditure in Britain on greatly expanding the welfare state has limited the possibilities for greater expenditure elsewhere, including on the military.

This is more generally true of Europe. In 2008, reports indicated serious problems of obsolescence with the *matériel* of the French armed forces. This crisis encouraged President Sarkozy to issue a new defence policy in 2008 intended to focus expenditure on high-spectrum equipment such as spy satellites, and to do so by cutting the size of the army, from a current strength of 120,000 to an operational force of 88,000, as well as the number of bases, in France and overseas. The transformation envisaged for the French military includes a smaller presence in francophone Africa, but, in contrast, the development of a base in Abu Dhabi, the first base in what was not a former French colony. This base is seen as providing a more valuable presence than the uncertainties of a vulnerable aircraft carrier: France had had serious problems with the reliability of its ageing carrier. Sarkozy's policy was met by bitter criticism, especially from within the military.

In 2013, a new defence budget brought further cuts: from 1.7 per cent of GDP to about 1.5 per cent. Moreover, Sarkozy's successor, François Hollande, confronted by a serious financial crisis, sought EU funds to help support the cost of France's deployment in the Central African Republic. This request also reflected France's argument, in its 2013 Defence White Paper, that the American 'pivot' or strategic balancing towards Asia, announced in 2011, meant that Europe was responsible for providing security in its immediate neighbourhood, notably in northern Africa. Developing France's traditional interests in North and West Africa and the Middle East, this White Paper offered a logic for intervention in Libya (2011), Mali (2013) and the Central African Republic (2013–14), and for pressure for intervention in Syria (2013).[17] Sarkozy had been in charge during the Libya intervention, and Hollande during the subsequent interventions.

In practice, the transformation of the European militaries was less than that in the USA. European commentators might like to think that this made the European militaries better able to handle counter-insurgency warfare, but, whether or not that was the case, there was certainly less of a capacity for force projection. Investment in the military was lower in Europe, and it was only a relatively minor goal as far as the EU was concerned, notably with its leading economy, Germany, where the politicians were disinclined to engage with difficult military issues. There was also a fundamental difference between the European (modest) commitment to network-enabled capability and the American to network-centric warfare.[18]

The Georgia crisis of 2008 did not lead to any change in European preparedness. The pressures of domestic political presents took precedence, not least as assumptions about social welfare clashed with economic realities in the context of a serious recession. Defence cuts were repeatedly a consequence. In 2008–10, sixteen of the twenty-six European NATO states cut their military expenditure. Whereas, in 1990, the European members of NATO accounted for 34 per cent of its military spending, by 2011 the percentage had fallen to 21 per cent. Aside from the USA, only four of the twenty-eight members met NATO's defence-spending target of 2 per cent of GDP: Britain, France, Greece and Albania.

The 2011 Libya campaign indicated serious weaknesses in NATO military capability and that for a nearby operation that did not involve the commitment of land forces. Much of the initial air operation was mounted by the USA.

At the same time, the choices made by individual European states reflected the differing priorities arising from geopolitical, strategic, political and institutional legacies and interests. The British and French decisions to maintain their nuclear deterrents are a prime example, while the case of the two British super-carriers contracted in 2008 provides a good instance. The essential logic is political (Britain showing the flag) and institutional (a prominent navy), and, despite support from operational analysis and military-industrial policy, not military. Although the carriers are supposedly 'future proofed' for the next generation of unmanned planes, the increased sophistication of unmanned aircraft, such as the Reapers purchased from the USA and employed by the British over Afghanistan since 2007, raises questions about the practical need for manned aircraft, certainly as an ordnance-delivery system as opposed to, for example, for transporting troops.

Moreover, although they will be difficult to sink, improvements in missiles underline the vulnerability of the projected carriers. Missiles combine with threats from submarines and mines in providing enhanced anti-access area denial (A2/AD) capabilities, a major restriction on naval power. In the case of carriers, it may well be the case that many naval units will have to be used to protect them, which suggests a degree of inflexibility built into protecting what will probably become an obsolescent technology.

2013 expenditure figures

The annual defence budget review published by IHS Jane's Aerospace, Defence and Security on 4 February 2014 provided important information on expenditure, trends and projections. There are issues with the figures, notably the reliability of information for certain states, particularly China, and also the effects of variable exchange rates as the data is given in billions of dollars. For 2013, the top ten in expenditure were:

USA	582.4
China	139.2
Russia	68.9
UK	58.9
Japan	56.8
France	53.1
India	46.2
Germany	44.7
Saudi Arabia	42.9
South Korea	31.6

For 2014, there were estimates that Saudi Arabia's expenditure would exceed Britain's, but the top three places remained the same. Saudi defence spending rose from $3.8 billion in 2009 to $8.4 billion in 2013, by when Saudi Arabia was the world's second-biggest spender on defence equipment. In 2014, Saudi Arabia settled a final price for the seventy-two Eurofighter jets it had agreed to buy from Britain's BAE Systems in 2007. This deal was an aspect of the attempt by BAE, Britain's biggest arms manufacturer, to focus sales on growth markets in order to offset demand from the USA and Britain that was weakened by withdrawal from Iraq and Afghanistan and public spending cuts. In 2012, 44.2 per cent of BAE's revenues came from the USA, 21.2 per cent from Britain, 10.4 per cent from the rest of Europe, 14 per cent from Saudi Arabia and 6.7 per cent from Australia. However, BAE's revenue from the American Defense Department fell successively in 2010, 2011 and 2012. The global defence export market was worth $63 billion annually by 2013, with the USA, Russia, France and Britain, in order, being the biggest exporters.

The military burden looks different if the percentages of the GDP spent on defence are considered, although there are also issues with the reliability of the figures. For 2013, the highest, in order, were (in billions of dollars):

Afghanistan	13.8
Oman	11.7
Saudi Arabia	8.0
Iraq	7.2

There were major geographical shifts. Total European defence spending in real terms fell by an average of 2.5 per cent annually in 2010–13, whereas Asian defence spending was 11.6 per cent higher in 2013 than in 2010, with China, Japan and South Korea being responsible for most of the increase. Indeed, in

2013, the Asia-Pacific region accounted for 24 per cent of the $1.538 trillion spent in the world, with predictions of 28 per cent by 2019. The US share, which had peaked at about 42 per cent in 2010, fell to 37.9 per cent in 2013, in part due to the rise in expenditure elsewhere and in part due to American cutbacks. In February 2014, a significant reduction in the size of the American army was announced, reducing it to its lowest level since World War Two.

Chinese expenditure was forecast to rise by 7 per cent per annum in 2014 and 2015, so that, by 2015, it would exceed that of Britain, France and Germany combined. Chinese expenditure and moves put pressure on other Asian powers in a context of regional concerns about stability. Chinese threats in the East China Sea helped ensure that Japan increased its defence budget in 2013 after a decade in which a protracted recession had ensured no real rise in expenditure. This increase was linked to the more assertive policies of the Abe government that gained power in December 2012 and also reflected decreased confidence in the extent to which Japan could rely on American support in any confrontation with China.

In the face of concerns about China, India abandoned a plan to cut its military expenditure in order to help deal with its budget deficit. Indonesia sought to modernise its military, planning to increase its budget in 2014 by 9 per cent to $7.3 billion. China's procurement made other regional powers appear weak, and thus vulnerable. Whereas Taiwan's military expenditure was half that of China's in the early 2000s, by 2013, as a result of the growth of the latter, it was a tenth of the size. The Philippines, which has competing maritime claims in the South China Sea and which regards China as menacing, had a defence budget of only $1.8 billion. Even Singapore, which has a far more effective military, spent only $9.7 billion in 2013. This vulnerability increased concern about the extent to which the USA would be willing and able to fulfil defence commitments.

Imperial powers?

The rivalry of the major powers will in part reflect their competition through lesser allies and protégés, as during the age of 'high imperialism' in the late nineteenth century and, even more, during the Cold War. There will also be a degree of competition in terms of trying to enforce control, or at least influence, in their own particular 'sphere', and thus of demonstrating power. Indeed, the dynamic and unsettled relations between major powers and instability is instructive. Empires, strong states of the past, played a role in suppressing local instability within or near their territories, for example controlling local tribal conflicts and limiting piracy. The Ottoman Empire in the Arab world and that of Austria in the Balkans provided examples in the late nineteenth century.

In speculating on future developments, it is appropriate to look at the patterns of the past. They suggest that chaos will not be tolerated by larger powers that have the will to stop it by imposing their imperial rule, formally or informally. Thus, just because we are leaving the era of European empires (excluding Russia), and because American experiments in imperial governance are in eclipse after the Iraq and Afghanistan interventions, does not mean that the idea of empire has been abandoned forever.

Conclusions

It has never been possible to invest for all eventualities, and defence planning has always involved the prioritisation of tasks and risks. This prioritisation requires a high level of skill and leadership on the part of military planners and governmental ministers and advisers, and the range of current and possible tasks has pushed this further to the fore. A firm sense of the national interest is an important part of the equation, but so also is an understanding of how best to define that in terms of practicality, and how to prioritise the latter with reference to a presentation of the national interest.

Turning to the more distant future, and considering technologies that are in early stages at the present, it is possible that different types of combatants will be created in the form of robots, cyborgs and clones. It is also likely that advances in knowledge of the brain and in genetic engineering may alter what can be expected from human warriors. Increased knowledge may also provide opportunities for action against combatants. At a different level, the possibility of using electromagnetic pulses may be developed in order to provide tactical, operational and strategic capabilities.

Some of the discussion of the long term may appear fantastical, but the world of robotics is already present to a degree in the form of automatic weapons that may be controlled from a distance, including weaponry on airplanes not themselves under the control of a pilot. Moreover, it would be very surprising if there is no military application of advances in other fields, such as genetic engineering. Such developments might not alter the political paradigms of warfare, but they could certainly alter the conduct of war.

Notes

1 R. Kagan, *The Return of History and the End of Dreams* (New York, 2008).
2 A.I. Johnston, *Cultural Realism: Strategic Culture and Grand Strategy in Chinese History* (Princeton, New Jersey, 1995).
3 T. Delpech, *Savage Century: Back to Barbarism* (Washington, 2007), p. 133.
4 D.M. Jones, N. Khoo and M.L.R. Smith, *Asian Security and the Rise of China: International Relations in an Age of Volatility* (London, 2013).
5 C. Norrloff, *America's Global Advantage: US Hegemony and International Cooperation* (Cambridge, 2010).
6 A.S. Erickson, *Chinese Anti-Ship Ballistic Missile (ASBM) Development: Drivers, Trajectories and Strategic Implications* (Washington, 2013).
7 A.S. Erickson, 'China's Near-Seas Challenges', *National Interest*, 129 (Jan./Feb. 2014), p. 63.
8 X. Li, *A History of the Modern Chinese Army* (Lexington, Kentucky, 2007).

THE RIVALRY OF MAJOR POWERS?

9 T. Yoshihara and J.R. Holmes, *Red Star over the Pacific: China's Rise and the Challenge to US Maritime Strategy* (Annapolis, Maryland, 2010); A.L. Friedberg, *A Contest for Supremacy: China, America, and the Struggle for Mastery in Asia* (New York, 2012).

10 BP data (June 2008).

11 F.K. Chang, 'China's Naval Rise and the South China Sea: An Operational Assessment', *Orbis*, 56 (winter 2012), pp. 23–24; A.S. Erickson, A.M. Denmark and G. Collins, 'Beijing's "Starter Carrier" and Future Steps', *Naval War College Review*, 65 (2012), pp. 26–27.

12 R.C. Rubel, 'The Future of Aircraft Carriers', *Naval War College Review*, 64, no. 4 (autumn 2011), pp. 19–26.

13 D.W. Barno, N. Bensahel and T. Sharp, *Hard Choices: Responsible Defense in an Age of Austerity* (Washington, 2011).

14 M.D. Cavelty, 'Cyberwar', in G. Kassimeris and J. Buckley (eds), *The Ashgate Research Companion to Modern Warfare* (Farnham, 2010), pp. 123–44.

15 S. Chesterman and C. Lehnardt (eds), *From Mercenaries to Market: The Rise and Regulation of Private Military Companies* (Oxford, 2007); C. Kinsey and M.H. Patterson (eds), *Contractors and War: the Transformation of US Expeditionary Operations* (Stanford, California, 2012).

16 B.M. Linn, *The Echo of Battle: The Army's Way of War* (Cambridge, Massachusetts, 2007), pp. 240–41.

17 F.S. Larrabee *et al.*, *NATO and the Challenges of Austerity* (Santa Monica, California, 2012); L. Simón, 'The Spider in Europe's Web? French Geostrategy from Iraq to Libya', *Geopolitics*, 18 (2013), pp. 403–34.

18 G. Adams and G. Ben-Ari, *Transforming European Militaries: Coalition Operations and the Technology Gap* (London, 2006).

8

INTO THE FUTURE

Weak states and 'small wars'?

'Everyone will know their place. Whoever dares to harm, stir up or set traps in this country we will come to break those hands.' The promise of the Turkish Prime Minister, Recep Tayyip Erdogan, to his supporters reflected the extent to which force, or the prospect of force, is a major element in domestic politics across much of the world. The likelihood that this role for force may lead to internal conflict is accentuated by the many factors threatening stability.

Resources

Alongside the emphasis on reasons for conflict between major military powers, comes the likelihood that most wars will go on being different in character, with the themes discussed in chapter 4 continuing to be pertinent. Looking to the future, there are structural changes in the world that suggest that more disputes will arise, while, unless we understand the security agendas of the marginalised, we eventually undermine our own security.

The first structural change relates to population increase, which provides a Malthusian vista of conflict derived from numbers exceeding resources, while also, as in Algeria, Palestine and Rwanda, ensuring a large percentage of young men able to fuel conflict. And not only there. The speed with which armies were created in the 1990s in areas with new states, such as the former Yugoslavia and the Caucasus, was a testimony to the ability to give rapid effect to bellicose plans. Moreover, once used to violence, it is extremely difficult, as the militias in Congo have shown, to re-integrate people into society. This is a pessimistic reflection as far as the future of Zimbabwe is concerned. Yet, many states with a high population growth rate, for example Senegal and Zambia, do not suffer from civil war.

While it is true that birth rates in many countries are falling, and that the rate of aggregate global population growth is expected to fall after mid-century, it is nevertheless the case that the intervening growth is still seen as formidable, as is total growth after mid-century. Projected figures reflect not only the entry into fertility of current children, but also improvements in public health and medical care that lead to a rise in average life expectancy, as well as the continuation in many countries of cultural restraints on restricting family sizes and on the use of contraception.

If the rise in population is one aspect of the modern Malthusian dilemma, another is provided by the extent and acceleration of climate change. This change is abundantly displayed by indicators such as melting glaciers, while climate change and population increases interact to produce such indicators as shrinking lakes, for example Lake Chad and the Aral Sea. Climate change will be massively asymmetrical in its consequences. These changes also have direct military consequences as they threaten individual and collective security. The melting of the Arctic ice cap is leading to new commitments in the Arctic, for example by Canada, as new trade routes and mining opportunities are opened up (and contested). In January 2014, Canada and Russia quarrelled over the situation in the Arctic, while China's interest in developing links with Iceland reflects its interest in possibilities there.

The rise in world population has tremendous resource implications, which will remain the case even if growth rates slacken, because, aside from the rise in overall demand for employment and resources, there will also be a continuation in the rise in per capita demand. Indeed, belief in a likely fall in population growth rates generally presupposes such a rise, as it asserts a virtuous linkage of economic growth and falling population. An alternative, predicated on rising levels of fatal diseases, is not anticipated, with the possible exception of AIDS in parts of sub-Saharan Africa, although the disruption caused by such diseases may well be a challenge for armed forces in the future. This role would be somewhat ironic, as troops have been a prime means of transmission of HIV (the prelude to AIDS) in the region: the widespread conflicts of the 1990s and 2000s, particularly the intervention of a number of states in the civil war in Congo, ensured that the numerous rapes and the support for large-scale prostitution by which soldiers spread HIV were extensive in their geographical range. The devastation wrought by AIDS and the very different threats conjured up by the SARS outbreak are such that it is possible that research effort will be devoted in some states to ensuring that pandemics could be a source of political intimidation and military assault on opponents.

Across the world, rising per capita demand is seen as a function, both cause and consequence, of economic growth and development, but these themselves are a cause of instability, because, despite important and continuing technological improvements in productive efficiency (for example the quantity of water or fuel used in manufacturing processes), economic growth also places major demands upon available resources. In addition, irrespective of economic growth, demand rises because of important social shifts, for example the move of much of the world's population into urban areas, which will continue. This move from rural areas is linked to a decline in former patterns of deference and continuity, both within families and communities, and more generally. In urban areas, there is a stronger willingness to reject parental aspirations and living standards, a decline in self-sufficiency, and an increased exposure to consumerist pressures.[1]

A particular problem posed by population growth and social change is that a high percentage of the population will be not only young but male. Across the world, there is a disproportionate number of males born and surviving childhood, and this creates problems in terms of the poorly socialised nature of this young male population, not to say its excessive energy and repressed sexual drive. A heavily partisan interest in sport is one manifestation, but bellicosity can be another. The availability of masses of young male labour may pose a deleterious effect, due to the need to take them into the labour force in order to secure stability.

The problem of excessive young males is accentuated by selective abortion and infanticide problems affecting women, which is a particular issue in China and India, but not only there. By 2030, it seems that there might be 20–30 million Chinese men without a chance of finding a bride due to the 'one child policy' and the abortion of millions of female fetuses thanks to ultrasound. This imbalance could have a powerfully destabilising influence. More generally, across the world, there are about 100 million 'missing' women. In the Islamic world, the discrepancy between male and female numbers, as well as social and cultural hostility to assertiveness by women, helps fuel opposition to modernisation and Westernisation, both of which are regarded as conducive to an unwelcome degree of female independence. Moreover, demographic pressures may be affected by variations in ethnic growth rates within particular countries, for example Muslim Arab/Asian populations in Europe.

Demand for resources may lead to an abandonment of the general principle that frontiers are inviolable. This principle is seen as a means to continued peace, one that is characteristic not only of the developed world but also of the Third World, especially in both Africa and Latin America. Instead, the search for energy and water may well encourage the seizure of territory between and within states, which will certainly trigger conflict. For example, anxiety over water availability may well accentuate disputes over both source areas and those through which rivers flow. Clashes between Turkey, Syria and Iraq over the Tigris and Euphrates basin; or between regional powers over the Jordan, the Mekong, and the Nile; or in Kashmir over the Indus are all possible. Alongside climate change, population rises threaten water availability; although other factors also play a role, notably inappropriate farming regimes and inefficient irrigation systems.

Across the world in 2007 there was a global average of 8,900 cubic metres of water annually per capita, and, due largely to the rising population and to environmental changes, that average is predicted to fall to 6,000 cubic metres by 2050. There are estimates that about 1.8 billion people will suffer from water insecurity by 2080. The regional situation for water availability is very varied. Good in South America, it is especially bleak in the Middle East and South Asia, putting great pressure on both fresh surface water and ground water.

The extent to which river flows cross international borders exacerbates the situation by making water allocations a key issue. Thus, Turkish plans to build dams on the Rivers Tigris and Euphrates, and to divert water for use in Turkey, are unacceptable to Iraq and Syria. In 1990, they threatened war when Turkey halted the flow of the Euphrates in retaliation for Syrian support for the Kurdistan Workers' Party (PKK) insurgency group. Sudanese and Ethiopian plans to dam the Nile led to a reported Egyptian willingness to attack in 1994 and 2013, respectively. There is growing competition over the Mekong. Sensitivity over water supplies, much of which come from southern Malaya, and the experience of a water shortage as an issue when conquered by Japan in 1942, results in Singaporean plans, in the event of conflict, for advances in order to seize these supplies. Water shortage, alongside hunger, is a key problem in Darfur.

Forests, and the land and resources they offer, provide another site of contest. For example, in 1999, paramilitary Chilean Special Forces police were deployed against Mapuche Indians who were in dispute with the powerful forestry industry. States will take a view on environmental issues not only because they seek resources themselves, but also because they feel that environmental degradation elsewhere challenges their interests. Climate change indeed greatly increases the problems of water availability and management.[2]

For many across the world, violence is a better option than economic development or, indeed, as a case of the economics of plunder, seizure and expropriation, is a form of such development. More generally, demands for goods and opportunities will be a cause of dispute and instability in families, communities and countries. This instability will probably be accentuated because, by 2007, more than 80 per cent of the world's population was living in countries where income differentials are increasing. Just as higher rates of unemployment tend to be linked to crime (although this can be cushioned by social welfare, and most of the unemployed are not criminous), so a sense of poverty, whether absolute or relative, encourages alienation.

A feeling of violence, or at least the use of force, is a response, as with squatting on rural land, such as the *Movimiento Sin Tierra* in Bolivia in 2003. Across the world, about 2.6 million people live on less than $1 a day. Rising demands for goods and opportunities will increase volatility in many states, and this will be particularly so in those that cannot ensure high growth rates and the widespread distribution of the benefits of growth, or cannot dampen or control expectations.

This situation is an additional reason why the global economic and financial crisis of 2008 was of particular concern, but, already in 2007, the introduction of petrol rationing in Iran (which lacks the necessary refining capacity) had led to riots. In 2008, food shortages and prices resulted in disturbances in over thirty states. The interaction of this situation with opposition to

135

authoritarian regimes was crucial in the unrest and disturbances of 2011 described as the Arab Spring. From another angle, the extent to which the serious economic problems of 2008–13 were not accompanied by revolution is notable.

Conflict creates poverty, but poverty encourages conflict, including the oppression on which such economically incompetent regimes as North Korea and Zimbabwe rely. Endemic unemployment provides arms for hire. Just as damaging is the threat of decline into poverty, and, even more, of the relative poverty that will be felt by those who are comparatively well-off but have not had their expectations realised, a group that may include sections of the military. In Manila, the attempted coup of 2003 in part rested on dissatisfaction among troops with their pay. The move to smaller militaries makes it easier to address this issue, but in some countries resources or corruption do not permit the necessary payments.

More generally, the relationship seen from 1990 to 2007 – of about 220,000 people killed in inter-state wars, compared to over 3.6 million dying as a result of conflict within states – is likely to continue. There are obviously problems with definitions and measurements; for example, how far should the violence in Iraq from 2004 on be classified as an aspect of the 2003 war, or how many people in Congo or Sudan would have died of disease and malnutrition whether or not there had been war? Nevertheless, the trend is clear.

The spiral of economic weakness, social breakdown and political instability poses problems not only for states but also for companies seeking to operate in such countries. This situation is more generally significant because much of the world's raw material production and reserves is located in unstable states. As a result, production and shipment facilities have to be protected, whether shipping in the Strait of Malacca, oil platforms off the Nigerian coast, oil survey ships off the Somali coast, oil pipelines in the Caucasus, or copper mines on Bougainville. A UN Security Council Resolution in 2008 allowed naval forces to move into Somali waters against pirates, and a large-scale naval deployment followed. This led, by 2013, to a decline in pirate attacks. The deployment included not only the Western naval powers and India, but also China, which proved willing to execute pirates.

Protection needs have led to a major rise in private military companies providing corporate stability. These companies play a crucial role protecting not only assets but also the transfer of capital flows for their clients.[3] Such private security is particularly important in Africa and is a fast-growing industry that benefits from a lack of regulation that is also very troubling.[4] Private security is also significant in Latin America, not least as a protection against kidnapping. It is also seen in the USA, with gated communities and shopping centres both protected by security services. Large numbers are employed as a result. The War on Terror accentuated this process, but, in the USA, as in Latin America, it reflected longer-term trends, notably social strains and concern about the widespread distribution of firearms.

In many countries, economic growth may well not serve to assuage internal tensions, while there may well be no political or ideological cohesion within the state to encourage the élite to develop policies of sharing benefits or arranging welfare provision. In certain countries, the resulting tensions may interact with a hostility to the élite's modernising ideology and policies, leading to an internal dissatisfaction that might easily escalate into civil conflict. This conflict could take several forms, including violence against particular ethnic groups, but it will reflect the precariousness of government structures and the difficulty of developing systems of mutual benefit. In turn, the political and governmental challenge will be to try to ensure that struggles for benefit take place as non-violently as possible. This task will be one for all states, but may also lead to more international peacekeeping missions with all the problems they entail for militaries who find themselves in long-term policing and garrison operations.

This schematic account, like the idea of 'war among people' as the pattern for future conflict,[5] is more true for some parts of the world than for others. By 1999, 95 per cent of the rise in the global population was occurring in 'developing countries', whose people often lacked adequate housing, sanitation and health services, and were increasingly conscious of their relative deprivation. This encouraged both migration and tension. Moreover, it was estimated in 1999 that nearly a billion people were illiterate, which again can increase volatility.

Furthermore, there was a political 'impoverishment' in that the means to press for significant change peacefully within the political system were often absent. This absence was an aspect of the problem of the failed state, a problem that was far more common than the conventional use of the term would suggest. Indeed, from this perspective of political 'impoverishment', many states were failures, particularly, but not only, some of those in the Third World.

The resulting politics leads to grievances and clashes over resources, both of a conventional type, most obviously land and water (as in Kenya in the winter of 2007–8), and of a more 'modern' type, such as quotas in educational opportunities, housing and government jobs (as in India), and the allocation of economic subsidies. The two types can combine and can have varied regional and ethnic dimensions. Thus, Indian groups in Highland provinces of Ecuador can draw on a regional and ethnic dynamics for opposition, as in 2006 when their protests led the government to impose a state of emergency.

The threat of disorder

Weak states and 'small wars' are classically understood in terms of the non-Western world, but this approach needs to be reconceptualised as it is increasingly the case that weakness appears to be a characteristic of modern government and that this weakness can lead to a type, or degree, of conflict that can be referred to in terms of 'small wars'. Tension approaching to confrontation, or even conflict, within countries may be seen as increasingly likely as governments find it more difficult to persuade dissenting groups not to turn to violent opposition. In France, the Arche exercises to prepare the military to cope with serious internal disaffection reflected governmental concerns about stability; the emphasis in France in the 2000s was on autonomous EU military operations or 'civilian–military' intervention operations within NATO, and in the early 2010s on power projection into Africa. However, the French military will be needed if the police prove unable to control large-scale civil disorder. Indeed, the problems that have occurred in the *bidonvilles* near Paris serve as a reminder that it is mistaken to think of large cities as posing a problem only in the Third World. Already in the early 2010s, France has deployed troops to deal with lawlessness in Marseille.

In theory, modern states are far better able to control and suppress discontent, as they have the capacity to create a surveillance society in which the government possesses considerable information about every one. Furthermore, the nature of the modern salaried workforce and (through social security) non-workforce is such that most people cannot afford to break from this surveillance society. Aside from information, the security resources at the disposal of governments are impressive. Their internal control forces, whether military or police, have communications and command and control capabilities that are far greater than those enjoyed even thirty years ago.

Yet, aside from the argument that the increase in the number of states has itself led to weaknesses, both internal and in terms of more border and other foreign disputes,[6] there are also widespread crises in respect for government as well as a process of social atomisation that poses significant challenges. Potentially, this situation will be accentuated by the danger, within many countries, that the decline of a civic nationalism will be matched by the rise of group, notably sectarian, enthusiasms. In some cases, these enthusiasts will be unwilling to accept the disciplines of democracy: subordination to majority opinions, and mutual tolerance against the background of the rule of law.

There are also the issues posed by autocratic governments and their limited capacity to control once their intimidatory methods break down. This was seen in Ukraine in 2014 as the government unsuccessfully sought to use force to suppress dissent. Kiev's police chief, Valeriy Mazan, claimed, 'The so-called peaceful protest actions have long ago turned into combat action.' At the same time, the special police forces used by the government freely used violence. In the event, the government fell in the face of the persistence of public protests, only for the new government to face a regional insurrection.

Whatever their capacity for surveillance, it is unclear that most states will be able to suppress violent opposition, in part due to the difficulty of the task, and in part as a result of the serious constraints affecting the response of most. Thus, peacekeeping as a military task will interact with what has been seen as the possible breakdown, or, at least, reconceptualisation of the state. This situation is more serious because of the widespread distribution of firearms. In 2007, it was estimated that there were about 875 million firearms in the world, of which civilians owned 650 million.

In part, the reconceptualism of the state to reflect the trans-national identities, interests and concerns of part of the citizenry is an issue. It is certainly the case that, in both strong and weak states, there are strong trans-national loyalties that, while not new, have become more insistent as a result of technological change, greater migration and more concern about co-religionists. People who live in networked societies can be acutely concerned about developments elsewhere, and this commitment reduces the capacity of the vertically structured state to contain the aspirations of their people, let alone to direct them. One consequence is that conflicts may spill from one country to another. Another is that volunteers will travel in order to take part, as with the jihadis who went to Syria and Iraq from across the Islamic world in the early 2010s.

Weaponry on the cheap

There is also a clear military dimension. The ready availability of weapons directly contributes to disorder and civil conflict. This ready availability in part reflected the end of the Cold War, and the massive amount of weaponry produced during it, and, in some cases, the profits from crime, notably gun crime. In 2004, hand grenades could be purchased in Mogadishu market for $10 and howitzers for $20,000. The ease with which weapons could be made also lessened the role of states in the supply and control of arms.

IEDs provided a key example, one relevant not only to military campaigns, in which capacity they have already been discussed, but also as a reminder of the variety of narratives possible with technology. Used with deadly effect, these devices became more effective with experience in manufacture and use. Cheap, so that six roadside bombs could be obtained in Afghanistan for about $100 in the early 2010s, these devices were made locally, which greatly reduced the vulnerability of supply networks. The lack of metal content made detection harder, as did the constantly changing nature of the devices. Increased explosive content, including up to 900 kilograms of explosives in individual bombs, ensured that these devices could destroy protected fighting vehicles, such as the British Warrior and the American Stryker. In turn, vehicles were upgraded, and new ones designed, in order to provide a measure of protection, not least the use of V-shaped hulls to project outwards the kinetic energy of an exploding bomb. Nevertheless, the size of the explosive charge available posed a formidable challenge.

There was also a degree of convergence on the part of governments and insurgent forces, as less expensive and less sophisticated weaponry was employed by the former. For example, in 2013, Syrian government forces began using improvised 'barrel bombs' dropped by helicopter on rebel-held areas.

Conclusion

In a sense, all modern states, whatever their character and form of government, are weak, or may have weakness thrust upon them.[7] This is an ironic, but important, counterpoint to emphasis on the technological enhancement of the military. The interplay between the two will be an important dimension to the future of war and should be far more central to the literature than is currently the case. Resources are a key part of the equation; at once, a cause of conflict and, very differently, a means to pursue it.

This duality can also be seen with the cultural dimension of warfare. Again, cultural elements both helped to explain warfare and also were important to the operation of militaries. These elements also made it likely that the equations of relative capability and likely outcome represented by military planning and operations were challenged by opponents, notably in asymmetrical warfare. Thus, the cultural dimension was central to the unpredictability of conflict. This dimension is one way to express the idea that political factors are broadly based and in part rest on the factors that affect the perception of success.[8]

Notes

1 T. Homer-Dixon, *The Upside of Down: Catastrophe, Creativity and the Renewal of Civilisation* (Washington, 2007).
2 N. Mabey, *Delivering Climate Security: International Security Responses to a Climate Changed World* (London, 2008), pp. 80–81.
3 C. Kinsey, *Corporate Soldiers and International Security: The Rise of Private Military Companies* (Abingdon, 2006), p. 121.
4 S. Armstrong, *War PLC: The Rise of the New Corporate Mercenary* (London, 2008), p. 250.
5 R. Smith, *The Utility of Force: The Art of War in the Modern World* (London, 2005).
6 J.-L. Dufour and M. Vaisse, *La guerre au XX siècle* (2nd edn, Paris, 2003), p. 217.
7 P. Bobbitt, *Terror and Consent: The Wars for the Twenty-First Century* (London, 2008).
8 J. Black, *War and the Cultural Turn* (Cambridge, 2012).

9

CONCLUSIONS

The literature on recent, current and future warfare is dominated by the language of change and modernisation. As is the general pattern in modern culture, change and modernisation are equated with improvement. Relative performance or promise is defined according to these emphases, as are the conflicts seen as worthy of attention by scholars, and therefore, in a circular sense, as contributing to their analyses. Such an approach, however, begs the question of what is a modern, let alone a more modern, style of military operations?

Leaving aside the argument that violence and war are becoming less common,[1] an argument that can be queried, and particularly if the emphasis is on civil wars, Western commentators do not generally define as modern the operations of non-Western forces, whether current or recent, regulars or irregulars. These 'small wars', some of which are far from small, are slighted, although, in practice, conflicts such as those in Congo and Sri Lanka are as, if not more, typical of the circumstances of warfare around the world, than the Iraq invasion of 2003. In 2004, for example, Congo saw conflict in its borderlands and an attempted coup in the capital by elements of the Presidential Guard. Similarly, in 2008, there was a coup in Mauritania.

The problems posed to regional peace by 'small wars' led to the deployment of international peacekeepers as a major military activity for many armies, although, again, this peacekeeping, if it does not involve Western forces, tended and tends to be slighted. In 2003 and 2004, the UN and the African Union agreed to deploy 53,000 troops as peacekeepers in Liberia, Sierra Leone, Congo, Ivory Coast and Burundi, and on the Ethiopia–Eritrea frontier; although, in practice, the numbers deployed were fewer, and mostly all from South Africa. The same problem of willingness to deploy troops, as opposed to promises, also occurred in the case of UN forces in Darfur. In July 2007, the UN authorised 26,000 troops for this operation, but, a year later, fewer than 1,000 had been provided.

This lack of troops was despite the use of such military service to help sustain the cost of armies. Indeed, on one level, peacekeeping entailed developed countries paying for UN troops who were overwhelmingly from poorer

141

states, for example Bangladesh. This was an important aspect of the global economics of war.

However, other elements were involved in peacekeeping, notably concern about regional security. Thus, in late 2013, Senegal had over 2,000 troops in operations across Africa, including in Ivory Coast, Mali, Guinea-Bissau, Congo and the Darfur region of Sudan. The deployment in Mali in 2013, made in accordance with a UN resolution, saw not only French forces but also African forces from the Economic Community of West African States (ECOWAS) and Chad.

Considering most armies in the world since 1990, and also looking to the future, it is unclear that the central narrative and related analysis that has been dominant for so long, which focused on 'high-tempo' symmetrical warfare between states, is appropriate. Instead, it is apparent that it is necessary to devote more attention not only to 'small wars' but also to issues such as counter-insurgency, let alone civil control. It is also crucial to consider the world as it is, one in which the bulk of the population lives in cities, which will probably prove the prime sphere for land operations in the future.[2]

Yet, at the same time, as the discussion in chapter 7 indicated, it may well be the case that interest in counter-insurgency has now been pushed too far in the West, as, aside from the failures of COIN, various agendas of great power confrontation can be outlined which require different doctrines, capabilities and force structures.[3] The Russian attack on Georgia in 2008 highlighted this point, as, even more, did speculation in 2013–14 that China might push a confrontation with Japan over conflicting claims in the East China Sea to the point of conflict.

In all cases, there is the customary danger of present needs crowding out future options. This process is particularly understandable given the extent to which these needs are posed in the shape of difficult crises and the problems arising from serious financial constraints. The net result is likely to be a more profound weakness when confronting a different military crisis in the future. Responsibility will lie not only with the priorities reflected by these constraints – a target of criticism by military commentators – but also with the military's frequent tendency to focus on the present and to fail to give sufficient weight to alternative challenges. Thus, in one light, this work is a call for more strategic thinking and thinking about strategy, and by military and non-military alike.

Overall, any need for reconceptualisation suggests a multiple approach to military modernity, and an emphasis on its diversity. Such an approach does not accord with technological triumphalism, nor indeed with the tendency of governments and militaries to over-estimate their own ability to achieve success while underestimating the problems of transition to whatever is defined as modern. Technological triumphalism, whether or not expressed in terms of the RMA, provides a crucial aspect of this tendency. So also does the emphasis on bureaucratic models of military activity, those most focused on control and least on contingency.[4]

A different perspective for relativism in the judgement of military developments is offered by the reflection that the standard models explaining how change occurs pretend to an inappropriate objectivity. The action–reaction and task–response models suggest that military effectiveness is, in large part, a matter of responding rapidly to events and to the needs set by clearly and ably defined goals. However, this assumption underplays the extent to which perception is integral to both. A similar problem is posed by the notion that the spread of the methods of a paradigm, or leading power, notably the USA, creates a cultural space, or region of similar activity and norms, in warmaking, and, indeed, bridges such spaces as this spread takes place.

In place of this notion, the emphasis should be on how the selective character of borrowing military ideas and practices, both within and between such regions, reflects the need to employ with care analytical terms such as 'modern' or 'Western' warfare as if they readily described an inherent reality or process of emulation and diffusion. The same is true of other terms such as Oriental or non-Western or Muslim.[5]

This emphasis on the need to employ analytical concepts with care is not the sole conceptual point of relevance. There is also the problem posed by the assumption that perfect rationality is possible in the selection of appropriate weaponry, tactics, strategy and doctrine. Such a point can be taken further by asking questions about the tendency to assume that confrontations, and therefore military tasks, are predictable, with corresponding consequences for doctrine, training and procurement. Moreover, decisions for war represent assessments of need and risk that reflect cultural factors. Ideas are located in a context of suspicion and hatred that cannot be adequately discussed in an alternative context of state and other actors understood as optimal rational decision-makers.

Looking to the present and future, terrorism and resource struggles are two important instances of actual and possible unpredictabilities. The varied challenges they pose include the need for military reconfiguration from deterrence-orientated structures and doctrine to a response-orientated situation. This transformation could, and can, be seen as necessary both to advance the interests of individual states, such as Britain and the USA, and also, were it to be possible, to help sustain a world order based on whatever is understood as co-operation and progress. Yet, the transformation to more responsive and, thus, active forces and doctrines can also be seen as likely to ensure a high level of confrontation, if not conflict, not least because there is no agreement on the character and goals of such an order. The latter point challenges liberal attempts to create an order based on legal codes centred on human rights, as well as more neo-realist interpretations focused on power.

The value of military history

There will be varied responses to the arguments in this book, but, whether supportive or critical, hopefully all will draw on the need for 'evidence-based' analysis. It is, of course, possible to test ideas through war gaming, but history, for the recent as well as the more distant past, also provides a key frame of reference and source of evidence, not least because it serves as a reminder about unpredictability in developments and results. Military history of course serves a variety of purposes, including institutional education, academic scholarship, popular interest, commercial opportunity and collective myth-making. All and each needs to be considered when the subject is evaluated, and to judge one by the standards of another is not necessarily helpful. Indeed, it can be positively misleading.

The call to teach military history, which is a central conclusion to this book, might seem to shrink the options to the educational process. That is not, however, in practice the case, for the teaching of military history, understood in the widest sense, embraces the question of the nature and sustaining of civic militarism, and also, indeed, overlaps with the issue of commercial opportunity.

To approach the subject in another typology, one that draws heavily on the role and resonance of civic militarism, there is also the question of the point of reference. The question 'Why teach military history?' can be approached in the abstract, but it also depends on the country and society that is in the forefront. The issue is different, or, at least appears very different, in Sweden or Israel, Spain or Estonia, Ireland or South Korea. As a reminder of the variety of social contexts and needs, in many states, indeed, the teaching of military history is an aspect not simply of civic patriotism, a task that, in 2008, Victor Davis Hanson chided many American academics for slighting,[6] but also of a wider social engagement that owes something to conscription. This engagement is seen, for example, in Finland, Israel, Singapore and Switzerland. In these cases, as also more generally, the teaching of military history fulfils pedagogic purposes, but also helps in fostering the engagement of the civilian soldier, including the civilian reservist, a key element in conscription systems. Thus, morale, as widely conceived, plays a role in the reasons for teaching military history, and also in the content and tone of the teaching.

Conscription, like other aspects of a defensive military posture, can be unrelated to immediate threats, the case, for example, of Switzerland, but, usually, this is not the position. Thus, the teaching of military history, whether professional, educational or civic, is an aspect of a threat environment, and the assessment of value has to take note of this context. That, indeed, helps explain the role of military history in America's culture wars, as its downplaying is associated with a downplaying of the threat environment; and vice versa.

The prominence of the threat environment is also the case with societies, such as Iran and Myanmar in the 2000s, and North Korea today, where the politics of paranoia was crucial to the mobilisation of enforced consent on behalf of the government. In some states, moreover, such as Turkey, Pakistan, Indonesia, and, to a lesser extent, Brazil, the military present themselves as crucial to national integrity and identity. A functional element, moreover, is provided by the role of the military in providing employment and social mobility.

Considering these and other cases serves to underline the unusual, not to say eccentric, character of Western commitment in the discussion of military history and affairs, both to intellectual independence, and to academic and educational detachment from public politics. Indeed, on the world level, the pressure of public politics on education will probably become more salient as China rises in relative importance, not least as an economic–political model, and not only for parts of Asia and Africa. This point underlines the need to appreciate the diversity of national cultures within which military affairs are considered, with the teaching of military history presented as an aspect of the politics of these cultures.

The teaching of military history in the USA, by far the world's leading military power, is currently a matter of controversy. This controversy is not least due to the widely repeated charge that this teaching is being downplayed by the 'politically correct'. Indeed, it is widely argued that they are preventing the appointment of military historians in American universities and marginalising the subject as a whole. Is this true? Does it matter? Is, indeed, military history desirable? A question that is a 'politically correct' one. From the contrasting, 'non-politically correct', dimension, and the specific perspective of military change, not least technological change and the so-called Revolution in Military Affairs, is military history relevant? Does military history have a future?

An emphasis on social forces as the causes and agents of change, a dominant theme in modern historical work, can misleadingly make military history appear redundant or simply the expression of social developments and best understood in terms of 'war and society'. This, incidentally, is an approach that can help those who, as a different matter, see 'peoples' warfare' as bound to prevail over regular, professional forces, an approach that is of limited validity, but one that flourished during the period of so-called wars of national liberation, and was powerfully advanced in the USA by particular readings of the Vietnam War. However, insurrections do not necessarily succeed, as was shown, for example, in post-1945 Greece, the Philippines, Malaya, Kenya and Colombia, and in Iraq, eventually, in the late 2000s. It is still unclear whether the insurrection against the Assad regime in Syria in the early 2010s will succeed.

The relative diminution of military history thus reflects wider currents, including those both in society and in historical scholarship. In the former case, it is pertinent to note the degree to which the individualism, hedonism and atomisation of society associated with both 1960s *and* post-1960s values sapped general adherence to collectivist solutions and commitments. Thus, conscription, and the accompanying mental attitudes and social patterns, no longer commanded support. In part, this point is also highly relevant for the context of military history, at least compared to the 1950s.

In the case of historical scholarship, it is possible, when discussing the relative decline of military history, to point, as a cause, both to the rise of social history and cultural studies, and to the influence on historical work of perspectives derived from other social sciences, including anthropology and collective psychology. This process is not restricted to the USA, which indicates that locating the issue solely in terms of America's culture wars is inadequate. Instead, considering this relative decline requires a broader contextualisation that is alive to the interaction of American and international developments.

Turning more specifically to the history of war, there is a tension between military history as understood by many, but by no means all, of those who are interested in the subject, and the history of war. For many, particularly, but not only, in the non-academic world, military history is the history of war, a subject that should be about fighting, about battles and campaigns, troops, uniforms and weapons. This operational dimension is indeed important, and military history should not be demilitarised, but the operational dimension and the experience of combat do not constitute the complete subject. Indeed, part of the tension in the discussion of military history, not least among specialists, revolves not so much around its real or supposed neglect, but, instead, is in terms of how the subject is treated. Here, it is necessary to note differences among military historians. The operational historians and those who focus on battle, sometimes unfairly, but frequently all too accurately, referred to in terms of drum and trumpet history, are indeed neglected within the academic community, but those looking at wider dimensions, such as the staples of war and society, and war and the state, are generally assured of an audience there.

This situation is further the case because the 'history' in these cases is as much explored by sociologists, anthropologists and political scientists, as by those seen more conventionally as historians. In part, therefore, the discussion of military history today is a case of tensions among military historians and about the character of such history. This debate is not always explicit, but, in practice, exists not simply in terms of the content of the subject, but also of the way in which topics are pursued and presented, as well as of the powerful issues of patronage and appointment, and publication strategies. These latter issues are difficult to discuss, but are none the less important for that. Indeed, this importance can lend a shadowboxing character to public debate, with vague remarks about general attitudes when, in practice, it is the views of a small number of individuals operating in particular institutions that are crucial and at issue. Those of publishers are also extremely important, because, if the major presses do not publish military history, then it seems to lack scholarly weight. This situation makes it far more difficult for academics in this field to obtain posts in leading universities; and there is no doubt that that is a factor in the politics and culture of appointments.

Technological and cultural interpretations

It is easier to probe questions about the appropriateness of the standard approach to military history. This standard approach is characterised by a fascination with technology, both as a definition of capability and as an explanation of change, and by a focus on the Western way of war.[7] This fascination is linked to a concern with economic strength and development. The subject can, however, be treated in an overly reductionist fashion, as in the tendency to ascribe likely, if not inevitable, results to more powerful economies. This approach was seen in Paul Kennedy's influential *The Rise and Fall of the Great Powers: Economic Change and Military Conflict from 1500 to 2000* (1988), which encapsulated a widespread tendency.[8]

The West dominates attention not simply because it is indeed important in military technology and economic development, but because it is widely seen as setting global standards for effectiveness. This prospectus, however, is an aspect of a misleading tendency to dismiss non-Western military history as primitive. This tendency makes it more difficult to devise an appropriate doctrine for waging war with such powers, which is a key theme in this book.

These fundamental parameters of the subject are, in turn, linked to other issues. The fascination with technology and, more generally, with the material culture of war, contributes to a presentation of military history and success in future warfare in terms of revolutionary developments in warmaking, rather than of incrementalism, understood in general in terms of an evolutionary change based on trial and error. This preference is mistaken, as incrementalism is crucial, not least in terms of the response to allegedly revolutionary developments. The latter indeed have to be assessed, a response to them defined, and the response embedded in terms of procurement and training.

Responses to arguments of revolutionary developments in warmaking rest in part on an appreciation of the more complex nature of technological progress.[9] There is also the need, in assessing the effectiveness and, in part, relevance of technological factors, to consider what may be seen as cultural dimensions of warfare. In terms of conflict, it is clear that victory is obtained when one of the sides is persuaded that it has lost, and this involves more than just fighting. The cultural dimension is also present in the shape of very different responses to loss and suffering. Current conflicts around the world serve as an abrupt reminder that victory and defeat, suffering and loss, have very different meanings in particular contexts. Success in conflict, in part, depends on an accurate perception of these contrasts. A focus on military history and planning open to cultural dimensions is likely to be less overly determined than other accounts, not least because of the habitual emphasis on the material aspects of war. More generally, such an analytical approach serves as a reminder that the subject is far from 'closed' or 'done'.

The RMA: the redundancy of history?

The relevance of military history as a central aspect of the study of war was strongly challenged, directly and indirectly, by the belief in the RMA, which was employed within sections of the American military to deny the value of military history. It was claimed that the RMA, which is discussed in chapter 2, made military history redundant by moving warmaking forward, in a paradigm shift, to a new plane; the image varied.

Aside from the point that the RMA can be historicised by reference to other revolutions in military affairs, an approach on which there is a useful literature,[10] the claim that the RMA made history redundant, however, clashes with other analyses of military developments, notably the argument adopted in this study that military history throws light on the variety of military trajectories in the world as different societies have responded in contrasting ways to the opportunities and problems of their situation. This approach can be taken further if the emphasis in military development is placed on changes in 'tasking', in short on the goals and functions of the military, rather than a focus on capability, in particular on weaponry, a major theme in this book. Understanding the contrasting rationales of militaries, and how they rest on different strategic cultures, is important because this provides a way to appreciate the military drives of opponents. This analysis is particularly relevant for the West as force projection has become so important since the close of the Cold War. Military history, thus, has a direct value as an aspect of understanding the factors that mould capability as well as the reality of different strategic cultures. The latter provide a key concept in military studies, with military history proving a crucial aspect in the understanding of these cultures.[11]

Military history is also important as the repository of experience, and thus the background of training. Experience is particularly significant, because war, at the tactical, operational or strategic level, is about the management of risk, and experience helps define the understanding of risk. Furthermore, when two powers begin a war, each generally assumes that it can win, and at least one is wrong. History helps explain victory and defeat, and also shows that the balance between them was, and is, frequently very narrow. The military's expectation from history can be overly simplistic: they seem to want historians to indicate to them a range of alternatives and give them lucid explanations of outcomes. Nevertheless, historical 'lessons' can be valuable. At the tactical level, staff rides are a useful part of training, while historical operational exercises can indicate principles of manoeuvrist warfare, such as concentration and defeating opponents in detail (separately).

This presentation of past experience is a continuing process. For example, the need to make historical courses relevant can be seen with a stress on the history of joint warfare. Such operations, and associated doctrine, planning, command structures and procurement, became more important from the 1980s and, even more, 1990s, leading to a more integrated sense of military power, as well as to a questioning of former boundaries between tactical, operational and strategic perspectives and activities. The reconceptualisation of military power indicates the interplay of 'real world' experience in the reformulation of doctrine, a process that also alters the parameters of historical relevance. Thus, American interest in co-operating with local forces, seen in

CONCLUSIONS

Afghanistan in 2001, led the Army Command and General Staff College Press to publish in 2002 *Compound Warfare: That Fatal Knot*, a collection produced by its Combat Studies Institute on regulars and irregulars fighting in concert. The preface declared, 'Knowing how the dynamics of compound warfare have affected the outcome of past conflicts will better prepare us to meet both present crises and future challenges of a similar nature.'

Reference to history is also widespread elsewhere. For example, in 2000, Alain Richard, the French Minister of Defence, declared, 'The place of history is fundamental in the formation of officers, in order to illuminate their actions and their role in society.' In 1994, the French Ministry of Defence had been responsible for the foundation of a *Centre d'études d'histoire de la Défense*, based at Vincennes from 1995.

A more specific cause for historical debate was provided by the extent to which history was used to provide a frame of reference for debating military options. Thus, before the Iraq War of 2003 and the parliamentary vote in 2013 over military action against Syria, there was much reference in Britain by critics of action to the 1956 invasion of Egypt, the Suez Crisis, and by supporters to the Munich Crisis of 1938. In this, as in many other cases, 'history' served as a box from which words and images could be pulled for citation. This practice was seen, moreover, as the frame of reference offered, by outside commentators (sometimes well informed and often not), for American military activities in Iraq from 2003 apparently moving from being the rapid success of the Gulf War of 1991 to the intractable commitment of the Vietnam War. In turn, in 2007, President George W. Bush cited the chaos in South-East Asia that followed American withdrawal from Vietnam in 1973 as a reason for America continuing to persist in Iraq. Compared to this questionable, if not somewhat crude, practice (although a speech is not the place for an informed debate), part of the value of military history is that it should offer the possibility of a more sophisticated usage of references, not least in terms of the public debate.

Summary

Claims that a historical perspective on war is irrelevant are misguided, although, as discussion of the RMA indicated, they reflected a powerful impulse within modern American military culture that drew on a wider practice in the West. Indeed, for at least a quarter-millennium, it has been customary to emphasise the importance of particular devices, approaches, insights and developments by stressing their novel character and consequences; and the search for turning points and revolutionary developments has been an important aspect of Western intellectual culture. This intellectual culture rests on a broader engagement with technology as modern culture.[12]

The emphasis on innovation has indeed had multiple advantages, and to argue that military history should abandon its customary focus on the new and

149

CONCLUSIONS

revolutionary might seem counter-intuitive, especially if cutting-edge technology is regarded as the great force multiplier, as indeed is frequently the case. Military realities, however, are both too complex and too dependent on previous experiences to make a focus simply on change, let alone revolutionary change, helpful. In addition, as this book demonstrates, the complexities of military realities must be amplified by considering the range of different military circumstances, societies, cultures and environments around the world. Each of these terms is valid. They overlap, but they also capture the extent to which there is difference around the world and that this difference is not a passive recipient of technological prowess, nor overcome by the latter.

An emphasis on variety and on continuities captures the role of limitations, especially of Western tactical, operational and strategic military effectiveness and limitations with regard to non-Western environments; although, of course, continuity does not imply an absence of change. Such an understanding, of both continuity and change, underlines the crucial value of a historical approach. The argument of this book is that it has a lot to offer for the current debate about Western military effectiveness and possibilities.

Notes

1 S. Pinker, *The Better Angels of Our Nature: The Decline of Violence in History and Its Causes* (London, 2011).

2 D. Kilcullen, *Out of the Mountains: The Coming Age of the Urban Guerrilla* (Oxford, 2013).

3 M.J. Mazarr, 'The Rise and Fall of the Failed-State Paradigm: Requiem for a Decade of Distraction', *Foreign Affairs*, 93,1 (Jan./Feb. 2014), pp. 113–21.

4 H.S. Rothstein, *Afghanistan and the Troubled Future of Unconventional Warfare* (Annapolis, Maryland, 2006).

5 P. Porter, *Military Orientalism: Eastern War Through Western Eyes* (London, 2009); T. Barkawi and K. Stanski (eds), *Orientalism and War* (London, 2012).

6 V.D. Hanson, 'Why Study War?', *Army History*, 68 (2008), pp. 26–32.

7 T.G. Mahnken, *Technology and the American Way of War since 1945* (New York, 2008); J. Black, *War and Technology* (Bloomington, Indiana, 2013).

8 For a critique of Kennedy, J. Black, *Great Powers and the Quest for Hegemony: The World Order since 1500* (London, 2008).

9 J. Black, *War and Technology* (Bloomington, Indiana, 2013).

10 M. Knox and W. Murray (eds), *The Dynamics of Military Revolution 1300–2050* (Cambridge, 2001).

11 L. Sondhaus, *Strategic Culture and Ways of War* (London, 2006); R.W. Barnett, *Navy Strategic Culture: Why the Navy Thinks Differently* (Annapolis, Maryland, 2009); K.D. Johnson, *China's Strategic Culture: A Perspective for the United States* (Carlisle, Pennsylvania, 2009).

12 C. Coker, *Warrior Geeks: How 21st Century Technology is Changing the Way We Fight and Think about War* (London, 2013).

SELECTED FURTHER READING

Unless otherwise stated, all books are published in London.

Allard, K. *Somalia Operations: Lessons Learned* (Washington, 1995).

Armstrong, S. *War PLC: The Rise of the New Corporate Mercenary* (2008).

Bacevich, A.J. and Imbar, E. (eds) *The Gulf War of 1991 Reconsidered* (2003).

Bahadur, J. *The Pirates of Somalia: Inside their Hidden World* (New York, 2011).

Barkawi, T. and Stanski, K. (eds) *Orientalism and War* (2012).

Barnett, T. *The Pentagon's New Map: War and Peace in the Twenty-First Century* (2004).

Beckett, I.F.W. *Modern Insurgencies and Counter-Insurgencies: Guerrillas and Their Opponents since 1750* (2001).

Black, J. *The Dotted Red Line: Britain's Defence Policy in the Modern World* (2006).

Bobbitt, P. *Terror and Consent: The Wars for the Twenty-First Century* (2008).

Bowden, M. *Black Hawk Down: A Story of Modern War* (New York, 1999).

Burk, J. (ed.) *How 9/11 Changed Our Ways of War* (Stanford, California, 2013).

Clark, W. *Waging Modern War: Bosnia, Kosovo, and the Future of Combat* (New York, 2002).

Cordesman, A.H. *The Lessons of Afghanistan* (Washington, 2002).

Cordesman, A.H. and Wagner, A.R. *The Lessons of Modern War, IV: The Gulf War* (Boulder, Colorado, 1996).

Creveld, M.V. *The Changing Face of War: Lessons of Combat, from the Marne to Iraq* (2007).

Echevarria, A. *Fourth-Generation Warfare and Other Myths* (Carlisle, Pennsylvania, 2005).

Ferguson, B. (ed.) *The State, Identity, and Violence: Political Disintegration in the Post-Cold War World* (2003).

Freedman, L. *The Revolution in Strategic Affairs* (Oxford, 1998).

Freedman, L. *Strategy: A History* (Oxford, 2013).

Gates, R. *Duty* (Washington, 2014).

Gates, S. and Roy, K. *Unconventional Warfare in South Asia: Shadow Warriors and Counterinsurgency* (Farnham, 2014).

Grau, L.W. and Billingsley, D. *Operation Anaconda: America's First Major Battle in Afghanistan* (Lawrence, Kansas, 2011).

Gray, C. *Another Bloody Century: Future Warfare* (2005).

Jane's World Navies (2008–).

Johnson, R. *A Region in Turmoil: South Asian Conflicts since 1947* (2005).

Johnson, R. *Oil, Islam and Conflict: Central Asia since 1945* (2007).

Kaldor, M. *New and Old Wars: Organised Violence in a Global Era* (Stanford, California, 1999).

151

SELECTED FURTHER READING

Lehman, J.F. and Sicherman, H. (eds) *America the Vulnerable: Our Military Problems and How to Fix Them* (Philadelphia, 2002).

Leonhard, R.R. *The Art of Maneuver: Maneuver-warfare Theory and AirLand Battle* (Novato, California, 1991).

Linn, B.M. *The Echo of Battle: The Army's Way of War* (Cambridge, Massachusetts, 2007).

Lonsdale, D. *The Nature of War in the Information Age* (2004).

McNamee, T. (ed.) *War without Consequences: Iraq's Insurgency and the Spectre of Strategic Defeat* (2008).

Mahnken, T.G. *Technology and the American Way of War since 1945* (New York, 2008).

Mandel, R. *The Meaning of Military Victory* (Boulder, Colorado, 2006).

Munkler, H. *The New Wars* (2004).

Olsen, J.A. *Strategic Air Power in Desert Storm* (2003).

Ovendale, R. *The Origins of the Arab-Israeli Wars* (4th edn, 2004).

Porter, P. *Military Orientalism: Eastern War through Western Eyes* (2009).

Record, J. *Beating Goliath: Why Insurgencies Win* (Dulles, Virginia, 2007).

Reeve, S. *The New Jackals: Ramzi Yousef, Osama bin Laden and the Future of Terrorism* (Boston, Massachusetts, 1999).

Ricks, T.E. *Fiasco: The American Military Adventure in Iraq* (New York, 2006).

Scales, R.H. *Certain Victory: The US Army in the Gulf War* (Fort Leavenworth, Kansas, 1993).

Shacochis, B. *The Immaculate Invasion* (New York, 1999).

Shapiro, I. *Containment: Rebuilding a Strategy against Global Terror* (Princeton, New Jersey, 2007).

Smith, R. *The Utility of Force: The Art of War in the Modern World* (2005).

Swain, R.W. *'Lucky War': Third Army in Desert Storm* (Fort Leavenworth, Kansas, 1994).

Utley, R. *The Case for Coalition – Motivation and Prospects: French Military Intervention in the 1990s* (Camberley, 2001).

Woodward, B. *Plan of Attack* (New York, 2004).

Yoshihara, T. and Holmes, J.R. *Red Star over the Pacific: China's Rise and the Challenge to U.S. Maritime Strategy* (Annapolis, Maryland, 2010).

INDEX

Abacha, General Sani 51–52
Abdullah, king of Syria 63
Abila, Laurent 49
Abiola, Moshood 51
Abkhazia 10, 26
Abu Sayyaf group 60
Abubakar, Abdulsalami 52
Aceh 46, 96
Advanced Warfighting Experiment 37
Afghanistan 42, 55, 78, 82–86; British
    forces 60, 72, 84–85; civil violence 105;
    counter-insurgency operations
    84, 86; cruise missile strikes 37–38;
    drone attacks 10; drug production
    and trafficking 100, 101; Iranian
    influence 73; ISAF operations after
    September 11 attacks 60; military
    expenditure 128; *Mujahideen* 27;
    NATO-ISAF operations in (2006–)
    83, 84, 85–86; and Pakistan 57, 59,
    73; roadside bombs 85, 139; Soviet
    operations in (1979–88) 1, 6, 23, 57;
    Taliban in 3, 4, 42, 56–60, 73, 83, 84,
    85–86; troop numbers in (US and
    coalition) 85, 86; US intervention in 1,
    3, 21, 37–38, 42, 56–60, 72, 85
    (airpower 58, 59; and ground operations
    58, 59; and local allies 59–60, 148–49;
    and Northern Alliance 58, 59;
    Operation Anaconda (2002) 59; troop
    numbers 85, 86); warlord rivalry 83
Afghanistan Islamic Party 57
Africa 43, 46–47, 82, 89–91; coups and
    military regimes 50, 51–52;

peacekeeping missions in 24, 25, 88,
    141–42; *see also individual countries*
African Union 141
Ahmed, Abdullahi Yusuf 91
Aideed, Mohamed Farah 21, 22, 64
air force 121; Iraq 14; Israel 99; United
    Arab Emirates 119; US 74, 122
air power 10, 11, 123; Afghanistan 58, 59;
    Gulf War (1990–91) 14–15, 15–16; Iraq
    (1998) 38; Iraq war (2003) 64–65, 66;
    Kargil conflict 44; Kosovo 32–33, 36;
    Libya (2011) 105, 106, 127
aircraft: F-111 121; F-22 Raptor 123;
    F-35 Joint Strike Fighter 74, 121,
    122–23; MiG-21 fighters 121; stealth
    bombers 14, 58, 105; *see also* drones;
    helicopters
aircraft carriers 10, 117, 118, 120, 122,
    126, 127
AirLand Battle doctrine 15
Al-Ahmar clan 96
al-Qaeda 22–23, 38, 61, 62, 63, 69, 91,
    96; and Afghanistan 22, 23, 56, 58, 59;
    African members of 24; September 11
    terrorist attacks (2001) 37, 54, 55; and
    Somalia 24; in Yemen 102
al-Saiqa 106
Albanians/Albania 32, 33, 34, 127
Algeria 60, 61, 132
Amin, Idi 48
Angola 42, 44, 49, 86–87, 104; and
    Congo 89; diamond wealth 86; oil
    wealth 86, 87
Anjouan 96

153

INDEX

Ansar Bayt al-Maqdas (Companions of Jerusalem) 61
anti-ballistic missile systems 17, 109, 112
Arab Spring (2011) 106, 136
Arafat, Yasser 35, 75
Arctic 133
Aristide, Jean-Bertrand 25
armed forces *see* air force; military; navies
Armenia 26, 118
armoured personnel carriers 65, 70
arms *see* weapons
Army After Next Project 37
artillery 44, 65, 70
Assad regime, Syria 52, 103, 106, 107, 111
Assam 46, 101
Association of South-East Asian Nations (ASEAN) 117
asymmetrical warfare 23, 56, 82, 140
attritional warfare 7
Aung San Suu Kyi 94
Australia 113, 116; cruise missiles 74; and Iraq war 63; and USA relations 112
Awami League 104
Azerbaijan 26, 118

Baathists 3, 67
Babangida, General 51
BAE Systems 128
Baghdad 63, 64, 66; 'Shock and Awe' attack on (2003) 64
Bahrain 106
Bali 60
Ballistic Missile Defence shield 109
ballistic missiles 17, 35, 115, 119, 122
Baluch Liberation Army 96
Baluchistan 96
Baluevsky, General Yuri 62
Bangladesh 52, 104
Bangladesh Nationalist Party 104
Barak, Ehud 75
Barre, Mohamed Siad 21
barrel bombs 139
Barrero, General Leonardo 101
Barrio 18 gang 102
Bashir, Omar al-88
Basra 66
beheading 46
Belarus 109
Bhutto, Benazir 84
bin Laden, Osama 22–23, 38, 46, 58, 59–60
biological weapons 99

Blair, Tony 60, 76, 84–85, 126
Blue Force Tracker system 9
Boko Haram movement 61, 96
Bolivia 135
bombs: barrel 139; cluster 58; improvised explosive devices (IEDs) 72, 139; Joint Direct Attack Munitions (JDAMS) 64–65; roadside 70, 85, 139
Bosnia 30–32, 65; civilian casualties 30, 31; Dayton peace agreement (1995) 31; ethnic cleansing in 32; humanitarian goals in 31–32; NATO forces in 30, 31–32; Operation Deliberate Force 31, 32; UN forces in 30, 31
Botswana 94
Bozizé, General François 92
Brazil 102, 144
brigade-based force 37
Britain: and Afghanistan 60, 72, 84–85; drone development 10, 73; and Gilbraltar 116; Iraq war troops 63; and Kosovo 32; and Libya 105; military cuts 125; military expenditure 125, 128; Northern Ireland operations 39, 69, 80; nuclear deterrents 126, 127; and Sierra Leone 93; super-carriers 127; and Syria 113
Brown, Gordon 85, 126
Bulgaria 20
Burma (Myanmar) 51, 94, 100, 118, 144
Burundi 48, 50, 91, 141
Bush Doctrine 63
Bush, George H.W. 13, 15, 17, 26, 36
Bush, George W. 8, 10, 37, 38, 54, 68, 115, 125, 149

Cambodia 73, 105
Canada 36, 39, 72, 113, 133
capitalism 18, 117
Caprivi Strip 45
Casey, General George 68
Castro, Fidel 51
Castro, Raoul 51
casualties 1; Congo 1, 90; 'friendly fire' 15; Gulf War (1990–91) 15; Iraq war (2003) 1; 'primitive' warfare 50; Sudan 1; *see also* civilian casualties
Caucasus 26–29, 132
Central African Republic 50, 78, 88, 92–93, 103, 126
Central Asia 26–27, 100; American bases in 56–57; *see also individual countries*

154

INDEX

Central Security Forces, Egypt 53
Centre d'etudes d'histoire de la Défense 149
Chad 21, 78, 88–89, 93, 142
Chalabi, Ahmed 67
Chávez, Hugo 95
Chechen Republic 27
Chechnya 27–29, 96
chemical weapons 99
children: abduction of 103; as fighters
    21, 47, 90, 103; killing of, Syria 107
Chile 52
China 9, 11, 23, 52, 103, 114–20; aircraft
    carriers 117, 118, 122; Civil War
    (1946–49) 1; economic growth 35,
    114; and India relations 110, 113; and
    Iran 119; and Japan 142; military
    autonomy in 95; military expenditure
    71, 118, 119, 128, 129; missile
    systems 74, 115, 119; navy 116–17,
    119; nuclear weapons 115; revisionism
    114–15, 116; Revolution in Military
    Affairs (RMA) 35; and Russia relations
    110–12; submarines 74, 118, 119;
    and Taiwan 113, 115, 116, 117; and
    USA relations 109, 113, 114–16,
    118, 120
Christian/Christianity 23, 43, 50, 89, 91,
    92, 93, 103
civil violence, and interventionism 103–7
civilian casualties: Afghanistan 86; Angola
    87; Bosnia 30, 31; Iraq 32, 68;
    'primitive' warfare 50; Somalia 21, 24;
    Sri Lanka 97; Syria 107
clash of civilisations thesis 91
climate change 133, 134, 135
Clinton, Bill 26, 30, 32, 36, 37, 115
cluster bombs 58
Coalition warfare 36; Gulf War (1990–91)
    16, 17
Cohen, William 71
Cold War 6, 13, 23, 49–50; continuing
    conflicts 42–43; end of 3, 6, 9,
    18–20, 112
Colombia 51, 100–101, 102, 145
Combined-Effects Munitions 58
command and control 9, 138; Iraqi 14,
    15, 64
communications technologies 9
Communism, collapse of 6
Comoros 50, 96
Companions of Jerusalem 61
compound warfare 149

Congo 48, 49–50, 87, 89–90, 93, 103,
    132, 141, 142; casualties 1, 90;
    Rwanda's ambitions in 89–90; UN
    intervention in 24, 141
Congo-Brazzaville 50
conscription 39, 124, 144, 145
contractor forces 71, 79
Conventional Armed Forces in Europe
    Treaty 109
conventional forces, limitations of 4
counter-insurgency (COIN) doctrine 8,
    70, 78–79, 142
counter-insurgency warfare 24–25, 79,
    126, 142; Afghanistan 84, 86; Iraq
    68–69, 72, 79; Russia 28
counter-terrorism 61–62
coups 50–53, 93, 141; failed 52, 93
crime/criminality 99, 100–102, 135
Croats/Croatia 30, 31
cruise missiles 16, 37–38, 58, 74, 122
Cuba 42, 51, 87
Cuban Revolutionary Armed Forces
    (FAR) 51
cultural dimensions of warfare 147
Czech Republic 20

Daghestan 28–29
Darfur 70, 88–89, 135, 141, 142
Dayaks 46
Dayton peace agreement (1995) 31
declinism 2
defeatism 2
Defence Regiments, Syria 53
defence spending *see* military
    expenditure
democracy/democratisation 18, 38, 51,
    114, 117, 138
deterrence 6, 20
diamond wealth, Angola 86
Dinka 88
Djibouti 78
Djindjic, Zoran 95
Dostum, Abdul Rashid 57, 82–83
drones 9, 10, 55, 58, 73, 76, 79,
    122, 123
drugs 100–101
Dudayev, Dzokhar 27–28

East Asian financial crisis (1997–98) 117
East Germany 20
East Pakistan 97
East Timor 45–46, 73, 104

155

INDEX

Eastern Europe 20; and Ballistic Missile Defence Shield 109; nationalism 23; *see also individual countries*
Economic Community of West African States (ECOWAS) 142
economic growth 133, 137; China 35, 144; India 113; USA 34–35
economic/financial crisis (2008) 135–36
economy, role of military in 52
Ecuador 51, 95, 137
Egypt 52, 98, 106; Central Security Forces 53; military coup (2013) 94; military courts 95; and water resources 135
El Salvador 42–43, 102
Elf-Aquitaine 48
Equatorial Guinea 52, 95
Erdogan, Recep Tayyip 132
Eritrea 43, 46, 91, 105
Estonia 27, 109
Ethiopia 21, 43, 46, 91, 105, 135
Ethiopian People's Revolutionary Democratic Front 43
ethnic cleansing 31, 32, 50
ethnicity, as key element in conflict 45, 47
Eurofighter Typhoon 121
Europe: militaries in 125–27; *see also* Eastern Europe; *and individual countries*
expeditionary warfare 3

failed states 46, 55, 137
Falklands War (1982) 1
Fallujah 72, 79
Farabundo/Marti National Liberation Front (FMLN) 42, 43
Fatah 97
Fatah Al-Islam 102
Fedayeen 64
Fiji 93, 104, 116
financial crisis: East Asian (1997–98) 117; global (2008) 135–36
firearms, ownership of 99, 102, 136, 139
Force XXI 36–37
force projection 7, 16, 19, 20, 56, 76, 127, 148; Gulf War (1990–91) 16
forestry, as site of contest 135
France: and Central African Republic 78, 92–93, 126; civil disorder 138; drone development 10; and Ivory Coast 77, 78, 93; and Kosovo 32, 33; and Libya 105, 126; and Mali 89, 105, 106, 126; military expenditure 126, 127, 128; military reductions 126; military

service 39; and Rwanda 48–49; and Syria 126
Free Papua Movement 45
Fretilin movement 45
'friendly fire' casualties 15
frontier disputes 104–5, 110–11
Fujimori, Alberto 51
Fur tribe 88

Gabon 78
Gaddafi, Muammar al-105–6, 112
Gadet, General Peter 88
Gandhi, Rajiv 97
gangs 93, 94, 100, 101, 102, 104
Gates, Robert 24
Gaza 75, 77, 97
genetic engineering 130
genocide, Rwanda 48, 49
Georgia 10, 26, 27, 60, 109, 118, 127, 142
Germany 9, 17, 84, 113, 127; East 20; and Kosovo 32, 33; military cuts 39; military expenditure 128; military service 39; unification of 20
Gilbraltar 116
Global Positioning Systems (GPS) 58, 64, 100
globalisation 23
Gorbachev, Mikhail 6, 23
Greece 33, 127, 145
grenades, rock-propelled 28, 65, 106
guerrillas/guerrilla warfare 4, 35, 55, 56, 74, 82; Aceh 96; Chechnya 27, 29; Sudan 44; Tamil 97; UNITA 87
Guinea 93, 103
Guinea-Bissau 142
Gulf War (1990–91) 1, 3, 13–18, 23, 25, 35, 36, 113, 149; air offensive 14–15, 15–16; casualties 15; Coalition warfare 16, 17; force projection 16; ground campaign 15; interoperability issues 16; logistics 16; post–war settlement 17; stealth and precision 14, 15, 16; tank warfare 16; US decision to end 17
gun ownership *see* firearms
Gutiérrez, Lucio 95
Gyanendra, king of Nepal 97

Habibie, Bacharuddin 45
Haiti 25–26, 51, 102
Hamas 74, 77, 97
Hanson, Victor Davis 144
hard power, US 24

156

INDEX

hearts and minds strategy 78
Heath, Edward 15
Hekmatyar, Gulbuddin 57
helicopter(s) 28, 34, 59, 65, 85, 100;
  gunships 35, 65
Helmand 84, 85, 86
Hemas 90
Herat 58
high-intensity conflict 7
high-spectrum capabiity 3
Hikmatyar, Gulbuddin 83
Himalayan frontier 110
HIV/AIDS 133
Hizbullah 4, 35–36, 56; drones 76; Iranian
  support for 35, 56, 76, 77; and Lebanon
  35–36, 75–77; rocket capacity 77; and
  Syria 76, 77, 107
Hollande, François 126
Hong Kong 111, 115
hostage-type situations 10
Houthis 73, 96
Humala, Ollanta 95
humanitarian goals 103; Bosnia 31–32;
  Haiti 25; Somalia 21, 25
Hungary 20
Huthi, Sheikh Hussein Badr Eddin al-102
Hutus 48, 49, 50, 89

imperialism 49, 129–30
improvised explosive devices (IEDs)
  72, 139
India 9; Border Security Force 101;
  and China relations 110, 112; civil
  violence 104; economic growth 113;
  military expenditure 98, 128, 129;
  nuclear weapons 98, 112, 113, 115; and
  Pakistan conflict 43–44, 98, 110, 111;
  Prevention of Terrorism Ordinance 74;
  and USA relations 112–13, 120,
  121–22; weapons procurement
  121–22
Indonesia 45–46, 52, 117, 144; New
  Paradigm of the Political Role of the
  Military 94
infantry 37, 70, 125
information technology 9, 36–37
information warfare 109
Institute for National Strategic Studies
  (USA) 38
insurgency 43–44, 79; Iraq 3, 4,
  67–69; Maoist, Nepal 97; *see also*
  counter-insurgency

Inter-Services Intelligence Agency (ISI),
  Pakistan 29, 60, 84
International Monetary Fund (IMF) 117
International Security Assistance Force
  (ISAF) 60, 83, 85–86
interoperability issues 39; Gulf War
  (1990–91) 16
interventionism 19, 55; civil violence and
  103–7
Iran 67, 72, 96, 98, 112, 124, 144; and
  Afghanistan 73; and China 119; and
  Hizbullah 35, 56, 76, 77; and Iraq war
  (2003) 66; Islamic Revolution (1979) 2,
  18, 23; nuclear programme 56, 77, 99;
  Revolutionary Guard 53; and Saudi
  Arabia 121; and Sudan 87; support for
  Shia-dominated Iraqi government 77;
  and Syria 103, 107; and USA 118
Iran–Iraq war (1980–88) 1, 2, 13, 15
Iranian Revolutionary Guard Corps 82
Iraq 78, 98, 135, 145; air-defence system
  14; armed forces 63, 65; civil violence
  in 105; civilian casualties 32, 68;
  invasion of Kuwait (1990) 1, 2, 13; and
  Iran war (1980–88) 1, 2, 13, 15;
  Japanese assistance with peacekeeping in
  73; military expenditure 128; no-fly
  zones 18; nuclear weapons 99; oil
  exports 13, 14; and Operation Desert
  Fox (1998) 18, 38; and Operation
  Provide Comfort (1991) 18; police 79;
  Republican Guard 53, 64, 65; Soviet
  support for 14; weapons of mass
  destructions (WMD) 11, 63; *see also*
  Gulf War (1990–91); Iraq, invasion and
  occupation of
Iraq, invasion and occupation of (2003–11)
  1, 3–4, 9, 15, 17, 18, 19, 39, 60, 63–73,
  113, 124–25, 149; air power 64–65, 66;
  artillery 65, 70; casualties 1, 32;
  contractor forces 71; cost of 71, 79;
  counter-insurgency 68–69, 72, 79; and
  de-Baathification 67; drone attacks 10,
  79; infantry 65, 70; insurgency 3, 4,
  67–69, 79; manoeuvrist warfare 63–64,
  66; Operation Al Fajr (New Dawn),
  2004 79; Operation Iraqi Freedom 63;
  Sons of Iraq groups 68; special forces 66;
  tanks 65, 66; terrorist challenge to 4;
  troop numbers 63, 66–67, 68–69,
  72; troop withdrawals 72; urban
  warfare 64, 66

157

INDEX

Irian Jaya *see* West Irian
Islamic Courts groups 61, 91
Islamic Jihad 75
Islamic jihadist internationalism 23
Islamic Movement of Uzbekistan 60–61
Islamic Salvation Front 61
Israel 3, 11, 56, 63, 113; air force 99;
  drone use 10, 73, 76; and Gulf War
  (1990–91) 17; and Hamas suicide attacks
  74, 75; and Lebanon 4, 14, 35, 75–77;
  influence of military in 95; nuclear
  weapons 99; and Palestine 35, 74–75;
  security wall construction 75; and
  Syria 77
Italy 32, 39
Ivory Coast 47, 50, 77–78, 89, 93, 103,
  141, 142

Jamaica 102
Janjaweed militia 88
Japan 9, 17, 113, 115–16, 117; atomic
  bomb attack on 6; and China 142;
  military expenditure 128, 129; and
  North Korea threat 73, 112; and
  peacekeeping operations 73; revisionism
  117; satellite surveillance 73; Self
  Defence Forces (SDF) 73; and USA 112
Jerusalem 74
Joint Direct Attack Munitions (JDAMS)
  64–65
Jonathan, Goodluck 94
Jordan 60, 61
Justice and Equality Movement, Sudan 88

Kabila, Joseph 93
Kabila, Laurent 89, 90, 93
Kabul 58
Kalimantan (Indonesian Borneo) 46
Kandahar 58, 83, 86
Kargil conflict (1999) 44, 98
Karimov, Islam 92
Karzai, Hamid 59, 82, 83, 84, 85
Kashmir 43, 46, 96, 98
Keegan, John 62
Kemal, Babrak 57
Kennedy, Paul 147
Kenya 91, 102, 103, 137, 145
Khan, Abdul Qadeer 98
Khan, Ismail 83
kidnappings 101, 136
Kiir, Salva 88
Kirkuk 66

Koang, Major-General James 88
Kosovo 10, 32–34, 35, 65, 114, 116; air
  offensive 32–33, 36; ethnic cleansing in
  32; land attack 33; NATO Operation
  Allied Force 32–33, 34; NATO
  peacekeeping force in 32
Kosovo Liberation Army 32
Kunduz 58, 83
Kurdistan Workers' Party (PKK) 135
Kurds 18, 66, 104
Kursk submarine 27
Kuwait 15, 17; Iraqi invasion of (1990) 1,
  2, 13

land power 11
laser weapons 123
Lashkar-e-Jhangvi 84
Latin America 82, 95, 136; crime rate
  101–2; *see also individual countries*
Latvia 109
Lebanon 4, 14, 35–36, 75–77, 78; gun
  ownership 102; and Hizbullah 35–36,
  75–77; Israel and 4, 14, 35, 75–77;
  Palestinian camps in 102
Lendus 90
Liberation Tigers of Tamil Eelam (LTTE)
  96–97
Liberia 24, 46–47, 93, 141
Liberians United for Reconciliation and
  Democracy 93
Libya 92, 98, 126; civil violence and
  intervention in (2011) 105–6, 112, 127;
  NATO air attacks on 105, 106, 127;
  nuclear weapons 99; rival militias 106
Libya Shields 106
limited warfare 4
Linebacker I and II campaigns, Vietnam
  15, 16
Lithuania 109
Liu Huaqing 116
logistics, Gulf War (1990–91) 16
London bombings (2005) 55
long-range missiles 7, 17, 98, 99
Lord's Resistance Army (LRA) 103
Los Angeles riots (1992) 39–40

Macao 111, 115
Macedonia, Republic of 34
McGarth, John 79
Machar, Riek 88
Madrid bombings (2004) 55
Madurans 46

INDEX

Mainassara, Ibrahim Bara 51
Malaya 145
Malaysia 117
Maldives 93
Mali 50, 89, 105, 106, 126, 142
Maliki, Nuri al-68, 72
Manila 136
manoeuvrist warfare 148; Iraq war (2003) 63–64, 66
Mao Zedong 35
Mara Salvatrucha 102
March 23 Movement (M23), Congo 90
martyrdom 61
Masalit tribe 88
Mauritania 50, 51, 52, 141
Mazan, Valeriy 138
Mazar-e Sharif 58, 83
mechanisation, ideology of 7
Mengistu Haile Mariam 43
Mexico: drug gangs 100; kidnappings 101; and US border, National Guard deployment on (2006) 80
Middle East 2
military 53, 144–45; control 94; coups 30, 31, 50–53, 93; and economy 52; European 125–27; and national identity and integrity 144; privatisation of 71, 123, 136; reductions in 36, 39, 125, 126; role in politics 94–95; specialist 123–25; US *see under* United States; *see also* air force; navies
military expenditure 7, 98–99, 127–29; Afghanistan 128; Britain 125, 128; China 71, 118, 119, 128, 129; France 126, 127, 128; Germany 128; India 98, 128, 129; Iraq 128; Japan 128, 129; NATO 127; Oman 128; Pakistan 98; Philippines 129; Russia 71, 112, 128; Saudi Arabia 128; Singapore 129; South Korea 128; Taiwan 129; United States (USA) 71, 128, 129
military history 143–50; and cultural dimensions of warfare 147; as repository of experience 148; and Revolution in Military Affairs (RMA) 147–49; technological approach to 147; value of 143–46
military operations other than war (MOOTW) 25
Military Professional Resources Incorporated 31
military regimes 50–53

military service 7, 124; complusory/ conscripted 3, 39, 124, 144, 145; France 39; Germany 39; Spain 39
Milošević, Slobodan 30, 32
Mindanao 60, 92
missiles *see* ballistic missiles; cruise missiles; long-range missiles
Mobuto Sese Soko 49, 87, 89
modernisation 7, 134, 141
Mohamed, Ali Mahdi 21
Mohammed, Atta 83
Moldova 27
morale: Iraqi armed forces 65; US military 72
Moro Islamic Liberation Front 92
Moro National Liberation Front 92
Morocco 61
Mosul 66
Mouvement patriotique de Côte d'Ivoire 93
Movement for the Emancipation of the Niger Delta 96
Movement for the Liberation of the Congo (MLC) 92
Movimento Popular de Libertação de Angola (MPLA) 42
Movimiento Sin Tierro 135
Mugabe, Robert 94, 103
Mujahideen 27
Mumbai bomb blasts (2008) 55, 60, 104
Mungiki gang 102
murders 101, 102
Museveni, Yoweri 48
Musharraf, Pervez 52, 59
Muslim Brotherhood 94, 95, 106
Muslim fundamentalism 26, 54, 91
Muslims 22–23, 27, 29, 37, 56, 60, 78, 84, 134, 143; Abkhazia 26; Algeria 61; Bosnian 30, 31; Central African Republic 50, 92–93; India 104; Ivory Coast 89; Kashmiri 43; Kosovo 32; Nigeria 92, 96; Pakistan 92, 98; Philippines 92; Somali 43; Sudan 44, 103; Thailand 91; Xinjiang 95–96; *see also* Shias; Sunnis
Mutually Assured Destruction (MAD) 6, 20
Myanmar (Burma) 51, 94, 100, 118, 144

Nagorno-Karabakh 26, 118
Najibullah, Mohammad 57
Namibia 45, 89
Nasheed, Mohammed 93

159

INDEX

Nasiriya 64
National Congress for the Defense of the People (CNDP), Congo 90
National Guard: Saudi Arabia 53; US 39–40, 71, 72, 80, 125
nationalism: Eastern Europe 23; Soviet Union 23
NATO-ISAF operations, in Afghanistan 83, 84, 85–86
NATO (North Atlantic Treaty Organization) 16, 23, 27; and Bosnia 30, 31–32; Georgia membership of 109; and Kosovo 32–33, 34; and Libya 105, 106; and Macedonia 34; military expenditure 127; military force reductions 36; Ukraine membership of 109
navies: Chinese 116–17, 119; Soviet 27
neo-conservatives 8
neo-liberalism 34
Nepal 47, 90, 110; Maoist insurgency 97
network-centric warfare 8, 36–37, 127
network-enabled capability 127
Nicaragua 43
Niger 50, 51
Nigeria 47, 50, 51–52, 61, 92, 93, 94, 96
1920 Revolution Brigades 69
non-Western warfare 1–2, 4
Noriega, Manuel 26
North Korea 52, 136, 144; nuclear weapons 56, 98–99; as threat to Japan 73, 112
Northern Ireland 39, 69, 80
nuclear deterrents 126, 127
nuclear weapons 3, 6, 7, 57, 120, 126; India 98, 112, 113, 115; Iran 56, 77, 99; Iraq 99; Israel 99; Libya 99; North Korea 56, 98–99; Pakistan 98, 115; USA 70
Nuer 88

Obama, Barack 10, 85, 86, 125
Obote, Milton 48
Oceania 42, 104
Ogaden war 21
oil 13, 14, 120; Angola 86, 87; Sudan 87, 88
Oman 128
Operation Al Fajr (New Dawn) (Iraq, 2004) 79
Operation Allied Force (Kosovo, 1999) 32–34, 65

Operation Anaconda (Afghanistan, 2002) 59
Operation Deliberate Force (Bosnia, 1995) 31, 32
Operation Desert Fox (Iraq, 1998) 18, 38
Operation Iraqi Freedom (2003) 63
Operation Joint Cause (Panama, 1989) 26
Operation Provide Comfort (Iraq, 1991) 18
Operation Restore Hope (Somalia) 21
Operation Uphold Democracy (Haiti, 1994) 25, 26
operational goals 11
Oriental warfare 2
Oslo Agreement (1993) 35
Ovimbundu 86

Pacific islands 93, 104, 116
Pakistan 52, 73, 94, 144; and Afghanistan 57, 59, 73; East 97; and India conflict 43–44, 98, 110, 111, 112; Inter-Services Intelligence Agency (ISI) 29, 60, 84; military regime 50; North-West Frontier Province (NWFP) 84; nuclear weapons 98, 115; Quetta riot (2004) 101; storming of Lal Masjd (Red Mosque) 92; and Taliban 59, 60, 62, 83–84, 85; US drone strikes in 10; Waziris–Uzbek rivalry in 61
Pakistan Muslim League 84
Pakistan People's Party 84
Palestine 35, 74–75, 78, 97, 132
Palestinian Liberation Organization (PLO) 35, 75
Palestinian refugees 74, 102
Panama 26
Papua New Guinea 104
Paraguay 93
paramilitary services 52–53, 82, 93
Patassé, Ange-Félix 92
Patriot missiles 15, 16, 17
peacekeeping 19, 137, 138; Abkhazia 26; in Africa 24, 25, 88, 141–42; Bosnia 31–32; Haiti 25; Iraq 73; Japanese assistance with 73; Liberia 47; Sierra Leone 47; Tajikistan 26
Peretz, Amir 76
Peru 51, 95
Petraeus, General David 68
Philippines 60, 92, 129, 145
pirate attacks 136
Poland 20, 109

160

police: armed 53, 79; Iraqi 79; Thai 53
politicians, lack of military experience 3
population: female 134; growth 132–33, 134, 137; young male 134
poverty 102, 135, 136
Powell, Colin 38
pre-emption 62, 63
precision munitions 14, 15, 16
Predator drone 10
Primeiro Comando da Capital 102
'primitive' warfare 50
private military companies 71, 123, 136
proxy wars 56, 59
Putin, Vladimir 29

Qaqa militia 106
Qatar 77, 105, 106, 107

Rally for Congolese Democracy 89
Ramadi 72
rapid deployment 37
remotely piloted vehicles (RPVs) 10
Republican Guard, Iraq 53, 64, 65
resource competition 132–37, 140, 143; Sino-Russian 111, 112
revisionism: Chinese 114–15, 116; Japanese 117
Revolution in Military Affairs (RMA) 3, 6–12, 34, 35, 36, 54–55, 63, 123, 142, 147–49
Revolutionary Armed Forces of Colombia (FARC) 100, 101
Revolutionary Guard, Iran 53
Richard, Alain 149
roadside bombs: Afghanistan 85, 139; Iraq 70
Robertson, George 32
robotics 130
rocket-propelled grenades 28, 65, 106
rogue states 55, 56, 62
Romania 20
Rouhani, Hassan 99
Rumsfeld, Donald 8, 67, 70
Russia 19–20, 114; and Abkhazia 26; and Afghanistan 56; and Chechnya 28–29; and China relations 110–12; and Conventional Armed Forces in Europe Treaty 109; and counter-insurgency warfare 28; economic difficulties 20; failed coup in 52; and Georgia 26, 29, 109, 118, 142; military exercises 109; military expenditure 71, 112, 128;

pre-emptive attacks 62; secret police 29; and South Ossetia 26; and Syria 103, 107; and Tajikistan 26; and Ukraine 27; and USA relations 109; *see also* Soviet Union
Rwanda 24, 47–49, 132; and Congo 89–90; genocide 48, 49; Japanese assistance to refugees 73
Rwanda Patriotic Army (RPA) 48, 49
Rwanda Patriotic Front (RPF) 48

Saddam Hussein 1, 2, 3, 13, 14, 17, 18, 19, 64, 67
Sadr, Moqtada al-68
Saleh, Ali Abdullah 96
Sandinistas 43
Sarkozy, Nicolas 126
SARS outbreak 133
Sassou-Nguesso, Denis 50
satellite surveillance 11, 15, 73
Saudi Arabia 13–14, 17, 77, 98, 106–7; and Iran 121; and Iraq war (2003) 63; military expenditure 128; National Guard 53; suicide bombings in (2003Ä4) 60; US forces in 23
Savimbi, Jonas 86, 87
Sawaiq militia 106
Scognamiglio, Carlo 39
Scottish separatism 125, 126
Scud missiles 17
Séléka rebel group 92
sea denial, doctrine of 116–17
sea power 11
security 38
Senegal 78, 142
separatist movements 82, 95–97; Baluchistan 96; China 95–96; former Soviet Union 26–29, 96; in Indonesian archipelago 45–46, 96; Nigeria 96; Tamil 96–97; Yemen 95, 96
September 11 terrorist attacks (2001) 37, 54, 55
Serbs/Serbia 3, 95; and Bosnia 30–32; and Kosovo 26, 32–34
Sevastopol naval base 27
Shabab groups 24, 61, 91
Shanghai Co-operation Organization 111, 118
Sharif, Nawaz 84
Sharif, Shahbaz 84
Sharon, Ariel 74, 75, 76, 95

161

INDEX

Shias 18, 22, 23, 65, 67, 69, 72, 73;
see also Hizbullah
Shinseki, Eric 37
Shoneham, Ernest 51
Sierra Leone 46–47, 50, 86, 93, 103, 141
Sinai 61
Singapore 61, 117, 121, 129
Singh, General V.K. 113
Sisi, General Abdel Fattah al-94
Slovenia 30
small wars 111, 137–38, 141, 142
soft power 78; US 24
Solomon Islands 104, 116
Somali National Movement 21
Somalia 20–22, 35, 42, 46, 55, 91, 103;
and Al-Qaeda 24; child fighters 21;
civilian casualties 21, 24; clan factions
21; and Ethiopia 91; Islamic Courts
groups 61, 91; *Shabab* groups 24, 61, 91;
UN intervention in (1992) 21–22, 25;
and USA 21–22, 24, 91
Soro, Guillaume 89
South Africa 94
South Asia 2, 43–44; *see also individual
countries*
South Korea 117, 128
South Ossetia 26
South Sudan 87–88, 103
Southern Sudan Independence Army 44
Soviet Union: and Afghanistan (1979–88)
1, 6, 23, 57; and Angola 87; and Cold
War 23; collapse of 6, 18, 22, 23, 34;
and Iraq 14; nationalism in 23; navy 27
Spain 95; and Gibraltar 116; military
service 39
special forces 66, 70
Srebrenica 31
Sri Lanka 96–97, 118, 141
stealth bombers 14, 58, 105
stealth technology 74
strategic goals 11–12
strength, assessment of 7
Stryker units 37
submarines 27, 118; Chinese 74, 118, 119
Sudan 43, 44, 70, 87–89, 121; casualty
figures 1; Comprehensive Peace
Agreement (2011) 87; cruise missile
strikes in 37–38; Darfur region 70,
88–89, 135, 141, 142; and Iran links 87;
oil 87, 88; South Sudan 87–88, 103;
and Uganda 103
Sudan Liberation Army 88

Sudan People's Liberation Army 44
Sudan People's Liberation Movement 87
Suharto, General 52, 94
suicide military operations 23
suicide terrorism 54, 60, 61–62; Hamas
74, 75
Sumatra 46, 96
Sunnis 22, 23, 67, 68, 69, 72–73, 77
super-carriers 127
surveillance capability 9–10, 11, 15, 73
surveillance society 138
synergetical warfare 109, 110
Syria 14, 17, 52, 56, 67, 98, 104, 126, 135,
145; Assad regime 52, 103, 106, 107,
111; barrel bombs 139; civil war (2013)
105, 107–8; civilian casualties 107;
Defence Regiments 53; and Hizbullah
76, 77, 107; and Israel 77; weapons of
mass destruction 67, 99

Taiwan 11, 111, 113, 115, 116, 117,
118; cruise missiles 74; military
expenditure 129
Tajikistan 26, 96
Taliban 26, 96; in Afghanistan 3, 4, 42,
56–60, 73, 83, 84, 85–86; Pakistani
support for 59, 60, 61, 83–84, 85
Tamil Tigers 96–97
tanks 118; Chinese 118; Gulf War
(1990–91) 16; Iraq war (2003) 65, 66;
Israeli, in Lebanon conflict 76
Taya, Maaonya 51
Taylor, Charles 47, 93
technology-driven warfare 9–12, 147
technology transfer 11
Tentera Nasional Indonesia (Indonesian
National Military) 52
terrorist states 55
terrorists/terrorism 37–38, 54–55, 82, 143;
in Iraq 4; rights of suspects 78; *see also*
counter-terrorism; suicide terrorism;
War on Terror; *and individual groups*
Thailand 52, 53, 91–92, 93, 105
Thatcher, Margaret 13
thermal-imaging laser-designation
systems 14
threat environment 144
Tibet 110
Tigré People's Liberation Front 43
Tikrit 66
Tito, Josip 30
Togo 50

162

INDEX

Tonga 104
total victory 7
Trans-Dniester Republic 27
Transformation process 8, 36
Treaty of Beijing (1860) 110
Trident II D-5 35
Tuareg 106
Tudjman, Franjo 30
Turkey 94, 144; and Gulf War (1990–91)
   113; and Iraq war (2003) 63, 66, 113;
   and Kurdish nationalism 104; suicide
   bombings in (2003) 60; and water
   resources 135
Turkmenistan 44
Tutsis 47–48, 50

Uganda 47, 49, 89, 90, 91, 103
Ukraine 27, 53, 94, 109, 118, 138
unemployment 102, 135
*União Nacional para a Independência Total de
   Angola* (UNITA) 42, 86, 87, 89
unilateralism, US 8–9
Union of Congolese Patriots 90
Union Solidarity and Development Party,
   Myanmar (Burma) 94
unipolar international system 6, 9
United Arab Emirates 121
United Kingdom *see* Britain
United Liberation Front of Asom 46, 101
United Nations (UN) 17, 19; Assistance
   Mission for Rwanda 48; and Bosnia 30;
   and Congo 24, 141; Development
   Programme 101; peacekeeping in Africa
   88, 141–42; and Somalia 21–22, 25;
   and USA relations; 19; weapons
   inspectors 11
United Self-Defence Forces of Colombia
   (AUC) 100, 101
United States (USA): and Afghanistan
   see under Afghanistan; air force 74, 122;
   AirLand Battle doctrine 15; and
   Australia relations 112; ballistic missiles
   35; bases in Central Asia 56–57; and
   Bosnia 30, 38; and China relations 109,
   113, 114–16, 118, 120; and Cold War
   23; counter-insurgency warfare 24–25;
   drone attacks, use of 10; economy
   34–35, 125; and Gulf War (1990–91)
   13–18, 25, 35, 36; and Haiti 25–26;
   hard power 24; and India relations
   112–13, 120, 121–22; and Iran 118; and
   Iraq war (2003) *see* Iraq, invasion and

occupation of; and Japan 112; and
Kosovo 32, 34, 35, 36, 38; and Liberia
24; Los Angeles riots (1992) 39–40;
military (Advanced Warfighting
Experiment 37; Army After Next
Project 37; brigade-based force 37; in
Europe 109; expenditure 71, 128, 129;
force reductions 36; information systems
36–37; institutional culture 24–25, 125;
morale 72; retention problems 72;
structure of 71–72; as volunteer force
39); militray history teaching in 145;
National Guard 39–40, 71, 72, 80, 125;
National Security Strategy (2002) 62;
neo-conservatives 8; neo-liberalism 34;
nuclear weapons 70; and Pakistan 10;
and Panama; 26; Plan Colombia
initiative 100; and Revolution in
Military Affairs (RMA) 6, 7–9; and
Russia relations 109; and Rwanda 48;
and Saudi Arabia 23; soft power 24;
and Somalia 21–22, 24, 91; Strategic
Assessment (1999) 38; and Sudan
37–38; surveillance satellites 11; and
Syria 111, 114; and UN relations 19;
unilateralism 8–19; and Vietnam 1, 15,
16, 21, 24, 25, 38, 145, 149; War on
Drugs 101; and War on Terror *see* War
on Terror; weapons procurement 121;
and Yemen 10, 102
unmanned aerial vehicles (UAVs)
   see drones
unmanned platforms 9–11, 127
urban warfare, Iraq 64, 66
urbanization 133
USS *Abraham Lincoln* 120
USS *Wisconsin* 16
Uzbekistan 27, 56, 60–61, 92
Uzbeks, in Pakistan 61

Vall, Colonel Ely 51
Venezuela 95, 102
Vietnam War 1, 15, 16, 21, 24, 25, 38,
   145, 149

Wahhabis 29
War on Drugs 101
War on Terror 38, 54–81, 101, 109, 136;
   Afghanistan 56–60; counter-terrorism
   61–62; Iraq and 63–73; outside
   Afghanistan 60–61
warlords, Afghan 83

163

INDEX

warrior ethos, decline of 7
Watada, Lieutenant Ehren 72
water resources 134–35
Waziris 61
Waziristan, Federally Administered Tribal Areas (FATA) 83, 84
weak states 137–38, 140
weapons: advanced 11, 115, 118, 119, 120, 123, 124; biological 99; chemical 99; laser 123; non-state ownership of 99, 102, 136, 139; precision munitions 14, 15, 16; procurement 120–23; ready availability of 139; *see also* artillery; ballistic missiles; bombs; cruise missiles; grenades; weapons of mass destruction (WMD)
weapons of mass destruction (WMD) 98; Iran 67; Iraq 11, 63; rogue states' acquisition of 56, 62; Syria 67, 99; *see also* biological weapons; chemical weapons; nuclear weapons
West Bank 75, 97
West Irian 45, 46
West Side Boys 93

Western narrative of military history 2
western New Guinea *see* West Irian
Westernisation 23, 134
Winograd Commission 76
Wiranto, General 94

Xi Jinping 114
Xinjiang 95–96

Yeltsin, Boris 28
Yemen 53, 55, 95, 96; gun ownership in 102; US drone attacks in 10, 102
young male population 134
Younis, Abdel Fatah 105
Yudhoyono, President 96
Yugoslavia: former 29–34, 132; *see also* Bosnia; Kosovo

Zaghawa tribe 88, 89
Zamana, Volodymyr 94
Zambia 94
Zenawi, Meles 43
Zimbabwe 49, 89, 94, 103, 132, 136